PENGUIN CLASSICS

SELECTED POEMS AND PROSE

PHILIP EDWARD THOMAS was born to Welsh parents in Lambeth, London, in 1878. Educated at Battersea Grammar School and St Paul's, Thomas showed early promise as a writer, and despite his father's hope that he would enter the civil service, he had already published his first book by the time he matriculated at Lincoln College, Oxford. While still an undergraduate, he met and secretly married Helen Noble, with whom he had a child, Merfyn, and later two daughters, Bronwen and Myfanwy. Having decided to live by the pen, he became an exceptionally prolific and widely published writer, but incessant overwork led to severe depression and, in 1911, a serious breakdown. In 1913 he met the American poet Robert Frost, with whom he formed a very close friendship and who urged him to try his hand at poetry, which Thomas considered the highest form of literature. He produced one hundred and forty-two poems in less than two years, which has established his lasting reputation as one of the great poets of the English language.

During this time he also enlisted and trained as an artillery officer, and, in January 1917, embarked for France. He was killed on the Western Front three months after arriving, by a shell at the beginning of the Battle of Arras.

ROBERT MACFARLANE is the award-winning writer of *Mountains of the Mind* (2003), *The Wild Places* (2007) and, most recently, *The Old Ways: A Journey on Foot* (2012), from which the foreword to this edition is taken. He is a Fellow of Emmanuel College, Cambridge.

DAVID WRIGHT (1920–1994) was born in Johannesburg and came to England aged fourteen to attend the Northampton School for the Deaf. His first poem was published shortly after graduating from Oriel College, Oxford, and he published poetry throughout his life, including *Moral Stories* (1954), *Monologue of a Deaf Man* (1958), *Metrical Observations* (1980) and *Elegies* (1990). He was both a remarkab'⋯⋯⋯⋯⋯⋯⋯⋯⋯⋯⋯⋯⋯⋯⋯ on-sible for, among others, ⋯⋯⋯⋯⋯⋯⋯⋯⋯⋯ ard

D1160898

John Trelawnay's *Records of Shelley, Byron and the Author*, *The Penguin Book of English Romantic Verse* and, with John Heath-Stubbs, *The Oxford Book of Twentieth-Century Verse*. He was also the author of a number of books on Portugal, a biography of Roy Campbell and a memoir, *Deafness: A Personal Account*.

EDWARD THOMAS

Selected Poems and Prose

Edited and with Notes by
DAVID WRIGHT

Foreword by
ROBERT MACFARLANE

PENGUIN BOOKS

PENGUIN CLASSICS

Published by the Penguin Group
Penguin Books Ltd, 80 Strand, London WC2R 0RL, England
Penguin Group (USA) Inc., 375 Hudson Street, New York, New York 10014, USA
Penguin Group (Canada), 90 Eglinton Avenue East, Suite 700, Toronto, Ontario, Canada M4P 2Y3
(a division of Pearson Penguin Canada Inc.)
Penguin Ireland, 25 St Stephen's Green, Dublin 2, Ireland (a division of Penguin Books Ltd)
Penguin Group (Australia), 707 Collins Street, Melbourne, Victoria 3008, Australia
(a division of Pearson Australia Group Pty Ltd)
Penguin Books India Pvt Ltd, 11 Community Centre, Panchsheel Park, New Delhi – 110 017, India
Penguin Group (NZ), 67 Apollo Drive, Rosedale, Auckland 0632, New Zealand
(a division of Pearson New Zealand Ltd)
Penguin Books (South Africa) (Pty) Ltd, Block D, Rosebank Office Park,
181 Jan Smuts Avenue, Parktown North, Gauteng 2193, South Africa

Penguin Books Ltd, Registered Offices: 80 Strand, London WC2R 0RL, England

www.penguin.com

This edition first published in Penguin English Library 1981
This edition, with a new foreword, published in Penguin Classics 2013
'Ghost', taken from *The Old Ways: A Journey on Foot*, first published by Hamish Hamilton, 2012

001

Foreword © Robert Macfarlane, 2012
Selection and editorial material © David Wright, 1981
The Acknowledgements, on p. xxxi, constitute an extension of this copyright page
All rights reserved

'The Road Not Taken' © Robert Frost, 1916
'The Road Not Taken' from *The Poetry of Robert Frost*, edited by Edward Connery Latham
Reprinted by permission of The Random House Group Limited

The moral right of the authors of the introduction and the editorial material has been asserted

Set in 10.25/12.25pt PostScript Adobe Sabon
Typeset by Jouve (UK), Milton Keynes
Printed in Great Britain by Clays Ltd, St Ives plc

Except in the United States of America, this book is sold subject
to the condition that it shall not, by way of trade or otherwise, be lent,
re-sold, hired out, or otherwise circulated without the publisher's
prior consent in any form of binding or cover other than that in
which it is published and without a similar condition including this
condition being imposed on the subsequent purchaser

ISBN: 978-0-141-39319-3

www.greenpenguin.co.uk

Penguin Books is committed to a sustainable
future for our business, our readers and our planet.
This book is made from Forest Stewardship
Council™ certified paper.

ALWAYS LEARNING   **PEARSON**

Contents

Poems

Foreword[*]

GHOST

Easter Sunday, 8 April 1917, the eve of the Battle of Arras. Thomas sits on an ammunition crate in his dugout, reading back through his diary. Reeking sack walls. Brown lamplight from a twin wick in a Swan glass chimney. A lid of skim-ice on the water in his mug.

Voices drift in. The men are singing 'Mr John Blunt': *And there came travellers, travellers three / Travelling through the night-oh . . .*

The diary is a Walker's back-loop pocketbook, bound in brown pigskin. There is an entry for the 'bright warm Easter day' just ending: a 5.9" shell had fallen two yards from Thomas as he stood in the forward-command post, but hadn't exploded; the blast from another had scratched his neck. On the final pages he has jotted notes for unwritten poems: 'The light of the new moon and every star'; 'The morning chill and clear hurts my skin while it delights my mind'; 'I never understood quite what was meant by God.'

Outside, the men are singing again: 'It's a Long Way to Tipperary'.

5.30 a.m. is zero hour. The offensive will begin with a creeping artillery barrage – the 'hurricane bombardment', as it's being called – which will prepare the way for the infantry assault on the German lines. Thomas and his battery will supply part of

* This foreword is taken from 'Ghost', the penultimate chapter of Robert Macfarlane's book *The Old Ways: A Journey on Foot* (Hamish Hamilton, 2012).

the barrage. For days his gunners have been practising with the new graze fuses, designed to vaporize barbed wire. The timing and aiming of the creep has to be precise: synchronized between batteries, and with the trajectories of each gun carefully calibrated according to its rate of barrel degradation when firing fast and hard, as they will be tomorrow.

Thomas has a long easy gait, rhythmic and swinging. A negligent lope, leisurely but rapid. He has blue eyes (or perhaps they are grey), tawny hair (or perhaps it is sandy, or perhaps just fair) and a fawnishness to his looks. He smells of tweed, peat and tobacco. He has large pockets tailored into his jackets, to carry maps, books and apples. He walks with a stick; hazel, sometimes ash, but holly best of all. He dislikes wearing a wristwatch. He walks usually with one-inch maps, which he consults by tucking his stick under his arm, spreading the map over his large hands, then refolding it and striding on, 'aware of some completely invisible track'. He tends to walk silently, even in company. His friend Eleanor Farjeon, who for years quietly loves him, says that after following a path with Thomas 'you would not walk [it] again as you did before. You would know it in a new way.'

From a young age, he is a compulsive walker, a 'wandering creature'. He's born in Lambeth, south London. His early experiences of walking are suburban: Wandsworth Common, Wimbledon Common. From a young age, too, he is a noticer. He keeps a journal of natural events. He remarks the date of the opening of the year's first violets, he plots the location of birds' nests, he records encounters (a heron taking an eel; a sparrowhawk's berserk pursuit of a starling) and phenomena (clouds that hang like pudding bags in the sky, heat mirages). He's a collector, too, mostly of flowers and eggs. He shins up trees to reach nests, always leaving one egg to encourage another clutch.

He develops an inclusive botanical vision that appreciates weeds as well as wild flowers. He prizes ragwort for the way its flowers show hard as brass. The overlooked and the unnoticed attract him: the 'flowers of rose-bay on ruinous hearths and walls' or 'the long narrowing wedge of irises that runs alongside and between the rails of the South-Eastern and Chatham Railway', almost into the heart of London.

He is introduced to Helen when they're both only seventeen. Helen knows almost immediately that her 'only peace would be to be needed by him', and so it proves to be. Their courtship is conducted mostly through walking. They walk fields and lanes and footpaths together: out at Merton, Richmond Park, Wandsworth Common. She can't at first tell a beech from a birch. She's short-sighted and finds it hard to pick out birds; he teaches her calls and songs so she can know without seeing. They press and label flowers: tormentil, bryony, harebell, bedstraw, milkwort. Thomas gallivants around, showing off his knowledge and ease in country lore. From a copse in Merton he retrieves a compact and mossy chaffinch nest, firm as a ball in the hand. At the Richmond Park heronry he scrambles up a Scots pine to bring down a blue-green heron's egg; a squashed sky-globe.

Helen feels lifted into a new world, doubly intimate with Thomas and with nature. '[I]t seems strange now,' she recalls years later, 'that there was ever a time when I could not recognize the beech's fine-textured skinlike bark, and the set of the trunk and branches like human limbs, and the beautiful curve that the leafy branches make, like a hand opened for giving.' It says much of Helen that she is able to perceive generosity in the form of a branch's curve.

When they first make love on the day of her twentieth birthday, it's inside a leafy glade in a hazel and beech thicket on Wimbledon Common. Thomas makes her a braid of white bryony and that evening gives her a ring, a fine gold signet ring with a red stone setting that had belonged to his great-grandfather, a Spanish sea captain.

They marry in secret, while Thomas is still an undergraduate at Oxford. They move around: lodgings in London, then the lease on a farmhouse in Kent. Their relationship is founded on her absolute love for him. But unconditional love is arduous to give, and even more arduous to receive. It can prompt – as it does in Thomas, over the years that follow – a cruelty on the part of the recipient. Such love, in its willingness to forgive all, in its eagerness to cherish faults as virtues, can come to seem like a declaration of insufficiency on the part of the recipient. You cannot match my love; your love will *always* fall short of mine. Added to this is the realization that the lover who loves you so much *cannot be hurt by you*; that their love is imperishable. Therefore you can try, almost guiltlessly, to hurt them. It becomes a challenge. As Thomas's melancholy tightens on him over the years, as the weasel-bite of his depression locks and deepens, he will hurt Helen increasingly. Her vulnerability, combined with the invulnerability of her love, conspire to encourage his emotional mistreatment of her.

Children come: a son, Merfyn, then a daughter, Bronwen. Thomas is often away from home in body (on long walking tours, researching books) or in mind (present, but writing). He churns out reviews in their hundreds, as well as book-length histories and biographies written to deadline. The work is hard, a bill-paying hackery that leaves him exhausted and despondent. His changes of mood are weather-like, and at times provoked by the weather. Heavy rain can leave him sluiced clean of depression, or more desperately waterlogged. When the black days arrive he lashes out at Helen, criticizing her plainness of mind or her lack of ambition. 'I hate my work,' he writes in a letter, 'I have no vitality, no originality, no love. I do harm.' Helen waits patiently 'to be let into the light again', and meets his cruelty with an unquerying acceptance of his right to be cruel.

So he administers self-punishment through hard walking: a way at once to macerate and to forget himself. Sometimes he leaves the house at evening and walks through the night, coming home haggard near dawn. At times he's settled by this motion; at times only further troubled.

When he's happy? Oh, then the days are fine. The house is filled with stories and rhymes. He sings while he bathes the children. Once they're dried and clothed he lets the children perch on his knees, takes his clay pipe from his mouth and any music that is in him comes forth. His voice is deep and his songs are various: Welsh folk songs, racy and ribald songs, rollicking sea shanties. Song is vital to Thomas: he is involved almost from the start in the English folk-song revival led by Cecil Sharp. He publishes *Poems and Songs for the Open Air*, an anthology of walking ballads and airs. Folk songs and foot-paths are, to his mind, both major democratic forms: collective in origin but re-inflected by each new singer or walker. Radical, too, in their implicit rebuke to the notion of private property. He admires 'Sumer Is Icumen in' more than anything by Beethoven. In his poem 'The Path' he will write of an old track to school through the woods that 'wind[s] like silver, trickles on'. It is smudged by moss and leaf-fall, but kept open by the feet of children. The path is a riverbed and the children the water, running 'the current of their feet' over it.

They leave Kent and move to Hampshire, to the village of Steep. First to Berryfield Cottage, and then to a house called Wick Green, which is reached by an ancient, deeply worn track, thick with rotted leaves. The track winds through beeches and yews to reach the long, low house, which sits several hundred feet up at the plateau edge and looks across to Chanctonbury Ring and the ridge line of the South Downs, seven miles distant. The house has been recently constructed on Morrisian principles. The planks and beams have been taken from local oaks. The nails, hinges and hasps have been forged in the village, the bricks cast nearby. Native stone has been used for the thresholds. When mists fill the valleys, they feel as if they are in a wooden galleon at sea, creaking in the swell.

Yet for all its magic, they can't fall in love with the house. They have always treated houses as animate, sounding them out for affinities or infirmities of spirit, and have already left one house for its cursedness, another for its tepidity. Thomas tries to settle: he digs a border by the door of his study and plants thyme, rosemary, lavender and old man's beard. But they soon realize that the hostile newness of Wick Green will make it impossible for them to be happy there, sturdy though it stands, magnificent though its position is. It's so high up that the wind shrieks in the gable room, the mists isolate it and the cold gnaws hard. Thomas's depression sharpens. He feels trapped by his work, trapped in his marriage, unhappy in his home. He longs to establish his own route in life.

He reacts to the disappointments of Wick Green by walking.

Treading the old paths seems to reduce the complexities of life, as if he has stepped into an archetype or allegory: track, forest, moon, traveller. He wanders far afield, even in heavy rain. Mostly the rain calms him because it deprives him of context. It desirably subtracts some part of him, taking away from him 'everything except the power to walk under the dark trees and to enjoy as humbly as the hissing grass'. Mostly, the 'tender loveliness' of his favourite landscapes offers compensations for his own lacks. At times, though – at the worst times – nature's beauty and exuberance feel to him like accusations. 'I am not a part of nature. I am alone. There is nothing else in my world but my dead heart and brain within me and the rain without.' What he has come to understand, painfully, is that one may too easily take the natural world as companion, friend and salve. Nature can cure but it can also be brutally mute, shocking in its disinterest: the river's seawards run, the chalk's whiteness, the hawk's swivelling stare. But he knows also that the acknowledgement of this refusal of relation might offer its own bracing reward, just as the delusion of response might also serve deep purpose – and that one might not need always to choose the one before the other.

During the Kent and Hampshire years, when Thomas is not walking he is reading about walking. Coleridge and Hazlitt, the nonconformists: path-following as dissent. Bunyan and the Puritan tradition: path-following as obedience. Cervantes and the picaresque, Malory and medieval chivalry, the *Mabinogion* and Wales and Giraldus Cambrensis. Cervantes, he notes approvingly, had 'the sense of roads'. Malory's *Le Morte d'Arthur* 'would have less vitality in its marvel if it were not for the roads'. He enjoys the story of Sir Launcelot, riding 'throughout marches and many wild ways'. Even Shakespeare he finds to be a path-writer who in *Cymbeline* 'gives a grand impression of wide tracts of country traversed by roads of great purpose and destiny'. He absorbs the nineteenth-century romance of the open road in Stevenson's *Songs of Travel*, Borrow's Romany fantasias, the *Rural Rides* of William Cobbett (whose sentences suggest to him the walking swing of an arm or leg) and the work of Richard Jefferies – above all Jefferies, Thomas's hero, whose style 'grew' to his use 'like the handle of a walking stick'; steadying and companionable, the stick taking the hand's mould. Yet Thomas stays sceptical about how one might, in a Rousseauian reverie, mistake walking for a 'primitive act, "natural to man"', and in this way feel falsely restored to 'a pristine majesty'.

Paths and tracks criss-cross his own work, figuratively and structurally. He writes of winding roads and he writes in winding syntax. He learns these reflexive habits from Hazlitt, who embeds walking as prosody to the depth of grammar. From Hazlitt, too, he learns the epistemological power of the proposition that is made and then part retracted. Again and again in Thomas's imagination, text and landscape overlap: 'The prettiest things on ground are the paths / With morning and evening hobnails dinted, / With foot and wing-tip overprinted / Or separately charactered.' The paths are sentences, the shod feet of the travellers the scratch of the pen nib or the press of the type. He understands that reading and walking expire into one another, that we carry within ourselves evolving maps of the world which are, as Wordsworth put it, '[o]f texture midway between life and books'.

Thomas starts to think, too, about thinking, and the ways in which the physical world might incite in us those kinds of knowledge that exceed cognition. In letters to his friend Gordon Bottomley he describes going beachcombing on the Suffolk coast and finding 'champagne corks, sailors' hats, Antwerp beer bottles, fish boxes, oranges, lemons, onions, banana stems, waterworn timber and the most exquisite flat & round pebbles, black, white, dove grey, veined, wheat coloured'. 'Not one [pebble] but makes me think or rather draws out a part of me beyond my thinking,' he writes to Bottomley. His observation of the difference between being made to think, and being drawn out beyond one's thinking, is tellingly precise; it records the transition from a perception exercised by the self upon the stones to the perception exercised upon the self by the stones.

Nature and landscape frequently have this effect on him: trees, birds, rocks and paths cease to be merely objects of contemplation, and instead become actively and convivially present, enabling understanding that would be possible nowhere else, under no other circumstances. 'Something they knew – I also, while they sang,' he will write of song thrushes in an early poem titled 'March'. He senses that the light-fall, surfaces, slopes and sounds of a landscape are all somehow involved in accessing what he calls the 'keyless chamber[s] of the brain'; that the instinct and the body (the felt smoothness of pebbles, the seen grain of light) must know in ways that the conscious mind cannot. Weather, in particular, is 'integral' to his thinking, as Eleanor Farjeon notices: 'Other people talk about the weather, Edward lived it.' Like Nan Shepherd thirty years later, he recognizes that weather is something we think *in* – 'the wind, the rain, the streaming road, and the vigorous limbs and glowing brain and what they created . . . We and the storm were one' – and that we would be better, perhaps, speaking not of states of mind, but rather of atmospheres of mind or meteorologies of mind.

He is slowly working out a model of thought – no, more than thought, of *self* – not as something rooted in place and growing steadily over time, but as a shifting set of properties variously supplemented and depleted by our passage through the world. Landscape and nature are not there simply to be gazed at; no, they press hard upon and into our bodies and minds, complexly affect our moods, our sensibilities. They riddle us in two ways – both perplexing and perforating us. Thomas knows this to be true because he has felt it on foot, with his feet, and Farjeon again, keenly, senses this: 'he walked with *himself*, with his eyes and his ears and his nostrils, and his long legs and his big hands.'

The challenge, of course, is how to record such experience – apprehended, but by definition unsayable – in language, using the 'muddy untruthful reflection of words'. Poetry is the form of utterance that can come closest; this he knows as a reader. But he has never written poetry, and has little reason to think he can.

Over the course of 1913, though, Thomas becomes friends with the American poet Robert Frost. They walk together in the fields and woods near Dymock in Gloucestershire, where Frost is living with his wife and where a group of poets has taken to gathering in order to wander, think and drink. Frost and Thomas tramp almost anywhere they wish 'on wavering footpaths through the fields', sometimes twenty-five miles in a day, discussing poetry, natural history and the coming war. Frost coins a new word for what he and Thomas do: 'talks-walking'.

It is Frost who encourages Thomas to make the move from prose into poetry. He is, Frost tells him, a poet behind the disguise of prose. It's Frost who takes lines from Thomas's travelogues and rearranges them as verse, so that Thomas can see what he's been doing all along without knowing it. Frost 'produced . . . the enharmonic change', Farjeon writes beautifully, 'that made [Thomas] not a different man, but the same man in another key'. Thus retuned, and with such encouragement, the poems start coming – tentatively, experimentally – the first finished on 3 December 1914.

War has been declared, though. The country has changed: disorganized trains, crowds at the stations, reservists being seen off by flag-waving friends. Thomas is sceptical of cheap nationalism, scornful of pompous martialism. But he is also anxious to fight: to prove his bravery, to defend a landscape he loves, to find the purpose that his life has been so unhappily lacking. Less than a year into the war, he finds himself at a crossroads. Frost and his family have already sailed for America; Frost is encouraging Thomas to emigrate to New England and find work there as a writer and a poet. Frost will help him make his way; they will be safe from the war at that distance. Helen is pleading with him to stay in Hampshire. But the army needs men, and Thomas has felt himself 'slowly growing into a conscious Englishman'. There's no obligation on him to enlist. At thirty-six he's old enough to sit the war out. He's married with children; it remains wholly honourable for family men not to fight. 'He could have been safe, if he had chosen to be,' Farjeon will later write.

It's the greatest decision of his life, and he imagines it as a separation of ways. He spends hours poring over his 'moral map', 'thinking out' his motives, when he 'ought to be reading or enjoying the interlacing flight of 3 kestrels'. On 7 December he begins a poem called 'The Signpost': a figure hesitates at a junction, unable to choose one or other of the paths. 'I read the

sign. Which way shall I go?' Now, if only he could take one
path and then retrace his steps and take the other . . .

In June 1915 Frost sends Thomas a draft of a poem he has
written called 'The Road Not Taken'. It was inspired, obliquely,
by the memory of walking with Thomas in the Dymock fields:
Thomas's eagerness, his wish to walk every path and his frus-
tration at crossroads, have been transformed by Frost into a
finely balanced metaphysical parable. 'Two roads diverged in a
yellow wood,' begins the poem:

> And sorry I could not travel both
> And be one traveler, long I stood
> And looked down one as far as I could
> To where it bent in the undergrowth;
>
> Then took the other, as just as fair . . .

Thomas is stung, seeing the poem as a parody of his indecisive-
ness over the question of the war. He interprets it as a spur,
feels it as a goad: *Hurry up, man, and make a choice; stop dith-
ering at the junction*. It's a drastic misreading of the poem, but
Thomas closes his mind to subtlety. He writes sharply back to
Frost. Within weeks he has made his choice. In early July he
draws up his will and enlists. On 14 July he passes his medical.
The King's shilling is taken: he is Private 4229 in the 28th Bat-
talion of the Artists Rifles, part of the larger London Regiment.
He has committed to a route, and the knowledge of its irrevers-
ibility reassures him.

Why, really, does he enlist? Impossible to say: another path
vanishing back into the distance, another track petering out.
One of so many things lost in the creases where the map folds.
He doesn't even know himself: 'Several people *have* asked me
[why I joined], but I could not answer yet.' To Gordon Bottom-
ley, the best he can do is characterize the decision as 'the natural
culmination of a long series of moods & thoughts'. He doesn't
even tell Helen in person, instead sending her a telegram from
London. 'No, no, no,' is all that she can say, 'not that.'

But he is writing so fast; a life's worth of poems torrenting from him now that he has set his face to France. Verse – from the Latin *vertere*, 'to turn'. He writes nearly sixty poems between enlisting and embarking for the Front. Sometimes a poem a day, quick and brilliant: 'Roads', 'When we two walked', 'The Lane', 'The Green Roads'. Some of these poems seem to know more of his own fate than he does; they draw out part of him beyond his thinking: 'the future and the maps / Hide something I was waiting for.'

Thomas's first proper posting is to Hare Hall Training Camp in Essex, where he works as a navigation instructor. In spare hours he writes poems, but covertly. He doesn't mind poets knowing he's a soldier, but he does mind soldiers knowing he's a poet. He's surprised by how much he likes aspects of army life: polishing his high trench boots – right hand stuck into the boot, left hand buffing across the toecap – until his own face looms in the shine. Surprised by how he enjoys the unvarying routines: teaching map-reading with a prismatic compass to the men of A Company, taking them out on foot-manoeuvres. Surprised by how much he likes Essex. Surprised by the absence of depression; 'black despair' has given way to 'calm acceptance'.

On top of a hill in Epping Forest he finds a run-down cottage called High Beech, where Helen and the children can live and which he can easily visit when he has furlough. When the snow falls during their first winter there, time slows and modernity retreats. 'It is fine and wintry here,' he writes in a letter. 'The hills look impassable and make me think they must have looked like that 2,000 years ago.'

In early December 1916 a call comes round for volunteers to go straight out to the batteries in France. Thomas is among the first to sign up. On 6 January he comes back to High Beech for his last days of leave before departing for the Front. He tries to behave as if nothing is wrong, but Helen can barely function. He studies maps with Merfyn, tries to show Helen how to take a bearing on his prismatic compass; she cries. They're sharp and bickery, then they quarrel openly, then she cries again, and then they are tender together. On the morning of his departure, the snow around the cottage is frozen iron-hard, with the footprints of birds set into it like hieroglyphs. Thomas gives Helen a book into which he has copied out all his poems. 'Remember that, whatever happens, all is well between us for ever and ever,' he tells her. A freezing mist hangs in the air.

Thomas walks away, the hard snow unmarked by his leaving feet. Helen stands at the gate and watches him go until the mist hides him. As he descends the hill, he keeps on calling *coo-ee!* to her, as if he were arriving rather than leaving. She answers him with her *coo-ee!* and they go on like that, call and answer, fainter and fainter.

The day before he's due to sail he hires a bicycle and pedals out from the transit camp in Kent in which he is billeted, to say goodbye to England. It is such a ride! Hedgeless roads over long sloping downs sprinkled with thorns, and covered with old tracks whose routes are marked by juniper. A clear pale sky. A faint sunset, a long twilight.

Embarkation: 29 January 1917. Thomas and his men march through the pre-dawn dark to the station. The air very cold, very still. Soldiers stamp their feet. He is one of seven officers commanding 150 men, who will work four 9.2" howitzers, and who together make up Number 244 Siege Battery.

The men sing 'Pack Up Your Troubles in Your Old Kit-bag'.

A freezing train to Southampton, where they wait until dusk. Thomas walks to pass the time and stay warm. Inland, an ice-scattered lake, birds diving, a dark wood beyond. Some of the men play rugby on a stretch of waste ground. As the light fails the seagulls seem to float rather than fly.

At 7 p.m. they board the *Mona Queen*, clumping up a sagging gangplank. The sea tumbles. Thomas rests rather than sleeps during the crossing, listens from his cabin to the men laughing and swearing.

Le Havre dock, 4 a.m. Light falling in slabs from the windows of tall pale houses and in arcs from the electric quay lights. They march through the town in fine falling snow. French sentries: hooded with long loose cloaks and carrying rifles with curved bayonets. Dinner is iron rations, supplemented with cheese and marmalade. They sleep that night in tents, twelve men in each,

each with two blankets against the cold. Subalterns sit up late by lanterns in the mess, censoring letters.

Days of waiting, hard clear nights. Troop ships arrive, black stark vessels from the north-west. Hospital trains pull in from the east, carrying men with shocking wounds. At last, on 4 February, they spend cold hours entraining the guns. When the job is done they all sit on bales of cotton on the railway platform and wait for the train to the front.

The men sing 'There's a Long, Long Trail'.

When the train at last arrives some of the men begin shouting in jest, 'All tickets!', 'All tickets please!' Then they fall quiet. At 11 p.m. prompt, the train lurches away and a yell of *HUR-RAY!* ripples down the train. Then silence again, even before they're clear of the bare platform with its trampled snow.

The train clacks past Alaincourt, past Amiens and on to Doullens. Thomas looks out of the window at the wooded chalk hills. He's back in the South Country already. Poplars in lines. Mistletoe in the branches. They're on the highest land in northern France and the roads are frozen.

Forwards to Mendicourt, where they billet in part-ruined barns. Enemy planes float over like pale moths, looking serene among the black shrapnel bursts. Thomas rigs up a table on which to do his paperwork. He remembers how one night on the Downs he had gazed up and wondered 'what things that same moon sees eastward about the Meuse'. Forwards again to Dainville along a shell-pocked track, to billets on the Arras road, near a graveyard with three recently arrived residents. Big-gun firing is audible now. There is the distant rickle of machine guns. From an observation post Thomas glasses the snowy broken land. Glinting wires, dead trees. A corpse under a railway bridge. The shell-holes make him think of tumuli and dew ponds. Paths everywhere: duckboard zigzags, wriggling little tracks, and medieval field boundaries now turned into sunken roads used to hide the movement of troops and supplies.

The officers dine on bully, cheese and white wine. Someone has brought a gramophone, its ribbed and flaring trumpet reminding Thomas of bindweed flowers. He writes letters home to Helen, up to five a week, finding it easier to inhabit his marriage lovingly at a distance.

The gramophone plays cheery tunes: 'Wait Till I'm as Old as Father' and 'Where Does Daddy Go When He Goes Out?'

Days pass. Cannonades thud away to the south, over near Ancre. An old white horse works a treadmill, tramping in patient circles. Farmers carry on as best they can. The gramophone plays Gounod's 'Ave Maria'.

Thomas comes to know this landscape as he has come to know all others: by walking and watching. He hadn't expected so much life in such a shattered place. Hare, partridge and wild duck in fields south-east of his guns. Grass just beginning to show green through melting snow. Black-headed buntings talking to each other, rooks cawing. Vegetation flopping over the edge of the trenches: dead campion umbels, rank grass-tangles, clots of thistles.

The gramophone plays 'Dormez-Vous', by the end of which they have all fallen silent.

He writes up the fighting book, sleeps badly. Star shells light up the night. When the big guns fire, he can feel the blasts quivering in his guts. His table and mantelpiece silt up with letters to be censored. One night the artillery falls silent. He can only hear machine guns and rifle shots. He lies, idly, toying with words and rhymes. Rifle and idle, vital and rifle. How odd that rifle fire can feel almost relaxing in comparison to the Berthas. The machine guns sound like someone knocking at a door.

He goes to Arras itself; it reminds him of Bath. White houses, shutters, domes, an empty white square. There's so much to recall home and the chalk counties. When sentries challenge him in the street, he answers with the password 'Sussex'. A mad captain takes his men behind the lines to drive partridges into the air, whistling and crying 'Mark over!', as though he were on a field shoot in Wiltshire. A strategic ridge to the west of his position, from which German snipers hunt, is called Telegraph Hill. One day Thomas looks up from his observation post to see kestrels hanging in pairs as they used to over Mutton and Ludcombe hills, except that above the kestrels wheel five planes.

He shifts billet to an abandoned big house, mirrors and paintings still on the wall. In the evenings he reads Shakespeare's sonnets or Frost's poetry. When the guns fire, he and his fellow officers cannot hear each other speak, and gulp like fish, trying to lip-read. He is adjutant to a ruddy colonel, ex-Raj, who refers fondly to the 'confoundedly cheeky . . . old Hun', even as his men are dying.

The gramophone plays 'Peer Gynt', its music drifting through the building.

He begins to experience the world as silent tableaux. German prisoners standing in the mud, one with his hand resting on another's shoulder. A turbaned Indian at a barn door, holding a sheep by a rope around its neck. A line of dark thin trees standing against the bright afternoon sky. One day in early March he sees the Royal Flying Corps lose four planes. The tank of the last burns white as the plane drops from the sky, both pilots scorched to death. The land an exhausted cinder.

The gramophone plays Chopin's 'Berceuse'.

244 Battery moves forward for their first shoot. The men tramp up the road whistling 'It's Nice to Get Up in the Morning' and 'The Minstrel Boy'. Six-inch guns snuffle. The field shells sing. Machine guns spatter. The wind blows the water in the shell-holes into close intersecting patterns, like that of a file's blade.

The gramophone plays 'Allan Water'.

One night, lying in bed, he becomes sure he will die there, by shell-blast, in that big room. It's the first time he has felt real fear – what a place to feel it! Should he die with his clothes on? Should he haul his bed to the window side of the room, or to the chimney side? Should he sleep upstairs where he might fall further if a shell strikes, or on the ground floor where he might be crushed? He has too much time to think: he wants to bite the day to its core. At dawn he listens to the thrushes.

The gramophone plays Ambrose Thomas's 'Mignon Gavotte'.

In early March there is snow again, fine snow and a fierce wind. Thomas is working on aerial reconnaissance, using photographs secured by the RFC boys, trying to fit them together into a meaningful pattern. Seen from above – the view of the hawk or the helmeted airman – the trench system resembles an intricate network of paths and holloways, leading from everywhere to everywhere. As well as the photographs he is using flash-spotting and new sound-ranging techniques involving triangulated microphones. All part of the effort to locate and destroy the German gun emplacements, hidden away behind ridges, including those camouflaged from aerial view.

The RFC wireless man reads *The Song of Hiawatha* aloud: 'Down a narrow path they wandered / Where the brooklet led them onward / Where the trail of deer and bison / Marked the soft mud on the margin . . .' Skylarks sing over no-man's-land. There is the noisy parley of starlings, and revolver reports from men hunting rats in the trenches.

He spends dangerous, dull days in observation posts, peering out with his field glasses through a hedge of elder and thorn in which sparrows and blackbirds chink. Action erupts in its casual baffling way, always expected but never anticipated. More of his home life slips from him. He is frustrated by waiting. He feels friendless. The mud sucks at his boots. On the morning of 14 March he is looking out towards no-man's-land when he sees a piece of burnt paper skipping towards him, whisking in the air. No, not paper. A bat, probably shaken from one of the last standing sheds in Ronville. He notices an old grey-green track that crosses no-man's-land, its path still visible even among the devastation. It must once have been a country way to Arras. How hard it is to erase a path! Deep green water has collected in one of the bigger shell-holes, and the skeletons of whole trees can be seen lying there. He writes home to Merfyn, asking him to oil up a bicycle so that the two of them can go out riding together when he returns in the summer.

The gramophone plays 'D'Ye Ken John Peel?'

The military and the natural are so compressed here that it becomes hard to sort the one from the other. When the Huns' guns fire above their heads into Beaurains, the shells come over like starlings returning, twenty or thirty a minute. He sees a great shell-burst stand up like a birch tree. When the larks sing he feels invulnerable. Buried seeds thrown to the surface by explosion and trench digging have resulted in surreal sprays of early spring flowers, growing among bones and mess tins.

Word is that the big push approaches. Thomas is keen to have a share in the great strafe when it comes. By mid-March, his guns are firing between 400 and 600 rounds a day, mostly at Vimy Ridge. He sights off targets and shell-fall using a lensatic compass, whose degree-plate tipples in the liquid of the instrument's dial.

On 24 March, Thomas goes out to the advance position on the front line at Beaurains. My 'new position, fancy, was an old chalk pit in which a young copse of birch, hazel etc. has established itself', he writes to Helen that day. 'I am sitting warm in the sun on a heap of chalk with my back to the wall of the pit. Fancy, an old chalk pit with moss and even a rabbit left in spite of the paths trodden all over it. It is beautiful and sunny and warm though cold in the shade. The chalk is dazzling. The sallow catkins are soft dark white . . .'

Late March and early April brings a run of clear serene winter mornings, and preparations for the spring offensive. The larks start singing at 5.15 a.m., the blackbirds follow at 6 a.m., the guns shortly afterwards. Thomas and his men fill sandbags for reinforcing their dugouts, readying for battle. Rubin and Smith, the two men with the best voices, sing duets from *The Bing Boys*. Thomas reads *Macbeth*.

Helen writes to an old friend, Janet Hooton – wife of Harry, the man to whom Thomas had dedicated *The Icknield Way*. He's still the poet, even out there, Helen tells Janet proudly, 'delighting in what beauty there is there, and he finds beauty where no one else would find it . . . My eyes and ears and hands long for him, and nearly every night I dream he has come and we are together once again.'

On 4 April they fire all day, 600 rounds dispatched, though almost nothing comes back in return. The artillery makes the air flap, a noise like that of loose sails in a gusty wind. Thomas's feet are constantly wet and cold. Fine green feathers of yarrow fletch the sods on the forward dugout. He reads *Hamlet*.

On the weekend of 7 and 8 April, they line up the heavy guns of the battery out on the old sunken road that runs parallel to the front. The German bombardment is unusually heavy. He composes a letter to Helen:

Dearest

Here I am in my valise on the floor of my dugout writing before sleeping. The artillery is like a stormy tide breaking on the shores of the full moon . . . The pretty village among trees that I first saw two weeks ago is now just ruins among violated stark tree trunks. But the sun shone and larks and partridge and magpies and hedge-sparrows made love and the trench was being made passage for the wounded that will be harvested in a day or two . . .

I slept jolly well and now it is sunshine and wind and we are in for a long day and I must post this when I can.

All and always yours Edwy

The gramophone plays 'Death of the Troll'.

Easter Monday, 9 April, the first day of the Battle of Arras, begins with a massive artillery barrage from the British – the hurricane bombardment. The air sags and beats with shell-rip. Thomas is in his observation post, watching the shell-fall, directing fire. In the wintry dawn light, behind the creeping barrage, the first waves of troops advance on the German lines.

The morning is a triumph for the British batteries. They disable most of the German heavy guns with their counter-battery fire, and their troops take the German infantry unawares. As the guns slow their fire the British soldiers emerge to shout and dance.

Thomas steps out of the dugout and then leans back into the doorway, to fill and light his clay pipe. Snow and red sun; a ridge sweeping away bare for miles. He has part filled the pipe when a stray German shell drops near him and the vacuum caused by its passing throws him hard to the earth.

His body is unwounded. Beside him lies his clay pipe, unbroken. He has been killed by a pneumatic concussion, his heart stopped still by a violent absence of air. The fatal vacuum has created pressure ridges on the pages of his diary, which resemble ripples in standing water.

Helen is sewing and Myfanwy is sitting nearby, filling in the pricked dots on a postcard with coloured wool, making a wild duck to send to France. Out of the window, Helen sees the telegraph boy stop on his bicycle and lean it against the fence. He hands the telegram over. She reads it in silence. He waits to see if a reply is wanted. 'No answer,' she says.

   Helen writes to Frost. She cannot tell which tense to use. 'For a moment indeed one loses sight and feeling. With him too all was well and is. You love him, and some day I hope we may meet and talk of him for he is very great and splendid.'

The contents of Thomas's pockets are returned to Helen in a box. There is the diary, and inside it a photograph, a loose slip of paper and a creased letter. The letter is from her to him. The photograph is of her. The slip of paper has addresses and names written on one side, and on the other, three jotted lines in pencil:

   Where any turn may lead to Heaven

   Or any corner may hide Hell

   Roads shining like river up hill after rain.

What was Thomas seeing as he wrote those last verses in his Arras notebook? The old ways of the South Country, or the shell-swept support roads that wound to the Front? Both, perhaps, folded together, the one kind of path having led in its way to the other.

                                   Robert Macfarlane, 2012

Acknowledgements

I should like to thank the staff of the London Library, Mr Alistair Elliot of the University Library, Newcastle-upon-Tyne, and Mr David Burnett of the University Library, Durham, for their help and kindness in obtaining books by Edward Thomas and allowing me to see some of his ms. letters.

For permission to reprint copyright material, the following acknowledgements are made:

Extracts from *Letters from Edward Thomas to Gordon Bottomley*, edited by R. George Thomas (1968) and *The Collected Poems of Edward Thomas*, edited by R. George Thomas (1978) are reprinted by permission of Oxford University Press.

Extracts from *The Childhood of Edward Thomas* (Faber and Faber Ltd, 1938) and *Collected Poems of Edward Thomas* (Faber and Faber Ltd, 1949) are reprinted by permission of Mrs Myfanwy Thomas.

Note on the Selection

This selection of Edward Thomas's prose and poetry has been arranged as nearly as possible in chronological order of writing.

David Wright, 1981

Selected Poems
and Prose

PROSE

From 'A Diary in English Fields and Woods'[1]

April 1, 1895. Heronry at Richmond Park – on a harsh blowing day. Nests chiefly in firs, also in beech and oak, and almost invariably built among the crowning branches; differing much in bulk – some are huge with the layers of succeeding years, others lightly built in the manner of wood-pigeons. One nest was a yard thick, of large twigs, the hollow for the eggs, however, being no broader or deeper than usual. In general the eggs are laid in a shallow depression, roughly lined with mosses and light grasses or branchlets. The number of the herons has decreased, the keeper thinks, since the long frost, when the ponds were ice-bound and abandoned by moor-hen and wild duck; at which season the birds are much abroad in foraging, at the river-side or remote marshlands, and a prey to every gunner. Not more than five or six nests could we then make out. One contained six eggs, an unusual number; like a wild duck's in size and colour, but rough and chalky in the surface of the shell, as many sea-birds' are: they had been laid, probably, in the middle of last month, and would be hatched in two weeks hence. Another nest had only one egg, others were empty yet. Rising at our approach, the birds wheeled, their legs held parallel to their tails and close to the body, disturbing the banded wood-pigeons from the oaks under. When about to alight, the legs are dangled awkwardly as if seeking a perch, and their cries are loud and hoarse, varied by gentler metallic calls and coughings not bird-like. We learnt that the colony is the result of a forced migration from the neighbouring Park of Bushy.

Hedge-sparrow laying: in a low-built nest with the willow 'palms' over it: following the blackbird, thrush, and robin.

Swans resorting to their nests in the parks.

April 6 Chiffchaff singing, our earliest visitor, late this year; accompanied by the gentler willow-wrens; while the Norway wanderers, fieldfares, are still here.

Blackbirds and thrushes laying and building; new nests discovered each day since the earliest in mid-March.

Horse-chestnuts green with half-breaking buds; preceded only by the elder (always early: once noted on February 1). Hawthorn following, lime also in the groves, and blackthorn with its flower before the leaf.

April 12 Cuckoo at Wimbledon crying in the oaks; and below him the first wood-anemones, flushed white. Young rooks and thrushes in the nest.

April 13 Swallows, house-martins, and sand-martins come to Wandsworth Common in fine blue weather.

April 15–17 London to Marlborough Forest on foot. Swallows' and cuckoos' voices along the road westward. Whitethroat has come, singing and chattering with his 'I did it, I did', ceaselessly.

Jackdaws building in hollow beeches, and in rain-worn knot-holes.

Squirrels' drays, or 'huts', as they are locally known, contain new-born young.

Snipe bleating over water-meadows near Hungerford. This sound, which is most loud when the bird is in full flight, circling upward or hovering, makes the air vibrate, and seems to be caused by the play of wings. Peewits make a similar noise in their sharpest turns, diving and ascending; their joints seem to creak.

Loud laughter of the green woodpecker; clarion song of the missel-thrush; 'whit-whitting' of the nuthatch up the beech-bole.

Many jackdaws' nests lined luxuriously with down and deer's fur.

SWINDON[2]

May 27 True May forget-me-nots in the wet hollows, and densely among the waterside rushes: some flowers, pure white with the blue trembling through as in the lining of a shell.

White bryony in flower: green-ribbed blossoms among its many-angled leaves, that fling themselves, as it were, aloft on airy tendrils.

May 28 Young whitethroats gaping in the nest.

Yellow iris coming into flower in the broad reed beds at Coate[3] among its willow-islets.

May 29 Herb bennet or avens blossoming; its yellow flowers succeeded by bright deep-red plumes, bristling all over.

May 31 Honeysuckle in flower.

Moorhens and coots still laying at Coate.

Mowing begins on the broad billowy meadow that slopes to the forget-me-nots at the southern water's-edge of Coate Reservoir:[3] near it, in the water now, is the hollowed oak; and on shore an old crab-tree whose bark the cattle have rubbed to a polished red – to it the chaffinch comes for horsehair in the chinks. All along the shore is a row of young willows where the house-martins linger with the bank-swallows and preen their plumes and twitter. Out in the 'mere' pike leap: in the deeps at the edge of the vast weeds that root, twenty feet deep, in the cold bed of the pond, there are great tench. Hither, on a summer's day, the keepers stroll and chat with the fishers, and talk of the pheasants that do well this year. The keepers are from Burderop on the hill – great woods of oak and ash and lesser larches, with violet and wind-flower and primrose in spring – in whose midst is the low dormer-windowed cottage of Richard Jefferies' 'gamekeeper', overbrowed by walnut-trees, whose fruit the old keeper used lately to give the boys of the countryside.

June 1 Opposite the old house of Richard Jefferies, on the Coate Road just beyond the stile which leads a path aside to the reservoir, I met an old dame who had lived there in the old low house since a time considerably before the birth of Jefferies. She talked willingly of Jefferies; of his wanderings at all hours and on every side: and of the fact that she, in younger days, prepared the single-windowed cheese-room at Coate Farm for use as his study. The family has left the village: Jefferies himself visited it little after his marriage. The martins that built in the eaves of the old lady's cottage she called affectionately 'my birds'.

Ragged-robins and water-cress in flower together.

Sainfoin blossoming.

Nest of young swallows; and near it, in the barn, an old swallow's nest had been altered by a great tit, and crammed with his own customary moss and feathers.

The last cuckoo-flowers.

June 5 The first wild rose of the summer.

Several nightingales have ceased to sing.

At one time sand-martins built at the very edge of Swindon old town in 'the Quarries'; but frequent blastings and the invasion of starlings and sparrows have exiled them.

June 6 The sand-martins here certainly are not, as Gilbert White described them, 'rather mute' and not 'of a sociable turn'; they are garrulous, though in gentler tones than swallows, with whom also they associate. Neither are they shy, seeking unfrequented banks; for in London, in a busiest suburb, they occupy drain-holes in the upright cement wall of a railway embankment, past which trains are incessantly whistling towards and from a great junction.

June 7 Yarrow blossoming from the stones of the field-roads, and at path-sides: cockscomb out in the thin mowing grass.

Elder in flower, its scent thickest after rain when the petals whiten the sward under: the flower-clusters were noticeable, bosomed in young leaf, as soon as the March buds burst.

Hemlock in flower along the brook.

House-martins beginning to lay: thus late, because earlier nests had been blown down.

Lesser field convolvulus in flower: braiding the driest paths, even on ploughed land, unsown: and creeping about the barren sea-beach.

Common mallow flowering in dry places.

June 12 Blackberry-bramble blossoming; humming already with many bees.

Cuckoo sings, but broken-voicedly.

June 16 Wild parsnip flowering: found more in the midst of the fields than at the hedges, like parsley.

Curious crying of the young rooks – a faltering 'ka-wa-wa', in attempting the grave 'caw'.

Bee, burying himself in the larkspur blooms, each one of which he looks into in turn.

Meadow-sweet flowering: at the margins of canal and brook – sometimes actually in the water, with the lesser skull-cap and its upturned leaves.

June 17 Common arrowhead in blossom; growing in dense beds, where the moorhen builds, and under which the pike lurk: its leaves and tough, easily penetrable stems, hold the angler's line or hooks.

Nightingale hatches her eggs under a bramble: and her mate stops singing and begins to scold with a harsh 'bit-bit' or a wistful 'wheet-torr', in which both birds join deep in the underwood.

Spotted orchis blossoming with poppy, tormentil, chamomile and coltstail, among the railway metals on dry soil.

Shivering drawl of the common bunting, as if the dust of the roadsides, which he loves, had got into his throat: he sings on the telegraph wires or bare posts by preference: quite a short song, betraying his relationship to the reed-bunting, and in a lesser degree to the larks.

June 18 The chiffchaff is now the commonest singer, with the willow-wren, and he sings on to September; the garden-warbler is silent with the nightingale, and the talkative whitethroats and sedge-birds are more often quiet than before; the cuckoo now is hardly a voice, and it is strange how few know his low flight and long-tailed figure as he journeys, now silent as a rule.

Stonecrop with mallow on the dry ha-ha wall.

June 19 Stonechats in the furze occupy the blackened sprays and cry from them 'whee-chuck-chuck' on the windy warren-hill.

'Brook betony' or figwort blossoming purple above its square stems.

June 20 Pied flycatcher's nest lodged ten feet high against an elm-bole: four pale-blue spotless eggs. The nest was built outwardly of crumpled hawthorn-leaves, as the nightingale's is of oakleaves: lined with hairs.

Nightingales follow us through the copse where their nest is hid: the young birds are abroad within a fortnight after hatching.

June 22 Branched water-plantain in flower.

Young cuckoo, fledged in a hedge-sparrow's nest, abroad.

Flowering-rush puts out a bunch of rosy flowers from the abrupt top of its stem after the manner of certain kinds of narcissus.

Greenfinches laying.

June 23 Swifts dip in brook and pond as they fly: but more rarely than swallow and sand-martin.

Bird-voices heard at midnight: –

Corncrake intermittently.

Sedge-warbler.

Nightjar: with his rattling drilling cry, long, and seldom musical – though it has something in common, from its ease and liquidity, with the nightingale.

Larks rise singing in the darkness, before the stars are gone: followed by the swallows as the east grew white (but not for half an hour did the swallows fly, they only twittered on the oaks that overlook their barns): later came the shrieking of a peacock, yellow-ammers singing, hedge-sparrow, rook, and wren. All night the rabbits pattered in the wood.

June 27 Water-vole swims out to an arrowhead bank, nips a stalk, and returns with it trailed behind. He feeds frequently on a flag-platform of his own construction, much resembling a moorhen's nest. Beaver-like he nibbles the tallest reed through at its thick base, and feeds upon it at his ease when it has fallen flat.

June 30 Grass of the rising aftermath or 'lattermath'[4] beautifully green after a quickening rain, while the thistled pastures are grey.

July 1 Narrow-leaved water-parsnip in flower.
   Nuthatch flings himself through the air with powerful jerky strokes.

July 5 Last cry of the cuckoo.
   Yellow-ammer yet sings.
   Sparrows flocking in the unmown fields: as they rise their combined wings sound like a horse shaking himself in the meads.
   Peewits flocking: in much the same numbers as will be seen henceforward until March.

July 7 Teasel plumes purpling.

July 11 Eyebright blossoming with wild thyme, bird's-foot lotus, and rest-harrow on the hot downs.
   Hips large and reddening; here they are 'peggles', blown through hollow wild-parsnip stalks, called 'peggle-shooters'.
   A tender sky, stroked, as it were, by winds into ripples of grey.

July 14 Tall willow-herb, capped with fresh red flowers, crowding in the ditches, where their grey stalks outlast the winter with a thin cottony plume aloft.

Yellow lady's bedstraw, lowly, thick on the banks and square wastes, with a faint smell of autumn.

July 16 Larks, already banded, fly skipping across the clover, with but a chirrup of song.

July 18 Linnet has eggs newly laid; also blackbird.

Linnets lay on until the end of August, together with swallows: wood-pigeons even later.

July 20 Small insects throng very high in the twilight air: slight rain does not beat them down, and the swallows do not descend.

SWINDON, WILTS

February 25, 1896 In a corner of the garden at the rear of Coate Farm we find a round brick summer-house, with conical thatched roof, circular window opening south, low doorway, and a seat running round the interior: this house was built by Richard Jefferies alone with his own hands, and is that mentioned in 'Wild Life in a Southern County'.

Beeches and firs of the isolated hilltop clump at Liddington all blown to a leaning angle by the west wind; in the valley also the same wind has bowed many pines.

'Oont land', a land of many moles, near the old 'castle' or encampment at Liddington; acres of land ruffled by great mole-heaps.

Hare's form, where there is no grass – a slot in the ground, deep at one end for his hind-quarters.

Limes ruddy with leaf-buds.

Flocks of yellow-ammers in the fir-trees.

February 26 The hare in his form rises slowly bit by bit, and returns, as carefully, after a stretch of his hind-legs or reconnoitre.

February 27 South wind breaks up the ice; house-flies hum over an inch of thawing ice.

February 28 Leaves bursting on bramble and brier.
Starlings have got the visiting plover's whistle by heart already.

February 29 Stout dock-stems hide each a spider in their hollows.
Bow-legged beetles begin to climb clumsily about the grass, in sable-bright armour: they move the second leg of one side with the first and third on the opposite side at each step.
Moorhens' feet, treading the mud like 'ski' on snow, leave broad-arrow prints.

March 1 Larks have paired, and fly, hover, and feed in couples; resorting often to the roadsides.

March 2 At the passing of a kestrel starlings and fieldfares rise in fright to meadow elms, squealing long after the threat is past.
Dog's mercury flowering.

March 3 The first violet.
Kestrel buffeting in the air with two rooks, who rival him in adroitness but not in speed.
Hares prefer to face the apparent and combatable danger of men and dogs to the treacherous net, scented though unseen, by a gateway: they bolt between the legs of the poachers and dogs – the latter being slow, and fit only for driving game.
Water-voles have faint winding 'runs' on the beds of streams, worn as they swim, according to their habit, at the very bottom of the water; the 'runs' are rapidly erased by the water.

March 4 Golden plover manoeuvre for an hour at a time – ascending high and wandering far. But their 'wedge' formation is carefully observed; and even when split up aloft, by a wind or varying strength, several wedges appear side by side.
Rooks advanced in their building; but twenty birds, some of

them strangers, quarrel loudly over the three nests which were all that were necessary before to the diminutive colony.

Elms glow startlingly rust-red with flowers in sunlight.

At evening a new sound is heard, the hissing of fallen rain through the grassblades into the earth.

March 5 'Tump' means a small mound. 'Tumps' are formed in meadows by the piling of roots and blades of a coarse tufty grass called 'bull-polls'; sweet grass soon covers the mound, and it then resembles a tumulus.

March 6 Rabbits out on the windy side of the hedge in storm at night.

Kestrel sways in the lightest wind, like a ship on a calm sea; beats along the hedge, up and down in small curves, hovering at the summit of each – sometimes at the height of only a yard or two. Starlings pass him fearlessly.

March 8 Kingfishers up and down the brook together; building at some distance. They give a high-pitched squeal, particularly on alighting, when they bob their heads nervously.

March 9 The first tortoise-shell butterfly zig-zagging out in the sunlight.

Kingfishers build in the hollow stem of an old willow, leaning like its neighbours threateningly over the stream, which has loosened the soil about their roots.

Willow-catkins hoary, green, and gold: the last on the upper boughs.

March 10 Moorhen's cry sounds as if uttered while the bird's mouth was full of water.

Water-vole occupies a heap of flood-wrack on the shore, caught by willow-boughs; there, in hiding, he curls up in a ball, and, shutting his eyes, may be touched or handled.

March 12 Though the weather is mild, the earth is bitterly cold, as the mole-catcher finds it.

Hawthorns fully in leaf.

Crab-tree leaf-buds burst.

Frogs spawning – on an approach they dive to the bottom-weeds of the water; while here a leg is upthrust, or a yellow mottled leg protrudes.

March 13 A dull warmth to-day which the chaffinch loves – in which he sings most and best.

Dumb-bell-shaped red ants occupy the wrinkling roots of a great water-dock; these roots reach an enormous size, are white within, and medicinal.

March 16 Bands of yellow-ammers and chaffinches still abroad.

Ground-ivy blossoms.

'Snow on the mountains', Alyssum saxatile, a fleecy show in cottage-gardens.

Common snake abroad.

Blackthorns flushed with blossom-buds.

March 18 Common moschatel in flower.

March 19 Wrens begin to build.

An old willowed garden, with elms around, where wildings are permitted – Wood sorrel, ivy-leaved toadflax, anemones, moschatel, pilewort, ground-ivy, climbing the rockeries.

Green curled fronds of hart's-tongue fern linger on the mounds as though fresh; as yet young shoots barely show.

March 21 Great tit has a little sweet song, like ' 'tis sweet – 'tis sweet'.

Chiffchaff arrives – one here, one there; singing always, even in flight; among others singing on the wing are – wren, pipits, buntings, linnet, robin rarely, whitethroat, cuckoo, and all the swallows.

An undertone of summer's insect-song has begun. Innumerable bees around the willow's 'palms', burying themselves in the gold.

Gnats thicken in the air, with finer music than the bees.

'Skaters' first out on the brooks; resting like a boat with outriggers; moving like boat and oarsman in one.

Caterpillar abroad on a grass-blade – beautiful with orange, black, dun, and blue in stripes and spots.

Nine-angled coltsfoot leaves begin to show; as a rule, after the flowers.

Always a sweet tender ending to the lark's song, as he pauses in his fall to the sward, 'hear it – hear it – hear it'.

A richness, now first felt, in the atmosphere, as if the sun drew fragrances from the earth.

The grass fairly ripples with the sweet small life of creatures in shining mail – flies and beetles.

Tortoise-shell butterfly at the coltsfoot blossom; but he would not touch it when gently placed between the leaves of a book – though bees will follow a garland into a house.

March 22 Peewits always alight with slowly closing wings, as if conscious of grace and colour; so, too, gulls settling in the sea.

March 23 Nest of five thrush's eggs; date of first laying – 19th.

Willows and crab-trees nearly in full leaf at Coate.

Wood anemones, delicately flush, blossom at Burderop.

Hazels coming into leaf.

Flags show a foot above the water of the brooks.

Hairy bittercress in white flower; petals almost hid by long seed-pods.

March 24 First blossoms of red-robin and cowslip.

Brimstone and peacock butterflies abroad.

Wood-pigeons travelling still in troops.

Fieldfares gather, clattering in the elms at noon, and in the larches with their chains of alternate leaf and flower.

Blackbirds are laying; robins also, and hedge-sparrows.

Tender still air of the twilight; when 'the gentleness of rain was in the wind'.

Bats begin to flit.

March 25 Marsh-marigolds flowering.

March 26 Elms in leaf.
Flowers of wood-sorrel.
Blackthorn bloom.

March 27 An early cuckoo-flower.
Water-crickets stirring.
Purple periwinkle in flower.

March 28 Orchard trees lit with blossom.
Chestnuts coming into leaf.

March 29 Deep-red blossom clusters on the ash; odorous of the earth, or of peeling bark.
Missel-thrushes sing on Wandsworth Common.
Dull, dry days, but calm beautiful nights.

March 30 Gorse-thorns, like fir-needles, form a friable mat of soil on the surface; gorse wastes almost as much as the bramble, in the number of its lesser branches which decay each year.
Poplar-twigs daily more jagged with breaking leaf-buds.

To Gordon Bottomley.
From Bearsted.[5]

March 17th, 1904

It is not easy for me to think about the future, even about next month. It all seems so improbable, and every day seems to be the last, so tired and unconcentrated am I. But now I promise myself that I will leave here for Cartmel on or about April 13 or 11. It is most pleasant to think of, and I thank you and all yours for asking me. You know I am no traveller. I am always wanting to settle down like a tree, for ever. But I have, except my body and clothes, already spent so much life at Cartmel that I feel I am not untrue to myself in taking them as well. You will let me have an hour or two a day for work, won't you? It may be quite unavoidable.

You will find me, I fear, somewhat hard of speech and hearing in the matters you and I really care about. For all my life I have been in the hands of those who care for other and even opposite things; and they have tried to teach me – or by my own imitative nature I have tried to learn – to say much and smartly about things I care nothing for. Perhaps after all they are the only things one can ever sum up and be satisfied with in conversation. And this reminds me of what you say about your own isolated position away from fellow artists. I know well the desire and the apparent need; for work that depends always and entirely upon a man's own invention and impulse always lets the artist down into deep waters of misery now and then, and at those times I have sought the company of many and various men, and yet I have always been alone and unaided; all I have got from them has been experiences which I never use. I have talked my soul empty to a man who (as I had not the wit to discover) answered me with his tongue, not one man but a score: I suppose, as I hinted just now, that my talk was obscure – 'in clouds of glory' if you like. Well, are you likely to have better luck? Your work seems to me to be a far lonelier flower than mine, and other artists might change you or swamp you, but couldn't help you to develop. – I think – for the mere health of the brain, a variety of social intercourse should be good: and I wish you were able to try it. But with me, social intercourse is only an intense form of solitude, and as solitude is what I have to avoid, the means are yet to be found. Does this uncomfortable talk comfort you at all?[. . .]

I am glad you like 'the rapture of the fight'. I hardly ever do. I look forward to writing and look back upon it joyfully as if it were an achievement and not an attempt – very often. But while I write, it is a dull blindfold journey through a strange lovely land: I seem to take what I write from the dictation of someone else. Correction is pleasanter. For then I have glimpses of what I was passing through as I wrote. This very morning the sun was shining, wide and pale gold and warm as it has done for two weeks, and the church bells suddenly beginning to ring were at one with it, a part of Spring, and they set me writing; for I could not go out, as I have a touch of Helen's illness and am over-weak; but at once, I became dull with the dulness of ecstasy (I suppose).

From Beautiful Wales[6]

A FARMHOUSE UNDER A MOUNTAIN

Having passed the ruined abbey and the orchard, I came to a long, low farmhouse kitchen, smelling of bacon and herbs and burning sycamore and ash. A gun, a blunderbuss, a pair of silver spurs, and a golden spray of last year's corn hung over the high mantelpiece and its many brass candlesticks; and beneath was an open fireplace and a perpetual red fire, and two teapots warming, for they had tea for breakfast, tea for dinner, tea for tea, tea for supper, and tea between. The floor was of sanded slate flags, and on them a long many-legged table, an oak settle, a table piano, and some Chippendale chairs. There were also two tall clocks; and they were the most human clocks I ever met, for they ticked with effort and uneasiness: they seemed to think and sorrow over time, as if they caused it, and did not go on thoughtlessly or impudently like most clocks, which are insufferable; they found the hours troublesome and did not twitter mechanically over them; and at midnight the twelve strokes always nearly ruined them, so great was the effort. On the wall were a large portrait of Spurgeon,[7] several sets of verses printed and framed in memory of dead members of the family, an allegorical tree watered by the devil, and photographs of a bard and of Mr Lloyd George. There were about fifty well-used books near the fire, and two or three men smoking, and one man reading some serious book aloud, by the only lamp; and a white girl was carrying out the week's baking, of large loaves, flat fruit tarts of blackberry, apple, and whinberry, plain golden cakes, large soft currant biscuits, and curled oat cakes. And outside, the noises of a west wind and a flooded stream, the whimper of an otter, and the long, slow laugh of an owl; and always silent, but never forgotten, the restless, towering outline of a mountain.

The fire was – is – of wood, dry oak-twigs of last spring, stout ash sticks cut this morning, and brawny oak butts grubbed from the copse years after the tree was felled. And I remember how we built it up one autumn, when the heat and business of the day had almost let it die.

We had been out all day, cutting and binding the late corn. At one moment we admired the wheat straightening in the sun after drooping in rain, with grey heads all bent one way over the luminous amber stalks, and at last leaning and quivering like runners about to start or like a wind made visible. At another moment we admired the gracious groups of sheaves in pyramids made by our own hands, as we sat and drank our buttermilk or ale, and ate bread and cheese or chwippod (the harvesters' stiff pudding of raisins, rice, bread, and fresh milk) among the furze mixed with bramble and fern at the edge of the field. Behind us was a place given over to blue scabious flowers, haunted much by blue butterflies of the same hue; to cross-leaved heath and its clusters of close, pensile ovals, of a perfect white that blushed towards the sun; to a dainty embroidery of tormentil shining with unvaried gold; and to tall, purple loose-strife, with bees at it, dispensing a thin perfume of the kind that all fair living things, plants or children, breathe.

What a thing it is to reap the wheat with your own hands, to thresh it with the oaken flail in the misty barn, to ride with it to the mill and take your last trout while it is ground, and then to eat it with no decoration of butter, straight from the oven! There is nothing better, unless it be to eat your trout with the virgin appetite which you have won in catching it. But in the field, we should have been pleased with the plainest meal a hungry man can have, which is, I suppose, barley bread and a pale 'double Caermarthen' cheese, which you cut with a hatchet after casting it on the floor and making it bounce, to be sure that it is a double Caermarthen. And yet I do not know. For even a Welsh hymnist of the eighteenth century, in translating 'the increase of the fields', wrote avidly of 'wheaten bread', so serious was his distaste for barley bread. But it was to a meal of wheaten bread and oat cake, and cheese and onions and cucumber, that we came in, while the trembling splendours of the first stars shone, as if they also were dewy like the furze. Nothing is to be compared with the pleasure of seeing the stars thus in the east, when most eyes are watching the west, except perhaps to read a fresh modern poet, straight from the press, before any one has praised it, and to know that it is good.

As we sat, some were singing the song 'Morwynion Sir Gaerfyrddin'. Some were looking out at the old hay waggon before the gate.

Fine grass was already growing in corners of the wrecked hay waggon. Two months before, it travelled many times a day between the rick and the fields. Swallow was in the shafts while it carried all the village children to the field, as it had done some sixty years ago, when the village wheelwright helped God to make it. The waggoner lifted them out in clusters; the haymakers loaded silently; the waggon moved along the roads between the swathes; and, followed by children who expected another ride, and drawn by Swallow and Darling, it reached the rick that began to rise, like an early church, beside the elms. But hardly had it set out for another load than Swallow shied; an axle splintered and tore and broke in two, near the hub of one wheel, which subsided so that a corner of the waggon fell askew into the tussocks, and the suspended horse-shoe dropped from its place. There the mare left it, and switched her black tail from side to side of her lucent, nut-brown haunches, as she went.

All day the waggon was now the children's own. They climbed and slid and made believe that they were sailors, on its thin, polished timbers. The grass had grown up to it, under its protection. Before it fell, the massive wheels and delicate curved sides had been so fair and strong that no one thought of its end. Now, the exposed decay raised a smile at its so recent death. No one gave it a thought, except, perhaps, as now, when the September evening began, and one saw it on this side of the serious, dark elms, when the flooded ruts were gleaming, and a cold light fell over it from a tempestuous sky, and the motion-less air was full of the shining of moist quinces and yellow fallen apples in long herbage; and, far off, the cowman let a gate shut noisily; the late swallows and early bats mingled in flight; and, under an oak, a tramp was kindling his fire . . .

Suddenly in came the dog, one of those thievish, lean, swift demi-wolves, that appear so fearful of meeting a stranger, but when he has passed, turn and follow him. He shook himself, stepped into the hearth and out and in again. With him was one whose red face and shining eyes and crisped hair were the decoration with which the wind invests his true lovers. A north wind had risen and given the word, and he repeated it: let us have a fire.

So one brought hay and twigs, another branches and knot-ted logs, and another the bellows. We made an edifice worthy of fire and kneeled with the dog to watch light changing into heat, as the spirals of sparks arose. The pyre was not more beautiful which turned to roses round the innocent maiden for whom it was lit; nor that more wonderful round which, night after night in the west, the clouds are solemnly ranged, waiting for the command that will tell them whither they are bound in the dark blue night. We became as the logs, that now and then settled down (as if they wished to be comfortable) and sent out, as we did words, some bristling sparks of satisfaction. And hardly did we envy then the man who lit the first fire and saw his own stupendous shadow in cave or wood and called it a god. As we kneeled, and our sight grew pleasantly dim, were we looking at fireborn recollections of our own childhood, wondering that such a childhood and youth as ours could ever have been; or at a golden age that never was? . . . The light spelt the titles of the books for a moment, and the bard read Spenser aloud, as if forsooth a man can read poetry in company round such a fire. So we pelted him with tales and songs . . .

And one of the songs was 'The Maid of Landybie', by the bard, Watcyn Wyn. Here follows the air, and a translation which was made by an English poet. The naïveté of the original has troubled him, and the Welsh stanza form has driven him to the use of rhymeless feminine endings; but I think that his version will, with the air, render not too faintly the song I heard.

THE MAID OF LANDYBIE

Air: Y Ferch o Blwyf Penderyn

I love a maid of Landybie
And it is she who loves me too.
Of all the women of Caermarthen
None is so fair as she, I know.
White and red are her cheeks' young roses,
The tints all blended mistily;
She is the only maid I long for,
And she will have no lad but me.

I love one maid of Landybie
And she too loves but one, but one;
The tender girl remains my faithful,
Pure of heart, a bird in tone.
Her beauty and her comely bearing
Have won my love and life and care,
For there is none in all the kingdoms
Like her, so blushing, kind, and fair.

While there is lime in Craig-y-Ddinas;
While there is water in Pant-y-Llyn;
And while the waves of shining Loughor
Walk between these hills and sing;
While there's a belfry in the village
Whose bells delight the country nigh,
The dearest maid of Landybie
Shall have her name held sweet and high.

LLEWELYN, THE BARD

And here is one of his imitative songs, reduced to its lowest
terms by a translator:[8]

She is dead, Eluned,
Whom the young men and the old men
And the old women and even the young women
Came to the gates in the village
To see, because she walked as beautifully as a heifer.

She is dead, Eluned,
Who sang the new songs
And the old; and made the new
Seem old, and the old
As if they were just born and she had christened them.

She is dead, Eluned,
Whom I admired and loved,
When she was gathering red apples,
When she was making bread and cakes,
When she was smiling to herself alone and not thinking
    of me.

She is dead, Eluned,
Who was part of Spring,
And of blue Summer and red Autumn,
And made the Winter beloved;
She is dead, and these things come not again.

APRIL

We had talked long into the night, and then as sleep came, out
of this darkness peered the early timorous warble of a black-
bird, and gradually all the birds in orchard, hedge, and wood
made a thick mist or curtain of innumerable and indistinguish-
able notes through which still crept the bolder note of that
same nearest blackbird. As the night lost its heaviness, though
not its stillness, the continuous mist of songs grew thicker and
seemed to produce or to be one with the faint darkness which
so soon was to be light. It seemed also to be making the land-
scape which I saw being made, when I looked out. There, was
the side of the hill; there the larches, the dark hedges, and the
lingering snow and the orchard: they were what I had seen
before, but changed and increased; and very subtle, plaintive,
menacing, vast, was the work, though when the light had fully
come, once more the larches, the hedges, and the orchard were
as if they had never been sung to a new order of beauty by the

mist of songs, and yet not the same, any more than a full coffin is the same as the lips and eyes and hands and hair, of which it contains all that we did not love. And still there were many songs; but you could tell who sung each of them, if you wished.

To Gordon Bottomley.
From The Weald.

July 24th, 1905

Helen has just gone away for two or three days with Mervyn and left me with Bronwen and myself.[9] I have lately been more miserable than ever in the intervals of entertaining numerous acquaintances and friends. [. . .] And now I have no money in the Bank, and I have laudanum inside me, and it is a fine sad evening, and I can no longer read a German on *The Development of the Feeling of Nature* and a Frenchman on Charles Lamb.

If only somebody who wanted to, would look after me – somebody strong and not too tender. For I am sure I get worse and worse (NB I haven't taken opium for several months until today) and no week – hardly a day – passes without my thinking that I must soon cease to try to work and live. But I am so irritable and restless that even if I go so far as to resolve not to work, in a few hours, out of sheer ennui I get down a review book and a little later perhaps write a review. If I have now and then ten oblivious minutes at sunset or midnight, I am very lucky: for at all other times, whether I am reading or writing or talking or trying to sleep, I am plagued by such little thoughts as how much I shall earn this week or what train I shall catch tomorrow or whether I shall have my letters by the next post, and such big thoughts as whether any thing is worth while, whether I shall ever again have hope or joy or enthusiasm or love, whether I could for any length of time be quite sensible in taking food, sleep, drink, etc., and whether if I could be I should be any better. You see – I must have some motive and to be honest, my responsibility to Helen and Mervyn and the dear and joyful Bronwen is not a motive. I must believe in myself or forget myself and I cannot. I get more and more self-conscious every day – of the little good in myself and work – of the much bad – of the futility of reviewing – of my insolence in Reviewing any book – of my way of doing things – my way of speaking – my very attitudes, dress, expression – Shall I ever have the relief of true and thorough insanity? Oh, for some one to help, instead of being surrounded by people who see that I have many things and am some things which they would like and therefore conclude that I ought to be happy or that I am 'affected' or wildly exaggerating, just because I can jest and walk a good many miles and do a good deal of work. But do not think I am foolish enough to believe that anyone will or could be expected to save me.

From The Heart of England[10]

LEAVING TOWN

Sunday afternoon had perfected the silence of the suburban street. Every one had gone into his house to tea; none had yet started for church or promenade; the street was empty, except for a white pigeon that pecked idly in the middle of the road and once leaned upon one wing, raised the other so as to expose her tender side and took the rain deliciously; so calm and unmolested was the hour.

The houses were in unbroken rows and arranged in pairs, of which one had a bay window on the ground floor and one had not. Some had laurels in front; some had names. But they were so much alike that the street resembled a great storehouse where yards of goods, all of one pattern, are exposed, all with that painful lack of character that makes us wish to rescue one and take it away and wear it, and soil it, and humanize it rapidly.

Soon a boy of nine years old came out of one house and

stood at the gate. At first he moved briskly and looked in every direction as if expecting to see someone whom he knew; but in a little while he paused and merely looked towards the pigeon, so fixedly that perhaps he saw it not. The calm silenced him, took him into its bosom, yet also depressed him. Had he dared, he would have shouted or run; he would have welcomed the sound of a piano, of a dog barking, of a starling coldly piping. While he still paused an old man rounded the corner of the street and came down in the roadway towards him.

The old man was small and straight, and to his thin figure the remains of a long black coat and grey trousers adhered with singular grace. You could not say that he was well dressed, but rather that he was in the penultimate stage of a transformation like Dryope's or Daphne's, which his pale face had not altogether escaped. His neglected body seemed to have grown this grey rind that flapped like birch bark. Had he been born in it the clothing could not have been more apt. The eye travelled from these clothes with perfect satisfaction – as from a branch to its fruit – to his little crumpled face and its partial crust of hair. Yet he walked. One hand on a stick, the other beneath a basket of watercress, he walked with quick, short steps, now and then calling out unexpectedly, as if in answer to a question, 'Watercresses!' No one interrupted him. He was hungry; he nibbled at pieces of cress with his gums, and so kneaded his face as if it had been dough. He passed the boy; he stooped, picked up a rotten apple, and in the act frightened the pigeon, which rose, as the boy saw, and disappeared.

The boy raised his head and watched. He saw the old man – as in an eloquent book and not with his own usually indolent eyes – and thought him a traveller. Yes! that was how a traveller looked – a strange, free man, hatless, walking in the road, ignoring puddles, talking carelessly to himself; from the country – such was his stick and the manner of his clothes; with something magnificent and comely in his hoariness; sleeping the boy knew not where, perhaps not at all, but going on and on, certainly not to church, but perhaps to places with mountains, icebergs, houses in the branches of trees, great waters, camels, monkeys, crocodiles, parrots, ivory, cannibals, curved swords. And the boy flushed to think that the quiet street was an avenue to all the East, the Pole, the Amazon . . . to dark men who wondered about the sunlight, the wind, the rain, and whence they came . . . to towns set down in the heart of forests and lonely as ships at sea. But whatever he was, the old man was more blessed than any one whom the boy had ever seen.

The old man was gone out of sight. The boy started to run and follow; but he stumbled and fell and uttered his intolerable longing in a fit of grave tears, while the street began to be bright and restless again.

I thought to follow him myself. But the next day I was still in that grey land, looking at it from a railway train.

The hundreds of streets parallel or at angles with the railway – some exposing flowery or neglected back gardens, bedrooms half seen through open windows, pigeon houses with pigeons bowing or flashing in flight, all manner of domesticities surprised – others a line of shop fronts and gorgeous or neat or faded women going to and fro – others, again, a small space that had been green and was still grassy under its encumbrance of dead trees, scaffolding, and bricks – some with inns having good names – these streets are the strangest thing in the world. They have never been discovered. They cannot be classified. There is no tradition about them. Poets have not shown how we are to regard them. They are to us as mountains were in the Middle Ages, sublime, difficult, immense; and yet so new that we have inherited no certain attitude towards them, of liking or dislike. They suggest so much that they mean nothing at all. The eye strains at them as at Russian characters which are known to stand for something beautiful or terrible; but there is no translator: it sees a thousand things which at the moment of seeing are significant, but they obliterate one another. More than battlefield or library, they are dense with human life. They are as multitudinous and painful and unsatisfying as the stars. They propose themselves as a problem to the mind, only a little less so at night when their surfaces hand the mind on to the analogies of sea waves or large woods.

Nor at the end of my journey was the problem solved. It was a land of new streets and half-built streets and devastated lanes.

Ivied elm trunks lay about with scaffold poles, uprooted shrubs were mingled with bricks, mortar with turf, shining baths and sinks and rusty fire grates with dead thistles and thorns. Here and there a man in a silk hat or a little girl with neat ankles and high brown boots stepped amidst the deeply rutted mud. An artist who wished to depict the Fall, and some sympathy with it in the face of a ruined Eden, might have had little to do but copy an acre of the surviving fields.

A north wind swept the land clean. In the hedges and standing trees, it sobbed at intervals like a bitter child forcing himself to cry; in the windowless houses it made a merrier sound like a horn. It drove workmen and passers-by to spend as much time as possible in 'The King's Head', and there the medley of the land was repeated. Irish and Cockney accents mingled with Kentish; American would not have been out of place. No one seemed to dislike the best room in the inn, where there was a piano, a coloured picture of Lord Roberts and of the landlord as a youth, an old print of snipe-shooting, some gaudy and fanciful advertisements of spirits, and no fire to warm the wallpaper which had once had a pattern characteristic of poor bathrooms.

I felt a kind of exalted and almost cheerful gloom as I stepped out and saw that it was raining and would go on raining. O exultation of the sorrowful heart when Nature also seems to be sorrowing! What strange merriment is this which the dejected mind and the wind in the trees are making together! What high lavolt of the shuffling heels of despair! As two lovers wounded and derided will make of their complainings one true joy that triumphs, so will the concealing rain and the painful mind.

The workmen had gone; faint lights began to appear through the blinds of the finished houses. There was no sunset, no change from day to night. The end of the day was like what is called a natural death in bed; an ill-laid fire dies thus. With the darkness a strange spirit of quiet joy appeared in the air. Old melodies floated about it on that mourning wind. The rain formed a mist and a veil over the skeletons round about, but it revealed more than it took away; Nature gained courage in the gloom. The rain soothed her as it will wash away tears on the lonely hills. The trees were back in Eden again. They were as before in their dim, stately companies. The bad walking was no annoyance. Once I came upon a line of willows above dead reeds that used to stand out by a pond as the first notice to one walking out of London that he was in the country at last; they were unchanged; they welcomed and encouraged once more. The lighted windows in the mist had each a greeting; they were as the windows we strain our eyes for as we descend to them from the hills of Wales or Kent; like those, they had the art of seeming a magical encampment among the trees, brave, cheerful lights which men and women kept going amidst the dense and powerful darkness. The thin, incompleted walls learned a venerable utterance.

The night grew darker. The sound of pianos mingled with the wind. I could not see the trees – I was entrapped in a town where I had once known nothing but fields and one old house, stately and reticent among the limes. A sense of multitude surged about and over me – of multitudes entirely unknown to me – collected by chance – mere numbers – human faces that were at that moment expressing innumerable strange meanings with which I had nothing to do. Had I said to one who entered an adjacent house that I was retrospectively a lodger of his, since I had once hidden for half a day in the hollow oak in his front garden, he would have stared. Here were people living in no ancient way. That they supped and slept in their houses was all that was clear to me. I wondered why – why did they go on doing these things? Did they ever sit up thinking and thinking, trying to explain to themselves why they were there, and then fall asleep in their chairs and awake still with the same goalless thought and so go shivering to bed? The window lights were now as strange to me and as fascinating as, to a salmon swaying by a bridge, the lights and faces of the poachers on the bank. As if it were new came back to me the truism that most men are prisons to themselves. Here was a city imprisoned deep, and I as deep, in the rain. Was there, perhaps, joy somewhere on account of those thousands of prisoners and lighted windows?

APPLE BLOSSOM

It is but an acre or two of sweet, undulating pasture, bounded
on two sides by tall hawthorn hedges, on the third by an ash
copse, on the other by an orchard of apple trees. The grass is
pure green, revealing here and there a purple orchis or dog
violet or blue self-heal, except where the crystal brook rushes
through it and gathers white and gold about its banks. Here no
shadow falls, or if it does the dew and blossoms break it up.
The leaning and interwoven apple trees make a white and
wine-filled sky by their dense clots of bloom. The swallows
embroider the air with their songs and their blue flight. A farm-
house walls are dusky red between the trunks. Overhead, the
dim blue sky lets a white cloud roll out at intervals like lilies
from a pool. And the blackbird perfects his song indolently; the
thrush thinks clearly, sharply aloud, with nothing long drawn
out; and the willow wren happily complains for ever – a voice
that has wings and must revolve continually through the land
to express for one or another the vague pains or pleasures of a
spring day.

To Gordon Bottomley.
From Minsmere.

February 26th, 1908

I laughed at your trying to find what Wagner and Beethoven
might have, out of their abundance, in common with me. But
my admirer, tho not a great intellect, did not link us except as
'influences' on him. I wish I believed you when you say I can
touch natural things 'with a large simple emotion'; but I can't,
knowing how I go about the world with a worried heart and a
note book . . . I believe you are right in preferring your own
aim and method to that of Conrad and others, simply because

you use verse, and hitherto prose has practically never been capable of transmuting matter, though it can help the mind of the reader to transmutations (as in De Quincey, Meredith and I forget). My mind at any rate refuses to be illuded by anything but verse – excepting a few short passages of prose. Poetry in verse is at one with the tides and the pulse; prose is chaos cut up into beds and borders and fountains and rusticwork like a garden. A merely great intellect can produce great prose, but not poetry, not one line. As you know! Forgive the commonplaces as of a ½d paper.

From The South Country[11]

'I TRAVEL ARMED ONLY WITH MYSELF'

The chief roads make south, south-east, south-west and west from London; almost the only road going east and west and not touching London is the old road known between Winchester and Canterbury as the Pilgrims' Way.

Most of the towns are small market towns, manufacturing chiefly beer; or they are swollen, especially in the neighbourhood of London, as residential quarters on lines of railway or as health and pleasure resorts on the sea. But any man used to maps will be wiser on these matters in an hour than I am. For what I have sought is quiet and as complete a remoteness as possible from towns, whether of manufactures, of markets or of cathedrals. I have used a good many maps in my time, largely to avoid the towns; but I confess that I prefer to do without them and to go, if I have some days before me, guided by the hills or the sun or a stream – or, if I have one day only, in a rough circle, trusting, by taking a series of turnings to the left or a series to the right, to take much beauty by surprise and to return at last to my starting-point. On a dull day or cloudy night I have often no knowledge of the points of the compass.

I never go out to see anything. The sign-boards thus often astonish me. I wish, by the way, that I had noted down more of the names on the sign-boards at the cross-roads. There is a wealth of poetry in them, as in that which points – by a ford, too – first, to Poulner and Ringwood; second, to Gorley and Fordingbridge; third, to Linwood and Broomy: and another pointing to Fordingbridge, to Ringwood, and to Cuckoo Hill and Furze Hill: and another in the parish of Pentlow, pointing to Foxearth and Sudbury, to Cavendish and Clare, and to Belchamps and Yeldham. Castles, churches, old houses, of extraordinary beauty or interest, have never worn out any of my shoe leather except by accident. I like to come upon them – usually without knowing their names and legends – but do not lament when chance takes me a hundred times out of their way. Nor have I ever been to Marlow to think about Shelley, or to Winterslow for Hazlitt's sake; and I enter Buriton many times without remembering Gibbon. They would move me no more than the statue of a man and a fat horse (with beribboned tail) which a grateful countryside erected to William III in the market square at Petersfield. I prefer any country church or chapel to Winchester or Chichester or Canterbury Cathedral, just as I prefer 'All round my hat', or 'Somer is icumen in', to Beethoven. Not that I dislike the cathedrals, or that I do not find many pleasures amongst them. But they are incomprehensible and not restful. I feel when I am within them that I know why a dog bays at the moon. They are much more difficult or, rather I am more conscious in them of my lack of comprehension, than the hills or the sea; and I do not like the showmen, the smell and look of the museum, the feeling that it is admiration or nothing, and all the well-dressed and fly-blown people round about. I sometimes think that religious architecture is a dead language, majestic but dead, that it never was a popular language. Have some of these buildings lived too long, been too well preserved, so as to oppress our little days with too permanent an expression of the passing things? The truth is that, though the past allures me, and to discover a cathedral for myself would be an immense pleasure, I have no historic sense and no curiosity. I mention these trivial things because they may be important to those who read what I am paid for writing. I have read a great deal of history – in fact, a university gave me a degree out of respect for my apparent knowledge of history – but I have forgotten it all, or it has got into my blood and is present in me in a form which defies evocation or analysis. But as far as I can tell I am pure of history. Consequently I prefer the old brick houses round the cathedral, and that avenue of archaic bossy limes to the cathedral itself with all its turbulent quiet and vague antiquity. The old school also close at hand! I was there after the end of the term once, and two boys were kicking a football in a half-walled court; it was a bright, cold, windy April afternoon; and the ancient brick was penetrated with their voices and the sound of the ball, and I thought there could be nothing lovelier than that court, the pleasant walls, and the broad playing fields in sight of a smooth noble hill and a temple of dark firs on top. I was not thinking of Winchester or of any one older than the fondest son of that 'mother, more than mother', and little of him; but was merely caught up by and with the harmony of man and his work, of two children playing, and of the green downs and windy sky.

And so I travel, armed only with myself, an avaricious and often libertine and fickle eye and ear, in pursuit, not of knowledge, not of wisdom, but of one whom to pursue is never to capture. Politics, the drama, science, racing, reforms and preservations, divorces, book clubs – nearly everything which the average (oh! mysterious average man, always to be met but never met) and the superior and the intelligent man is thinking of, I cannot grasp; my mind refuses to deal with them; and when they are discussed I am given to making answers like 'In Kilve there is no weathercock.' I expect there are others as unfortunate, superfluous men such as the sanitation, improved housing, police, charities, medicine of our wonderful civilization saves from the fate of the cuckoo's foster-brothers. They will perhaps follow my meanders and understand. The critics also will help. They will misunderstand – it is their trade. How well they know what I ought, or at least ought not, to do. I must, they have said, avoid 'the manner of the worst oleographs'; must not be 'affected', though the recipe is not to be had; must beware of 'over-excitation of the colour sense'. In slow course of years we acquire a way of expression, hopelessly inadequate, as we plainly see when looking at the methods of great poets, of beautiful women, of athletes, of politicians, but still gradually as fitted to the mind as an old walking-stick to the hand that has worn and been worn by it, full of our weakness as of our strength, of our blindness as of our vision – the man himself, the poor man it may be. And I live by writing, since it is impossible to live by not writing in an age not of gold but of brass.

BEECHES[12]

The beeches on the beech-covered hills roar and strain as if they would fly off with the hill, and anon they are as meek as a great horse leaning his head over a gate. If there is a misty day there is one willow in a coombe lifting up a thousand silver catkins like a thousand lamps, when there is no light elsewhere. Another day, a wide and windy day, is the jackdaw's, and he goes straight and swift and high like a joyous rider crying aloud on an endless savannah, and, underneath, the rippled pond is as bright as a peacock, and millions of beech leaves drive across the open glades of the woods, rushing to their Acheron.

A RETURN TO NATURE

I turn into my next inn with unusual hopes. For it was here some years ago that I met for the first time a remarkable man.[13] It was nine o'clock on a late July evening, and the haymakers, only just set free, came stamping into the bar. The last wagon-load stopped at the door while the red-whiskered carter stood, one hand on the latch, and drank his pint before leading his horses into the stall. After the haymakers, in their pale corduroys and dirty white slops, came a tall, spare, shock-headed man, not recently shaved, dressed in grey – grey coat, grey breeches and stockings, and a tall, hard felt hat that was old and grey. He called for sixpenny ale, and wiping the hay dust from his neck sat down beside me.

No, he is not here to-day. Perhaps he will never get out of London again.

I asked him the way to the nearest village and whether a bed was to be had there. He answered that it was some way off – paused, looked at me, drank from his tankard – and added in a lower voice that he would be glad if I would come and share his place. Such an unusual invitation enforced assent.

A quarter of a mile down the next by-way he opened a little oaken gate that slammed after us, and there, in a corner of a small, flat field, was his sleeping place, under an oak. Would I care to join him in fried bacon and broad beans and tea at six next morning?

He lit a wisp of hay and soon had a fire burning, and brought over some hay and sacks for the second bed. The lights of the farm-house shone on the other side of the little field behind lilac bushes. The farmhouse pump gave out a cry like a guinea fowl for a few minutes. Then the lights went out. I asked the name of the farm and he told me.

'I come here almost every summer for the haymaking,' he said, and detecting my surprise that it was not his first year of haymaking, he continued:

'It is my tenth summer, to be exact.'

He was a man of hardly over thirty, and I noticed that his hands, though small and fine, were rough and warty and dark. Thoughtlessly I remarked that he must find the winter hard if he travelled like this all the year round.

'Yes,' he said, with a sigh, 'it is, and that is why I go back in the winter; at least partly why.'

'Go back—?'

'Yes, to London.'

I was still perplexed. He had the air of a town-bred man of the clerkly class, but no accent, and I could not think what he did in London that was compatible with his present life.

'Are you a Londoner, then?'

'Yes, and no. I was born at the village of — in Caermarthen-shire. My father was a clerk in a coal merchant's office of the neighbouring town. But he thought to better himself, worked hard in the evenings and came to London, when I was seven, for a better-paid post. We lived in Wandsworth in a small street newly built. I went to a middle-class school close by until I was sixteen, and then I went into a silk merchant's office. My father died soon after. He had never been strong, and from the first year's work in the city, I have heard my mother say, he was a doomed man. He made no friends. While I was young he gave up all his spare time to me and was happy, wheeling me, my mother walking alongside, out into the country on every Sunday that was not soaking wet, and nearly every Saturday afternoon, too.

'It was on one of these excursions, when they had left me to myself a little while to talk more gravely than they usually did when we were out like that, that there was suddenly opened before me – like a yawning pit, yet not only beneath me but on every side – infinity, endless time, endless space; it was thrust upon me, I could not grasp it, I only closed my eyes and shuddered and I knew that not even my father could save me from it, then in a minute it was gone. To a more blessed child some fair or imposing vision might have risen up out of the deep and given him a profounder if a sadder eye for life and the world. How unlike it was to the mystic's trance, feeling out with infinite soul to earth and stars and sea and remote time and recognizing his oneness with them! To me, but later than that, this occasionally recurring experience was as an intimation of the endless pale road, before and behind, which the soul has to travel: it was a terror that enrolled me as one of the helpless, superfluous ones of the earth.

'I was their only child that lived, and my father's joy in me was very great, equalled only by his misery at the life which he had to lead and which he foresaw for me. He used to read to me, waking me up for the purpose sometimes when he reached home late, or if he did not do that rousing me an hour before breakfast. His favourite books were *The Compleat Angler* and *Lavengro*, the poems of Wordsworth, the diaries of Thoreau and the *Natural History of Selborne*. I remember crying – when I was twelve – with despair of human nature's fickleness to think that White, even though he was an old man, could have it in his heart to write that farewell to natural history at the end of his last letter to Barrington. My father read these books to me several times in a sad, hoarse voice – as it seemed to me, though when he paused he was happy enough – which I had often great trouble to endure as I got older and able and willing to read for myself. So full was I of a sense of the real wild country which I had never seen – the Black Mountains of Caermarthen I hardly recalled – that I became fanciful, and despised the lavish creeper that hung like a costly dress over the fence between our garden and the next, because the earth it grew in was not red earth but a black pasty compound, full of cinders and mortar and decayed rags and kittens. I used to like to go to the blacksmith's to smell the singeing hoof and to the tram-stables and smell the horses, and see the men standing about in loose shirts, hanging braces, bare arms, clay pipes, with a sort of free look that I could not see elsewhere. The navvies at work in the road or on the railway line were a tremendous pleasure, and I noticed that the clerks waiting for their trains in the morning loved to watch these hulking free and easy men doing something that looked as if it mattered, not like their own ledger work and so on. I had the same sort of pleasure looking up the street that rose from east to west and seeing the sun set between the two precipices of brick wall at the top; it was as if a gate opened there and through it all the people and things that saddened me had disappeared and left me to myself; it was like the pit, too, that opened before me as a little child.

'My father died of consumption. I was then just able to earn my own living, so I was left in lodgings and my mother returned to Wales. I worked hard at figures; at least I went early and stayed late and never stopped to talk to the others; yet I made frequent mistakes, and the figures swam in a mist of American rivers and English waterfalls and gypsy camps, so that it was a wonder I could ever see my Thoreau and Wordsworth and Borrow without these figures. Fancy men adopting as a cry the "right to work"! Apparently they are too broken-spirited to think of a right to live, and would be content only to work. It is not wonderful that with such a cry they do very little. Men cannot fight hard for the "right to work" as I did. My office was at the bottom of a pit. The four sides of the pit were walls with many windows, and I could hear voices speaking in the rooms behind and the click of typewriters, but could not see into them. Only for two or three days in June could I see the sun out of the pit. But in the hot days blue-bottles buzzed on my panes and I took care of them until one by one they lay dead upon the window ledge. There were no spiders and they seemed to have a good life. Sparrows sometimes flew up and down the pit, and once for a week I had the company of a black-and-white pigeon. It sat day after day in a hole in the opposite wall until it died and fell on to the paved yard below. The clouds sailed over the top of the pit. Sea-gulls flew over, all golden-winged, in October afternoons. I liked the fog when all the lights were lit, and though we did not know one another in the pit we seemed to keep one another company. But I liked the rain best of all. It used to splash down from all sides and make a country noise, and I looked up and saw the quaint cowls sitting like cats on the chimney-pots, and had ridiculous fancies that took me far away for a second or two.

'The worst time of all was two or three years after my father's death. I spent most of my poor earnings on clothes; I took the trouble to talk and smoke and think as much as possible like the other nine young men in the railway carriage that took me into the city; I learned their horrible, cowardly scorn for those who were poor or outlandish, and for all things that were not like those in their own houses or in those of the richer people of their acquaintance or envy. We were slaves, and we gilded our collars.'

'But the journalist and hack writer,' said I, 'is worse off. At least your master only asked for your dregs. The hack writer is asked to give everything that can be turned into words at short notice, and so the collar round his neck is never taken off as yours was between six in the afternoon and nine in the morning.'

'Ah, but it is open to you to do good or bad. We could only do bad. All day we were doing things which we did not understand, which could not in any way concern us, which had nothing to do with what we had been taught at school, had read in books or had heard from our fathers and mothers. When he was angry the head of the firm used to say we had better take care or a machine would supersede us in ten years instead of twenty. We had been driven out of life into a corner in an underground passage where everything was unnecessary that did not help us to be quick at figures, or taking down letters from dictation, or neat in dress and obedient to the slaves who were set over us. When we were out of the office we could do nothing which unfitted us for it. The head of the firm used to say that we were each "playing a part, however humble, in the sublime machine of modern civilization, that not one of us was unnecessary, and that we must no more complain or grow restive than does the earth because it is one of the least elements in this majestic universe." We continued to be neat when we were away from the office, we were disobedient to everything and everybody else that was not armed with the power of taking away our bread – to the old, the poor, the children, the women, the ideas which we had never dreamed of, and that came among us as a white blackbird comes in the winter to a barbarous parish where keeper and gardener and farmer go out with their guns and stalk it from hedge to hedge until, starved and conspicuous and rather apart from its companions, it falls to their beastly shot and is sold to one of the gentry who puts it into a glass case.

'Sometimes on a Saturday or Sunday I broke away in a vague unrest, and walked alone to the pretty places where my father and mother had taken me as a little boy. Most of them I had not seen for five or six years. My visits were often formal. I walked out and was glad to be back to the lights of the street, the strong tea, the newspaper and the novel. But one day I went farther than usual to a wood where we used to go without interference and, after finding all the blackbirds' and thrushes' and robins' nests within reach, boil a kettle and have tea. I had never in that wood seen any man or woman except my father and mother; never heard a voice except theirs – my father perhaps reading Wordsworth aloud – and the singing birds' and the moorhens' in the pond at the edge; it used to shut out everything but what I had learned to love most, sunshine and wind and flowers and their love. When I saw it again I cried: I really could not help it. For a road had been made alongside of it, and the builder's workmen going to and fro had made a dozen gaps in the hedge and trodden the wood backward and forward and broken down the branches and made it noisome. Worse than all, the field, the golden field where I used to lie among the buttercups and be alone with the blue sky – where I first felt the largeness and dearness and nearness of the blue sky as a child of eight and put up my hand in my delight to draw it through the soft blue substance that seemed so near – the field was enclosed, a chapel built; it was a cemetery for all the unknown herd, strange to one another, strange to every one else, that filled the new houses spreading over the land.

'At first I was for running away at once. But the sight made me faint-hearted and my legs dragged, and it was all I could do to get home – I mean, to my lodgings.

'However, I was quite different after that. I was ashamed of my ways, and now spent all my spare time and money in going out into the country as far as possible, and reading the old books and the new ones that I could hear of in the same spirit. I lived for these things. It was now that I knew my slavery. Everything reminded me of it. The return half of my railway ticket to the country said plainly, "You have got to be back at — not later than 10.39 p.m." Then I used to go a different way back or even walk the whole way to avoid having this thing in my pocket that proclaimed me a slave.'

A RAILWAY CARRIAGE

I left London as quickly as possible. The railway carriage was nearly full of men reading the same newspapers under three or four different names, when a little grizzled and spectacled man of middle age entered – a printer, perhaps – with a twisted face and simple and puzzled expression that probably earned him many a laugh from street-corner boys. As he sat down he recognized a sailor, a tall, ponderous, kind-faced man made in three distinct storeys, who supported his enormous red hands upon knees each fit to have been the mould of a hero's helmet.

'Well I never did, and how are you, Harry?'

They looked at one another kindly but with a question piercing through the kindness and an effort to divine the unknowable without betraying curiosity. The kindness did, in fact, melt away the almost physical obstacle of twenty years spent apart and in ignorance of one another.

'When did you leave the old place?' said the sailor.

'Soon after you did yourself, Harry; just after the shipwreck of the *Wild Swan*; twenty-one, twenty-two – yes, twenty-two years ago.'

'Is it so long? I could have sworn you had that beard when I saw you last', and the sailor looked at him in a way that showed he had already bridged the twenty-two years and knew the man.

'Yes, twenty-two years.'

'And do you ever go back to the old place? How's Charlie Nash, and young Woolford, and the shepherd?'

'Let me see—'

'But how is Maggie Looker?' broke in the sailor upon a genial answer in the bud.

'Oh, didn't you know? She took ill very soon after you went away, and then they thought she was all right again; but they could not quite get rid of the cough, and it got bad in the winter, and all through the spring it was worse.'

'And so she died in the summer.'

'So she did.'

'Oh, Christ! but what times we had.'

And then, in reminiscences fast growing gay – the mere triumph of memory, the being able to add each to the other's store, was a satisfaction – they told the story of a pretty country girl whom they had quarrelled over until she grew too proud for both; how heavy was her hair; how she could run, and nobody was like her for finding a wasps'-nest. Her boldness and carelessness filled them with envy still.

'I reckon we old ones would call her a tomboy now,' said the sailor.

'I should say we would.'

'Now, I wonder what sort of a wife she would have made?'

'Hum, I don't know . . .'

'Do you remember that day her and you and me got lost in the forest?'

'Yes, and we were there all night, and I got a hiding for it.'

'Not Maggie.'

'Not poor Maggie.'

'And when we couldn't see our way any more we lifted her up into that old beech where the green woodpecker's nest was.'

'Yes, and you took off your coat and breeches to cover her up.'

'And so did you, though I reckon one would have been enough now I come to think of it.'

'I don't know about that. But how we did have to keep on the move all night to keep warm.'

'And dared not go very far for fear of losing the tree.'

'And in the morning I wondered what we should do about getting back our clothes.'

'You wanted me to go because my shirt hadn't any holes in it.'

'But we both went together.'

'And, before we had made up our minds which should go first and call, up she starts. Lord, how she did laugh!'

'Ay, she did.'

'And says, "Now, that's all my eye and Betty Martin, boys"; and so did we laugh, and I never felt a bit silly either. She was a good sort of girl, she was. Man and woman, I never met the likes of her, never heard tell of the equal of her,' said the sailor musingly.

'Married, Harry?'

'No, nor likely to be, I don't think. And yourself?'

'Well, I was . . . I married Maggie . . . It was after the first baby . . .'

A small boy in a corner could not get on with his novelette: he stared open-mouthed and open-eyed, now and then unconsciously imitating their faces; or he would correct this mere wonderment and become shy and uncomfortable at the frank ways of these men talking aloud in a crowded carriage, and utterly regardless of others, about private matters.

A trim shop assistant pretended to read about the cricket, but listened and could not conceal his cold contempt for men so sunken as to give themselves away like this.

A dark, thin, genial, pale-faced puritan clerk looked pitifully – with some wrinkles of superiority that asked for recognition from his fellow-passengers – at these *children*, for as such he regarded them, and would not wholly condemn.

Others occasionally jerked out a glance or rolled a leaderless eye or rustled a newspaper without losing the dense veil over their individuality that made them tombs, monuments, not men.

One sat gentle, kindly, stupidly envying these two their spirited free talk, their gestures, the hearty draughts of life which they seemed to have taken.

All were botanists who had heard and spoken words but had no sense of the beauty and life of the flower because fate had refused, or education destroyed, the gift of liberty and of joy.

JUNE

It is curious, too, how many different kinds of Eden or Golden Age Nature has in her gift, as if she silently recorded the backward dreams of each generation and reproduced them for us unexpectedly. It is, for instance, an early morning in July. The cows pour out from the milking-stalls and blot out the smell of dust with their breath in the white road between banks of hazel and thorn. The boy who is driving them to the morning's pasture calls to them monotonously, persuasively, in turn, as each is tempted to crop the roadside sward: 'Wo, Cherry! Now, Dolly! Wo, Fancy! Strawberry! . . . Blanche! . . . Blossom! . . . Cowslip! . . . Rosy! . . . Smut! . . . Come along, Handsome! . . . Wo, Snowdrop! . . . Lily! . . . Darky! . . . Roany! . . . Come along, Annie!' Here the road is pillowed with white aspen-down, there more fragrant than pines with the brown sheddings of yew, and here thick with the dry scent of nettle and cow-parsnip, or glorious in perfect mingling of harebell and foxglove among the bracken and popping gorse on the roadside. The cows turn into the aftermath of the sainfoin, and the long valley echoes to their lowing. After them, up the road, comes a gipsy-cart, and the boy hangs on the gate to see the men and women walking, black-haired, upright, bright-eyed, and on the name-board of the cart the words: 'Naomi Sherwood, Burley, Hampshire.' These things also propose to the roving, unhistoric mind an Eden, one still with us, one that is passing, not, let us hope, the very last.

Some of these scenes, whether often repeated or not, come to have a rich symbolical significance; they return persistently and, as it were, ceremoniously – on festal days – but meaning I know not what. For example, I never see the flowers and scarlet-stained foliage of herb-robert growing out of old stone-heaps by the wayside without a feeling of satisfaction not explained by a long memory of the contrast between the plant and the raw flint; so also with the drenched lilac-bloom leaning out over high walls of unknown gardens; and inland cliffs, covered with beech, jutting out westward into a bottomless valley in the mist of winter twilights, in silence and frost. Something in me belongs to these things, but I hardly think that the mere naming of them will mean anything except to those – many, perhaps – who have experienced the same. A great writer so uses the words of every day that they become a code of his own which the world is bound to learn and in the end take unto itself. But words are no longer symbols, and to say 'hill' or 'beech' is not to call up images of a hill or a beech-tree, since we have so long been in the habit of using the words for beautiful and mighty and noble things very much as a book-keeper uses figures without seeing gold and power. I can, therefore, only try to suggest what I mean by the significance of the plant in the stone-heap, the wet lilac, the misty cliff, by comparing it with that of scenes in books where we recognize some power beyond the particular and personal.[14]

THE END OF SUMMER

All night – for a week – it rains, and at last there is a still morning of mist. A fire of weeds and hedge-clippings in a little flat field is smouldering. The ashes are crimson, and the bluish-white smoke flows in a divine cloudy garment round the boy who rakes over the ashes. The heat is great, and the boy, straight and well made, wearing close gaiters of leather that reach above the knees, is languid at his task, and often leans upon his rake to watch the smoke coiling away from him like a monster reluctantly fettered and sometimes bursting into an anger of sprinkled sparks. He adds some wet hay, and the smoke pours out of it like milky fleeces when the shearer reveals the inmost wool with his shears. Above and beyond him the pale blue sky is dimly white-clouded over beech woods, whose many greens and yellows and yellow-greens are softly touched by the early light which cannot penetrate to the blue caverns of shade underneath. Athwart the woods rises a fount of cottage-smoke from among mellow and dim roofs. Under the smoke and partly scarfed at times by a drift from it is the yellow of sunflower and dahlia, the white of anemone, the tenderest green and palest purple of a thick cluster of autumn crocuses that have broken out of the dark earth and stand surprised, amidst their own weak light as of the underworld from which they have come. Robins sing among the fallen apples, and the cooing of wood-pigeons is attuned to the soft light and the colours of the bowers. The yellow apples gleam. It is the gleam of melting frost. Under all the dulcet warmth of the face of things lurks the bitter spirit of the cold. Stand still for more than a few moments and the cold creeps with a warning and then a menace into the breast. That is the bitterness that makes this morning of all others in the year so mournful in its beauty. The colour and the grace invite to still contemplation and long draughts of dream; the frost compels to motion. The scent is that of wood-smoke, of fruit and of some fallen leaves. This is the beginning of the pageant of autumn, of that gradual pompous dying which has no parallel in human life yet draws us to it with sure bonds. It is a dying of the flesh, and we see it pass through a kind of beauty which we can only call spiritual, of so high and inaccessible a strangeness is it. The sight of such perfection as is many times achieved before the end awakens the never more than lightly sleeping human desire of permanence. Now, now is the hour; let things be thus; thus for ever; there is nothing further to be thought of; let these remain. And yet we have a premonition that remain they must not for more than a little while. The motion of the autumn is a fall, a surrender, requiring no effort, and therefore the mind cannot long be blind to the cycle of things as in the spring it can when the effort and delight of ascension veils the goal and the decline beyond. A few frosts now, a storm of wind and rain, a few brooding mists, and the woods that lately hung dark and massive and strong upon the steep hills are transfigured and have become cloudily light and full of change and ghostly fair; the crowing of a cock in the still misty morning echoes up in the many-coloured trees like a challenge to the spirits of them to come out and be seen, but in vain. For months the woods have been homely and kind, companions and backgrounds to our actions and thoughts, the wide walls of a mansion utterly our own. We could have gone on living with them for ever. We had given up the ardours, the extreme ecstasy of our first bridal affection, but we had not forgotten them. We could not become indifferent to the Spanish chestnut-trees that grow at the top of the steep rocky banks on either side of the road and mingle their foliage overhead. Of all trees well-grown chestnuts are among the most pleasant to look up at. For the foliage is not dense and it is for the most part close to the large boughs, so that the light comes easily down through all the horizontal leaves, and the shape of each separate one is not lost in the multitude, while at the same time the bold twists of the branches are undraped or easily seen through such translucent green. The trunks are crooked, and the handsome deep furrowing of the bark is often spirally cut. The limbs are few and wide apart so as to frame huge delicately lighted and shadowed chambers of silence or of birds' song. The leaves turn all together to a leathern hue, and when they fall stiffen and display their shape on the ground and long refuse to be merged in the dismal trodden hosts. But when the first one floats past the eye and is blown like a canoe over the pond we recover once more our knowledge and fear of Time. All those ladders of goose-grass that scaled the hedges of spring are dead grey; they are still in their places, but they clamber no longer. The chief flower is the yellow bloom set in the dark ivy round the trunks of the ash trees; and where it climbs over the holly and makes a solid sunny wall, and in the hedges, a whole people of wasps and wasp-like flies are always at the bloom with crystal wings, except when a passing shadow disperses them for a moment with one buzz. But these cannot long detain the eye from the crumbling woods in the haze or under the large white clouds – from the amber and orange bracken about our knees and the blue recesses among the distant golden beeches when the sky is blue but beginning to be laden with loose rain-clouds, from the line of leaf-tipped poplars that bend against the twilight sky; and there is no scent of flowers to hide that of dead leaves and rotting fruit. We must watch it until the end, and gain slowly the philosophy or the memory or the forgetfulness that fits us for accepting winter's boon. Pauses there are, of course, or what seem pauses in the declining of this pomp; afternoons when the rooks waver and caw over their beechen town and the pigeons coo content; dawns when the white mist is packed like snow over the vale and the high woods take the level beams and a hundred globes of dew glitter on every thread of the spiders' hammocks or loose perpendicular nets among the thorns, and through the mist rings the anvil a mile away with a music as merry as that of the daws that soar and dive between the beeches and the spun white cloud; mornings full of the sweetness of mushrooms and blackberries from the short turf among the blue scabious bloom and the gorgeous brier; empurpled evenings before frost when the robin sings passionate and shrill and from the garden earth float the smells of a hundred roots with messages of the dark world; and hours full of the thrush's soft November music. The end should come in heavy and lasting rain. At all times I love rain, the early momentous thunderdrops, the perpendicular cataract shining, or at night the little showers, the spongy mists, the tempestuous mountain rain. I like to see it possessing the whole earth at evening, smothering civilizations, taking away from me myself everything except the power to walk under the dark trees and to enjoy as humbly as the hissing grass, while some twinkling house-light or song sung by a lonely man gives a foil to the immense dark force. I like to see the rain making the streets, the railway station, a pure desert, whether bright with lamps or not. It foams off the roofs and trees and bubbles into the water-butts. It gives the grey rivers a dæmonic majesty. It scours the roads, sets the flints moving, and exposes the glossy chalk in the tracks through the woods. It does work that will last as long as the earth. It is about eternal business. In its noise and myriad aspect I feel the mortal beauty of immortal things. And then after many days the rain ceases at midnight with the wind, and in the silence of dawn and frost the last rose of the world is dropping her petals down to the glistering white-ness, and there they rest blood-red on the winter's desolate coast.

HISTORY AND THE PARISH

Some day there will be a history of England written from the point of view of one parish, or town, or great house. Not until there is such a history will all our accumulations of informa-tion be justified. It will begin with a geological picture, something large, clear, architectural, not a mass of insignificant names. It must be imaginative: it might, perhaps, lean some-times upon Mr Doughty's *Dawn in Britain*. The peculiar combination of soil and woodland and water determines the direction and position and importance of the ancient track-ways; it will determine also the position and size of the human settlements. The early marks of these – the old flint and metal implements, the tombs, the signs of agriculture, the encamp-ments, the dwellings – will have to be clearly described and interpreted. Folk-lore, legend, place-names must be learnedly, but bravely and humanly used, so that the historian who has not the extensive sympathy and imagination of a great novelist will have no chance of success. What endless opportunities will he have for really giving life to past times in such matters as the line made by the edge of an old wood with the cultivated land, the shapes of the fields, with their borders of streams or hedge or copse or pond or wall or road, the purpose and interweaving of the roads and footpaths that suggest the great permanent thoughts and the lesser thoughts and dreams of the brain . . . As the historic centuries are reached, the action of great events, battles, laws, roads, invasions, upon the parish – and of the parish upon them – must be shown. Architecture, with many of its local characteristics still to be traced, will speak as a voice out of the stones of castle, church, manor, farm, barn and bridge. The birds and beasts cannot be left out. The names of the local families – gentle and simple – what histories are in them, in the curt parish registers, in tombstones, in the names of fields and houses and woods. Better a thousand errors so long as they are human than a thousand truths lying like broken snail-shells round the anvil of a thrush. If only those poems which are place-names could be translated at last, the pretty, the odd, the romantic, the racy names of copse and field and lane and house. What a flavour there is about the Bassetts, the Boughtons, the Worthys, the Tarrants, Winterbournes, Deverills, Manningfords, the Suttons: what goodly names of the South Country – Woodmansterne, Hollingbourne, Horsmonden, Wolstanbury, Brockenhurst, Caburn, Lydiard Tregoze, Lydiard Millicent, Clevancy, Amesbury, Amberley (I once tried to make a beautiful name and in the end it was Amberley, in which Time had forestalled me); what sweet names Penshurst, Frensham, Firle, Nutley, Appleshaw, Hambledon, Cranbrook, Fordingbridge, Melksham, Lambourn, Draycot, Buscot, Kelmscot, Yatton, Yalding, Downe, Cowden, Iping, Cowfold, Ashe, Liss . . . Then there are the histories of roads. Every traveller in Hampshire remembers the road that sways with airy motion and bird-like curves down from the high land of clay and flint through the chalk to the sand and the river. It doubles round the head of a coombe, and the whole descent is through beech woods uninterrupted and all but impenetrable to the eye above or below except where once or twice it looks through an arrow slit to the blue vale and the castled promontory of Chanctonbury twenty miles south-east. As the road is a mere ledge on the side of a very steep hill the woods below it hurry down to a precipitous pit full of the glimmering, trembling and murmuring of innumerable leaves and no sight or sound of men. It is said to have been made more than half a century ago to take the place of the rash straight coach road which now enters it near its base. A deeply-worn, narrow and disused track joining it more than half-way down suggests that the lower part was made by the widening of an old road; but much of the upper half is new. Certainly the road as it now is, broad and gently bending round the steep coombe, is new, and it was made at the expense of the last of a family which had long owned the manor house near the entrance of the coombe. His were all the hanging beech woods – huge as the sky – upon the hill, and through them the road-makers conducted this noble and pleasant way. But near the top they deviated by a few yards into another estate. The owner would not give way. A lawsuit was begun, and it was not over when the day came for the road to be open for traffic according to the contract or, if not, to pass out of the defaulter's hands. The day passed; the contract was broken; the speculation had failed, and the tolls would never fill the pockets of the lord of the manor. He was ruined, and left his long white house by the rivulet and its chain of pools, his farms and cottages, his high fruit walls, his uncounted beeches, the home of a hundred owls, his Spanish chestnuts above the rocky lane, his horse-chestnut and syca-more stately in groups, his mighty wych-elms, his apple trees and all their mistletoe, his walnut trees, and the long bay of sky that was framed by his tall woods east and north and west.

AN UMBRELLA MAN

[. . .] It seemed that I had come upon the pure wild in this lane, for in a bay of turf alongside the track, just large enough for a hut and thickly sheltered by an oak, though the south-west sun crept in, was a camp. Under the oak and at the edge of the tan-gled bramble and brier and bracken was a low purple light from those woodside flowers, self-heal and wood-betony. A perambulator with a cabbage in it stood at one corner; leaning against it was an ebony-handled umbrella and two or three umbrella-frames; underneath it an old postman's bag contain-

ing a hammer and other tools. Close by stood half a loaf on a
newspaper, several bottles of bright water, a black pot of
potatoes ready for boiling, a tin of water steaming against a
small fire of hazel twigs. Out on the sunny grass two shirts
were drying. In the midst was the proprietor, his name revealed
in fresh chalk on the side of his perambulator: 'John Clark,
Hampshire'.

He had spent his last pence on potatoes and had been given
the cabbage. No one would give him work on a Sunday. He
had no home, no relations. Being deaf, he did not look for com-
pany. So he stood up, to get dry and to think, think, think, his
hands on his hips, while he puffed at an empty pipe. During his
meditation a snail had crawled half-way up his trousers, and
was now all but down again. He was of middle height and
build, the crookedest of men, yet upright, like a branch of oak
which comes straight with all its twistings. His head was small
and round, almost covered by bristly grey hair like lichen,
through which peered quiet blue eyes; the face was irregular,
almost shapeless, like dough being kneaded, worn by travel, pas-
sion, pain, and not a few blows; where the skin was visible at
all through the hair it was like red sandstone; his teeth were
white and strong and short like an old dog's. His rough neck
descended into a striped half-open shirt, to which was added a
loose black waistcoat divided into thin perpendicular stripes by
ribs of faded gold; his trousers, loose and patched and short,
approached the colour of a hen pheasant; his bare feet were
partly hidden by old black boots. His voice was hoarse and, for
one of his enduring look, surprisingly small, and produced
with an effort and a slight jerk of the head.

He was a Sussex man, born in the year 1831, on June the
twenty-first (it seemed a foppery to him to remember the day,
and it was impossible to imagine with what ceremony he had
remembered it year by year, during half a century or near it, on
the roads of Sussex, Kent, Surrey and Hampshire). His mother
was a Wild – there were several of them buried not far away
under the carved double-headed tombstones by the old church
with the lancet windows and the four yews. He was a labour-
er's son, and he had already had a long life of hoeing and

reaping and fagging when he enlisted at Chatham. He had kept his musket bright, slept hard and wet, and starved on thirteen-pence a day, moving from camp to camp every two years. He had lost his youth in battle, for a bullet went through his knee; he lay four months in hospital, and they took eighteen pieces of bone out of his wound – he was still indignant because he was described as only 'slightly wounded' when he was discharged after a 'short service' of thirteen years. He showed his gnarled knee to explain his crookedness. Little he could tell of the battle except the sobbing of the soldier next to him – 'a London chap from Haggerston way. Lord! he called for his mother and his God and me to save him, and the noise he made was worse than the firing and the groaning of the horses, and I was just thinking how I could stop his mouth for him when a bullet hits me, and down I goes like a baby.'

He had been on the road forty years. For a short time after his discharge he worked on the land and lived in a cottage with his wife and one child. The church bells were beginning to ring, and I asked him if he was going to church. At first he said nothing, but looked down at his striped waistcoat and patched trousers, then, with a quick violent gesture of scorn, he lifted up his head and even threw it back before he spoke. 'Besides,' he said, 'I remember how it was my little girl died— My little girl, says I, but she would have been a big handsome woman now, forty-eight years old on the first of May that is gone. She was lying in bed with a little bit of a cough, and she was gone as white as a lily, and I went in to her when I came home from reaping. I saw she looked bad and quiet-like – like a fish in a hedge – and something came over me, and I caught hold of both her hands in both of mine and held them tight, and put my head close up to hers and said, "Now look here, Polly, you've got to get well. Your mother and me can't stand losing you. And you aren't meant to die; such a one as you be for a lark." And I squeezed her little hands, and all my nature seemed to rise up and try to make her get well. Polly she looked whiter than ever and afraid; I suppose I was a bit rough and dirty and sunburnt, for 'twas a hot harvest and 'twas the end of the second week of it, and I was that fierce I felt I ought to have had my way ... All that night I thought I had done a wrong thing trying to keep her from dying that way, and I tell you I cried in case I had done any harm by it ... That very night she died without our knowing it. She was a bonny maid, that fond of flowers. The night she was taken ill she was coming home with me from the Thirteen Acre, where I'd been hoeing the mangolds, and she had picked a rose for her mother. All of a sudden she looks at it and says, "It's gone, it's broke, it's gone, it's gone, gone, gone", and she kept on, "It's broke, it's gone, it's gone", and when she got home she ran up to her mother, crying, "The wild rose is broke, mother; broke, gone, gone," she says, just like that,' said the old man, in a high finical voice more like that of a bird than a child ...

'Then my old woman – well, she was only a bit of a wench too; seventeen when we were married – she took ill and died within a week after ... There was a purpose in it ... It was then the end of harvest. I spent all my wages down at the "Fighting Cocks", and then I set out to walk to Mildenhall in Wiltshire, where my wife came from. On the way I met a chap I had quarrelled with in Egypt, and he says to me, "Hullo, Scrammy-handed Jack," with a sort of look, and I, not thinking what I did, I set about him, and before I knew it he was lying there as might be dead, and I went and gave myself up, and I don't mind saying that I wished I might be hanged for it. However, I did six months. That was how I came to be in the umbrella line. I took up with a chap who did a bit of tinkering and umbrella-mending and grinding in the roving way, and a job of hoeing or mowing now and then. He died not so very long after in the year of the siege of Paris, and I have been alone ever since. Nor I haven't been to church since, any more than a blackbird would go and perch on the shoulder of one of those ladies with feathers and wings and a bit of a fox in their hats.'

Labourer, soldier, labourer, tinker, umbrella man, he had always wandered, and knew the South Country between Ford-ingbridge and Dover as a man knows his garden. Every village, almost every farmhouse, especially if there were hops on the

land, he knew, and could see with his blue eyes as he remem-
bered them and spoke their names. I never met a man who
knew England as he did. As he talked of places his eyes were
alight and turned in their direction, and his arm stretched out
to point, moving as he went through his itinerary, so that verily,
wherever he was, he seemed to carry in his head the relative
positions of all the other places where he had laboured and
drunk and lit his solitary fire. 'Was you ever at H—?' he said,
pointing to the Downs, through which he seemed to see H—
itself. 'General —, that commanded us, lived there. He died there
three years ago at the age of eighty-eight, and till he died I was
always sure of a half-crown if I called there on a Christmas
Eve, as I generally managed to do.' Of any place mentioned he
could presently remember something significant – the words of
a farmer, a song, a signboard, a wonderful crop, the good ale –
the fact that forty-nine years ago the squire used to go to church
in a smock frock. All the time his face was moved with free and
broad expressions as he thought and remembered, like an ani-
mal's face. Living alone and never having to fit himself into
human society, he had not learnt to keep his face in a vice. He
was returning – if the grave was not too near at the age of
seventy-seven – to a primeval wildness and simplicity. It was a
pleasure to see him smoke – to note how it eased his chest – to
see him spit and be the better for it. The outdoor life had
brought him rheumatism, but a clear brain also and a wild pur-
ity, a physical cleanliness too, and it was like being with a
well-kept horse to stand beside him; and this his house was full
of the scent of the bracken growing under the oaks. Earth had
not been a kind but a stern mother, like some brawny full-
bosomed housewife with many children, who spends all her
long days baking and washing, and making clothes, and tend-
ing the sick one, and cutting bread and pouring out tea, and
cuffing one and cuddling another and listening to one's tale,
and hushing their unanimous chatter with a shout or a bang of
her enormous elbow on the table. The blows of such a one are
shrewd, but they are not as the sweetness of her nursing voice
for enduring in the memory of bearded men and many-childed
women.

Once or twice again I met him in later summers near the same place. The last time he had been in the infirmary, and was much older. His fire was under the dense shelf of a spruce bough in a green deserted road worn deep in the chalk, blocked at both ends, and trodden by few mortal feet. Only a few yards away, under another spruce, lay a most ancient sheep who had apparently been turned into the lane to browse at peace. She was lame in one leg, and often fed as she knelt. Her head was dark grey and wise, her eyes pearly green and iridescent with an oblong pupil of blackish-blue, quiet, yet full of fear; her wool was dense but short and of a cinder grey; her dark horny feet were overgrown from lack of use. She would not budge even when a dog sniffed at her, but only bowed her head and threatened vainly to butt. She was huge and heavy and content, though always all alone. As she lay there, her wool glistening with rain, I had often wondered what those eyes were aware of, what part she played in the summer harmonies of night and day, the full night heavens and cloudless noon, storm and dawn, and the long moist heat of dewy mornings. She was now shorn, and the old man watched her as he drank the liquor in which a cabbage and a piece of bacon had been boiled. 'I often thinks,' he said, 'that I be something like that sheep . . . "slightly wounded" . . . but not "short service" now . . . haha! . . . left alone in this here lane to browse a bit while the weather's fine and folks are kind . . . But I don't know but what she is better off. Look there,' he said, pointing to a wound which the shearer had made in one of her nipples, where flies clustered like a hideous flower of crape, 'I have been spending this hour and more flicking the flies off her . . . Nobody won't do that for me – unless I come in for five shillings a week Old Age Pension. But I reckon that won't be for a roving body like me without a letter-box.' In the neighbouring field a cart-horse shook herself with a noise of far-off thunder and laughed shrilly and threw up her heels and raced along the hedge. A bee could be seen going in and out of the transparent white flowers of convolvulus. The horse had her youth and strength and a workless day before her; the bee its business, in which was its life, among sunbeams and flowers; and they were glad. The old man

smacked his lips as he drained the salty broth, tried three times
to light his empty pipe and then knocked out the ashes and spat
vigorously, and took a turn up the lane alone in the scent of the
bracken.

From 'At a Cottage Door'[15]

The stream itself, in the midst of the town, was a black and at
times a yellow serpent in a cage of steep iron-bound banks,
watched by furnace, store-house, and factory. It was allowed a
mock liberty only to stray into other cages of steep-sided
wharves. The blackened labourer stood on the edge and spat at
it where it writhed deep below. A careless child or a desperate
man was engulfed by it on some night of fire and blackness, but
it remained sullen and regarded not the trivial offering. The
embrace with the sea was licensed, bridled, sternly watched by
tall cranes, a hundred ships, and the long bleached spine of a
breakwater where sea-faring men, idlers, and fluttering girls
walked up and down.

The courses of the avalanches from the opposite hills were
marked by white, dirty white, grey, and all but black, belts of
houses broadening out to the mass in the valley. At the broad
brow of the hills, in sight of the sea and of violet hills across the
sea, a few farm-houses and their outbuildings still shone, while
others mouldered grey and aghast and without tenants. Some
of their fields were still left between the streets, but their barbed
wire and patched hedgerows and walls imprisoned only an old
horse or two, a temporary flock of sheep or of lean American
steers on their way to the slaughter-house and the tables of the
town; and even where there were no houses straight lines of
streets were waiting to be built along. Across this tainted and
condemned grass, even between the houses, trotted narrow
brooklets over stony beds to their sepulchres in the town sewers.
The houses on the upper slopes were like Catherine Anne's,
though most were slated, not thatched. Fowls stalked or scut-

tered round about and through the open doors. The gardens were walled with once whitened stones and contained a few twisted apple trees. Old women of a former age stood on the doorsteps or moved busily in scanty undress, bareheaded. Old men pottered about, or leaned on their spades to talk or look out to sea or at the pigs. The smell of baking bread was blown from the doors. Their furniture, their Bible and theological works, were old. The curs were descended from sheep dogs that once herded the mountain flocks on these slopes. The road was still a watercourse, and the unnecessary tradesman could hardly ascend if he wished, except on foot. There was always a robin in the roadway, a wagtail in the glittering streamlet, often a rook on the square stone chimney, looking down at the town as if his ancestors had told him that it was new and might disappear any night – but as he saw that nothing was likely to happen immediately he turned his head, hopped into the air, and flew away over the hilltop.

The streets beginning on the hill-ridge ended in the thickest of the town, in a medley of steep criss-cross streets interrupted here and there by black squares of workshops with everburning furnaces and ever-smoking chimneys. Here every inch of the soil was covered with bricks, stones, cement, asphalte, iron-work, granite blocks. Not a tree or blade of grass was allowed to appear anywhere but in the graveyards, and even there the earth was plated almost entirely with tombstones. They were afraid of leaving any space unguarded lest Nature should show a regret, a curse or a warning. The river was unsightly, but must be tolerated alternately with insult and respect. But even here there was not an end of the 'country'. Through many open doors could be seen furniture like Catherine Anne's, and old women of her period. Thousands passed them many times a day, but they were built in days when everyone knew everyone else, and so the doors were still left open while the baking and the washing were done. The drunkard stumbled out of the crowd into the warm and rustic seclusion of his home. The child rushed out from the cradle he was tending and was swept along by the procession to meals or work. Women stood at doorways and talked, while one went on with her knitting or suckled her babe. A half-naked child wriggled through the crowd carrying tins of dough, for if they could not bake, at least they would knead and leaven their bread, at home. Many of the children were bare-legged and headed, dirty, hungry, and quick. Out of one or other of the houses would come a bent woman, wrinkled and foul, holding a shawl over her head, looking as if she had spent a thousand years in the cellar, crushed down in rigid, idle suffering like a toad embedded in an oak root. Such creatures, chiefly women, were not uncommon. They were small, grey-skinned, with clotted grey hair; they had scarred faces, had lost an eye and most of their teeth; they wore soiled print or black dresses, bedraggled like the plumage of a dead bird in the mud and in colour approaching the foul dust of the pavement and the garbage of the gutter. In appearance they were genuine autochthons. This earth of flagstone, asphalte, granite, brick, iron, and ashes, might have protruded such a monstrous birth on a night of frost, to prove that it was not yet barren in its age and ignominy. One such crone crawling out into the light, unclean, dull and yet surprised, had a look as if she had just been exhumed; she might have been buried alive in the foundation of the town for luck, and had now emerged to see what had been done. They were seen outside the taverns with their hands hidden under the remains of aprons, or were questing in the dustbins for food or unbroken glass; often they carried babies in whose shapeless faces was hidden the power to excel their grandmothers. When they were drunk in an alley a crowd of labourers and shopkeepers gathered to watch their waving arms and poisonous faces and hear their blazing curses screeched against some unlucky man. 'There will be murder,' said one. 'It is a shame that such things are allowed,' said another. None dared to enter the mouth of the alley. The crowd recognized that a different species, a chance-begotten, misdelivered, and curse-nourished spawn of humanity was living side by side with them, farther removed than slaves or domestic animals. It was sometimes proposed that if the streets were kept cleaner and the sewage improved this race might vanish, as if in fact it ate filth and lived in the drains. No one dared to interfere. Presently a woman rushed after the man into a house, and the door was slammed with a sound not of wood but of flesh and bone.

Such were not numerous; the majority were genuine villagers, but the minority was representative and it alone truly belonged to the place. They were villagers with a difference. One face expressed nothing but the abstraction caused by solitude in the midst of myriads. The next smiled with the intimacy of home or inn. Few had yet quite realized that they were living not at the edge of a field but in the bowels of a town, though most days it was impossible to hang clothes out to dry in the flagged or asphalted or trodden mud yards, since the air was so foul that it was worth while buying the head of a sheep fed in the neighbourhood for the sake of the copper in its teeth. Every house beheld chimneys and furnaces from one window, from another the masts of the docks or the sea and its little sails or the brown and the green hill side by side, over the ploughed sea of slate roofs. On pleasant days the smell of the sea, modified by the docks, mingled with the acrid smell and taste of smoke from the smelting of copper or the burning of carcases for manure; but at night either smell was drowned in that of fried fish. Every other house had a large window to expose fruit, vegetables, groceries, meat, 'herbal remedies', and above all fried fish, for sale. Every corner house was a tavern, its windows foul with breath and steam within and mud, rain, and fine ashes without. The houses were small, so that tavern and church and school were conspicuously islanded among the low roofs.

But, towards the river, away from the avalanches of buildings, the houses were high and supported on plate glass windows of immense size. The streets curved and doubled after a pattern created centuries ago by the neighbourhood of a castle whose Norman masonry was still hiding in fragments behind or within some of the shops. Inns and shops were old but with glittering new faces of glass, stone, ornamented tiles, and vast gold letters. The wires of telegraph, telephone, and electric light ran amongst and over antique stone and timber work. Every inch was obviously designed or converted to serve an immediate purpose; there was no largeness, no waste, nothing haphazard, no detail forgotten through the pursuit of some ideal; all was haste, grim and yet slatternly. Here and there an old house had been pulled down, and its place hidden by a temporary wooden fence, stuck over with advertisements in black, white, crimson, and blue, of drugs, infant foods, political meetings, auction sales, corsets, men's clothes, theatres – these last showing beauteous dishevelled adulteresses and heroic gentlemen in white shirts threatening them with revolvers – men in diving costume fighting for a bag of jewels at the bottom of the sea. Everywhere the ideal implicit was that of a London suburb. The shop walker came nearest to achieving this ideal: suave and superb in dress, manner, and speech, in all but salary, he had been metamorphosed from the son of a farmer, who spoke no English, into an effigy that put to shame the Pall Mall clubman, though he cost the nation incomparably less. Pity that he had so poor a world to shine in, and that his imitators resembled him no more than they did the figures exhibited in the tailor's advertisements, figures created merely to hold a cigarette between the lips and a whippy cane in the fingers. His clients included women bent on dressing extravagantly or even with aristocratic sumptuous modesty, at a low price; young men with white faces, riding breeches, cigarettes, and jaunty manners; sober farmers who had tired of wearing the same old homespun so thick that they shiver without it; wives who have come to town to sell butter and eggs; sailors who have just found a ship, sailors who have just been paid off, sailors who have called first at 'The Talbot Arms'; dark-eyed, clear-complexioned girls swaddled in blouses of red and black chequered flannel, blue and white flannel skirts, variegated or black and red flannel shawls, but, for all their natural and artificial plumpness, gay and continually chattering in musical voices as they move quickly about carrying well-scoured buckets of white wood on head or hips – women resembling wood-pigeons in their plumpness and quickness. All were buying what was very cheap, or very showy, or very new, or very much like something else, or much praised as a really good thing. Cattle and their drovers looked in at the gorgeous windows and spread over the streets where a dozen knots of old acquaintances were meeting for the first time since last market day. Young working men in black whose faces had clearly been of another colour recently but were now very white by contrast with dark eyes and black moustaches and hair, walked up and down the pavements doing nothing in a determined fashion and smoking, – men who might easily have been changed into starlings in an age of miracles. In nearly all, in men and women – except in the squalid hooded hags who crawled by, or the work girls beside them carrying younger sisters or bastards in shawls – the pallor, stiffness, and haste of the town were modified by country ways, a rolling walk as if on solitary roads, country gestures and speech and quiet eyes. Young and old of all classes mingled on an equality. There was no inharmonious element, it was a village crowd, and all were united by the fact that they had been peasant born and that they were now slaves to the town. They were fascinated by the charm of the town, which is, that it is there easy to fill the whole of life with a rapidly changing round of duties and necessities, where shops and all things are so convenient that life, as Catherine Anne had surmised, is swallowed up by its conveniences.

Hawthornden[16]

Hawthornden was always home to tea, except once, and it was a significant exception.

When he was about thirty-five Hawthornden moved out into the country, partly because rents were less and he could have a governess for his three children, and so put off for some years the difficulty of choosing a school; and partly, but this was unconsciously, because he had few friends left. As a young man, clever above the common, reckless (within certain limits) and open-handed, he had attracted men of very different types, both at the university and in his bachelor lodgings. But after he married, at twenty-eight, his friends never came to see him, except when they were definitely asked to dinner, though his wife was charming and clever and anxious to meet them, and though he was not too fond of her to attend to them. He seemed to have stiffened and chilled. His smile began to have an awkward catch in it. It was so awkward that it ought to have been dignified, but was not quite. And at the same time as his friends were neglecting him he was not making any progress in domesticity. He had decided against entering a profession, and as he could live on his private means, he was at home very much. But there he gave himself up chiefly to solitary reading, and saw his wife chiefly at meals, and, on evenings when he wished to go early to bed, after dinner. He had thought of writing, but he was squeamish and touchy, and had destroyed his early verses and prose with great care, burning them in his room one summer evening, with a tense, red face, and then, by an after-thought, preserving the ashes in a small cherrywood box. He read many books of almost every kind, except criticism. Criticism he had taught himself to hate, because it seemed to him absurd that the writing class should not only produce books, but circulate its opinion of them among people occupied – like himself – with the business of living at first hand, not at second hand. In the days before criticism life and literature had both been finer things. It was the men with no standards of taste at all who made the arts of the great periods. When there was no one to tell men what to put on their walls, how to build their houses, what to wear and what to read, the glorious things were being created which men instructed at every turn in these matters were content to imitate. Hawthornden sought to recover this freedom by allowing no middleman between art and himself as a human being. As it was, however, physically impossible to keep pace with modern literature without a guide, he neglected it without noticing that this was a concession; and as the old literature had been well sifted by the efforts of the very criticism he despised, he had little left but to enjoy, and he discovered, with some annoyance, that he read and thought – so far as he could express himself – very much like everybody else. Nevertheless, he continued to read abundantly, and for the sake of books put off year by year the problems which his own life offered him. He got out of touch with his wife, ignored her friends, and only by an insincere though determined effort, from time to time, succeeded in quieting her hysteria and relieving her melancholy. As to his children, he made spasmodic and more and more conscious efforts at pleasing and understanding them, and, observing that they could do without him, he plumed himself upon their ingratitude, and left them to the natural methods of his wife, of which he expressed his disapproval from time to time. Yet he was fond of the poetry of passion. He would look up from a poem sometimes and see his wife reading or embroidering, and then take his eyes away with a sigh and only the faintest dissatisfied recognition that he was becoming more and more incapable of being passionate himself and of meeting the passion of another. He also continued to sigh for the simple antique attitudes of the emotions in their liberty, and cursed a time when they could only be seen travestied on the stage. It was literature, nevertheless, and the stage, that had given him the standard which he unconsciously applied to scenes in life which he thought should have been heroical, for example, and were not. Nor was he shaken from his dim-pinnacled citadel of unreality by his one experience of something near tragedy at home. His wife rushed at him one day, with stiff, drawn, red-spotted face and staring eyes, and a shrill voice he had never heard before, to tell him that one of the children was injured. He drew her head to his breast and kissed her hair, and felt at first a kind of shame, then an instinctive disgust at the stains and rude prints of her grief. The same with beauty. He could not have defined it, but he had a standard which he applied to loveliness like a yard-wand, and never suspected that it was the standard that was wanting. It was expression that he feared in living beauty. He wanted the calm of antiquity – of death – of the photographs of celebrated women. A dark face, burning and wrenched with eagerness or delight, disturbed him, and – was not beautiful, because he had been at the trouble of putting aside the expression, and observing that the nose was too small, the eyes unequal, the lips too full, and so on.

He was fond of reading fairy tales and books for and about children, and had acquired strong opinions as to what they needed and liked. He was a great lover of liberty, of liberalism, of freedom for thought and action. He could be heard late at night reading aloud in a deep voice poems on liberty, and even at breakfast would relieve himself by muttering impressively –

> And in thy smile and by thy side
> Saintly Camillus lived and stern Atilius died.

The children looked up and said, 'What did you say, father?' or 'Do say some more like that'; but he stirred his tea, and made haste to leave the table for the study. He admired books of curious character and adventure such as Borrow's and adored the strange persons who frequented once upon a time, and perhaps even now, the inns and roads of England. He was indignant with civilization which threatened to extinguish such men, and used to cut from newspapers passages describing the efforts to chain up gypsies and tramps.

When he moved into the country he was prepared for adventures. Gypsies should be allowed to camp near his house and he would be familiar with them. He would invite the tramps into his study for a talk and a smoke. He used to sit by the roadside, or in the taproom of an inn, waiting for what would turn up. But something always stood in the way – himself. He grew tired of paying for a tramp's quart, and was disconcerted, now by too great familiarity and now by too great respect. When a tramp came to the back door, his maids or his wife reported it to him, and they sometimes had interesting fragments of a story to relate; for the women had human sympathies along with unquestioning commonplace views of social distinctions. Sometimes he saw the man coming or going, and formed romantic conjectures which made him impatient of what he actually heard. He thought at one time that perhaps his mistake was in keeping too near home; he would walk far over the hills, and stay away for a night or two. But it was always the same. He dressed negligently and carried a crooked stick, and when he complained of his failure to get at the heart of the wayfaring man, his wife flattered him by saying that any one could see what he really was, whatever his disguise; he liked the flattery, and remained discontented.

Perhaps his whole plan was wrong. He had bought many

maps, special walking clothes and boots, compact outfits, several kinds of knapsacks, rucsacs, haversacks, satchels, uncounted walking sticks, just as in other departments of his life he found himself buying pipes suitable for this purpose or that, half a dozen different species of lamps, pens, razors, hats and so on. He tried simplicity for a while, but this also meant a new outlay, and he was soon unfaithful.

Among the people of the neighbourhood he received a reputation for unconventionality. He was said to know the country and the people better than anyone. He was mistaken for a genius, a poet, an artist, a Bohemian, an eccentric millionaire, especially as he had a genuine dislike to parties and picnics and to the sound of men and women trying to put emotion into the words, 'Isn't the weather perfectly glorious?' by drawling them or emphasizing one word or each word in turn. He liked the mistake.

But one thing, above all others, gradually disturbed him. He was always home to tea.

He liked a certain kind of tea – the milk or cream of a precise quantity poured out first into his cup and then the tea on top of it, to scald it and produce a colour and flavour otherwise impossible. Then the sweet home-made cakes ... Once or twice he went into cottages for tea, to chat with the poor and see them *au naturel*. But he saw nothing, and was therefore keenly alive to the fact that the tea was bad, and the cakes all but uneatable – so that he had a second tea when he arrived home. Mrs Hawthornden was glad of this; she liked him to enjoy himself, and to praise her cakes. She made cakes regularly, and saw that they were of the kinds he preferred. When he started early for a long walk, she used to ask him when he would be back. 'Oh, I cannot possibly say!' he retorted at once; but added, on reconsideration, 'But perhaps by four or five.' He was rarely later than four, and she smiled. He made special efforts not to be back by five – dreading the habit – and yet at last walked so hard as to tire himself in the effort to reach home at that time. So at last, when his wife asked the question, 'When shall I expect you back?' he used to say, sometimes smilingly, sometimes with a submissive despair, sometimes with irritation,

'Oh, I am always home to tea!' When he was not punctual, he was proud – but regretted the cakes – and read Borrow with greater relish. But the next day he would find himself home again to tea, and eating too many cakes with equanimity. He knew they were too many, and the thought at length prevented him from enjoying them, but not quite from eating them; there was a relic of virtue in this inability to enjoy them, though he knew that it might have been greater. At times, in an ancient cathedral or in the midst of a tragic tale, he started with the thought that he was almost forgetting his tea, and then his pleasure was at an end. Lying awake at night, he reproached himself, 'You are always home to tea.' He was haunted by it, as men of noble families of old time were haunted by their fate, and in his moments of complacency it crept suddenly upon him.

One day he went out to a distant part of the country to explore a ruin. It was a fine August day, and he spent most of it in the castle. He left it late in the afternoon, and then began to run. There were several trains that he might have caught; nevertheless, he ran. That day he did not return to tea. His wife looked out a train, and expected him first by one and then by another. It grew dark, and he was not back. The afternoon had been hot, and he had run too fast for a man of his build. He was found lying beside the path. He had achieved his ambition. He had not only not come home to tea, but had ceased to think about tea, so far as can be known. He was dead.

The Attempt[17]

Several seasons had passed since Morgan Traheron had so much as looked at his fishing tackle, and now he turned over, almost indifferently, the reels and lines and hooks and flies which had been carefully put away in an old tool box of his great-grandfather's. He looked at the name 'Morgan Traheron' cut neatly inside the lid, and shivered slightly during the thought that one of his own name had bought it in 1776 at the iron-monger's and brazier's under the sign of the 'Anchor and Key' near Charing Cross, and that the owner had been dead nearly a hundred years. Cold, cold, must he be! Even as cold would be the younger bearer of that name, and he anticipated, in a kind of swoon, the hundred years that would one day submerge himself from all known friendliness of sun, earth, and man.

He was seeking, not any of the fishing tackle, but a revolver that lay amongst it, and a small green box containing only one ball cartridge. He had often thought of throwing the revolver away. His wife always looked wonderingly at him when he cleaned it once every year or so, but if she had urged him to throw it away he would have scoffed at the fear which he detected, all the more heartily because the sign of her concern inflated his vanity. She, lest she should provoke his mood in some way which even her consideration could not foresee, remained silent or asked him to tell again how he shot the woodpigeon fifty yards off, actually within sight of the game-keeper's cottage. It was a thrilling and well-told tale, albeit untrue.

It was not a mere accident that one ball cartridge was left.

Morgan took out the revolver and the cartridge and shut the box. The lock was stiff and the chambers would not revolve without the use of both hands. To fire it off, it would therefore be necessary to twist the loaded chamber laboriously round to its place and then force back the hammer to full cock. The bar-rel was brown from rust, but probably the ball would force its way through as it had done before. It was a cheap, ugly, repul-sive weapon; it impressed him with unsuitableness. He did not stay to oil it, but putting it in a pocket and the cartridge in another, he prepared to leave the house.

'Won't you take Mary with you, Morgan?' said his wife.

'Yes,' said Mary, his little daughter, laughing not so much because there was anything to laugh at as because she must either laugh or cry, and certainly the chance of a walk was nothing to cry for: 'Take me with you, father.'

'Oh no, you don't really want to come, you only say it to please me,' said Traheron, mild but hard.

'Yes, I am sure she . . . Good-bye, then,' said his wife.

'Good-bye,' said he.

The thought of kissing his daughter turned him back for a moment. But he did not; the act occurred to him more as a part of the ceremony of this fatal day than as a farewell, and he feared to betray his thought. She was the immediate cause of his decision. He had spoken resentfully to her for some fault which he noticed chiefly because it disturbed his melancholy repose; she had then burst out crying with long, clear wails that pierced him with self-hate, remorse, regret, and bitter memory.

Why should he live who had the power to draw such a cry from that sweet mouth? So he used to ask in the luxurious self-contempt which he practised. He would delay no more. He had thought before of cutting himself off from the power to injure his child and the mother of his child. But they would suffer; also, what a rough edge would be left to his life, inevitable in any case, perhaps, but not lightly to be chosen. On the other hand, he could not believe that they would ever be more unhappy than they often were now; at least, the greater poverty which his death would probably cause could not well increase their unhappiness; and settled misery or a lower plane of happiness was surely preferable to a state of faltering hope at the edge of abysses such as he often opened for them. To leave them and not die, since the child might forget him and he would miss many a passing joy with her, was never a tolerable thought; such a plan had none of the gloss of heroism and the kind of superficial ceremoniousness which was unconsciously much to his taste. But on this day the arguments for and against a fatal act did not weigh with him. He was called to death.

He was called to death, but hardly to an act which could procure it. Death he had never feared or understood; he feared very much the pain and the fear that would awake with it. He had never in his life seen a dead human body or come in any way near death. Death was an idea tinged with poetry in his mind – a kingly thing which was once only at any man's call. After it came annihilation. To escape from the difficulty of life, from the need of deliberating on it, from the hopeless search for something that would make it possible for him to go on living like anybody else without questioning, he was eager to hide himself away in annihilation, just as, when a child, he hid himself in the folds of his mother's dress or her warm bosom, where he could shut out everything save the bright patterns floating on the gloom under his closed eyelids. There was also an element of vanity in his project; he was going to punish himself and in a manner so extreme that he was inclined to be exalted by the feeling that he was now about to convince the world he had suffered exceedingly. He had thus taken up the revolver, and blurred the moment of the report by thinking intently of the pure annihilation which he desired. The revolver was the only accessible weapon that entered his mind, and he had armed himself with it without once having performed in thought what he had committed himself to do in fact before long.

As he mounted the hill by a white path over the turf, he felt the revolver strike against his hip at each stride. He was in full view of anyone who happened to be looking out from his home, and he pressed on lest the wavering of his mind should be seen. Recalling the repulsiveness of the weapon, the idea of a rope crossed his mind, not because it was preferable, but because it was something else, something apart from his plans which now had a painful air of simplicity.

When he was among some bushes that concealed him and yet still gave him a view of his house, he paused for breath. He half-longed for an invasion of sentiment at the sight of his home; but he was looking at it like a casual stranger, and without even the pang that comes when the stranger sees a quiet house embowered in green against which its smoke rises like a prayer, and he imagines that he could be happy there as he has not until now been happy anywhere. The house was mere stones, nothing, dead. He half wished that Mary would run out into the garden and compel him to a passionate state. His will and power of action were ebbing yet lower in his lifeless mood. He moved his eyes from the house to the elder hedgerow round it, to the little woods on the undulations beyond, to the Downs, and, above them, the cloudy sun perched upon a tripod of pale beams. Nothing answered his heartless call for help. He needed some tenderness to be born, a transfigured last look to keep as a memory; perhaps he still hoped that this answer that was not given to him could save him from the enemy at his side and in his brain; even so late did he continue to desire the conversion, the climacteric ecstasy by which life might solve its difficulty, and either sway placidly in harbour or set out with joy for the open sea.

He mounted the upper slopes and passed in among the beeches. He turned again, but again in vain. There was little in him left to kill when he reached the top and began to think where exactly he should go. He wished that he could hide away for ever in one of the many utterly secret mossy places known to him among beech and yew in the forsaken woods; the fox-hounds might find him, but no one else. But he must go farther. The sound of the discharge must not be heard in that house below. Almost with tenderness he dreamed of the very moment when his wife would hear the news and perhaps see his body at the same time; if only that could be put off – the announcement must not come to-day, not under this sun in which the world was looking as he had always seen it, though more dull and grey, but on some day he had not known, a black, blind day yet unborn, to be still-born because of this event so important to him. Who would find him? He did not like the thought that some stranger who knew him by sight, who had never spoken to him, should come across the body, what was left of him, his remains, and should suddenly become curious and interested, perhaps slightly vain of the remarkable discovery. If only he could fade away rapidly. Several strangers with whose faces he was familiar passed him in a lane, and he assumed a proud, hard look of confidence, as he hoped.

He quickened his steps and turned into a neglected footpath where he had never met anybody. He took out the revolver and again looked at it. It was just here that he had come in the hottest of the late summer to show his daughter cinnabar caterpillars, tigerish yellow and black, among the flaming blossoms of ragwort. The ragwort was dead now, blossom and leaf. He recalled the day without comment.

He was now hidden, on one side by a dense wood, on the

other by the steep slope of a hill, and before and behind by windings of the path which skirted the wood. He inserted the cartridge and with difficulty forced it into position; the brass was much tarnished. Now he revolved the chambers in order that the cartridge should be under the hammer, but by mistake he turned them too far; he had to try again, and, losing count of the chambers, was again defeated. Where the cartridge was he could not be sure, and he looked to see; its tarnished disc was hostile and grim to his eye, and he hid the weapon.

Moving on, he now looked down upon a steep wood that sloped from his feet, and then rose as steeply up an opposite hill. They were beech woods with innumerable straight stems of bare branch-work that was purple in the mass. Yews stood as black islands in the woods, and they and the briers with scarlet hips close to his eye were laced with airy traveller's joy, plumy and grey.

Traheron now turned the muzzle to his temple, first letting the hammer down for fear of an accident. He had only one shot to fire, and he could not feel sure that this would enter his brain. His ear, his mouth – the thought was horrible, impossible. His skin ached with the touch of the steel which was very cold. Next he turned the weapon to his breast, and saw that he had better pull the trigger with his thumb. The hammer was now at full cock, the cartridge in place. The hideous engine looked absurdly powerful for his purpose. The noise, the wound, would be out of proportion to the little spark of life that was so willing, so eager, to be extinguished. He lowered the weapon and took a last sight of the woods, praying no prayer, thinking no thought, perfectly at ease, though a little cold from inaction.

Suddenly his eye was aware of someone moving above the opposite wood, half a mile away, and at the same moment this stranger raised a loud halloo as if he had sighted a fox, and repeated it again and again for his own delight, feeling glad, and knowing himself alone. Traheron had been watching the wood with soul more and more enchanted by the soft colour, the coldness, the repose. The cry rescued him; with shame at the thought that he might have been watched, he raised the revolver and turned it to his breast, shut his eyes and touched the trigger, but too lightly, and breathless, in the same moment, he averted the barrel and hurled it into the wood, where it struck a bough without exploding. For a moment he dreamed that he had succeeded. He saw the man who found him pick up the revolver and examine it. Finding but one cartridge in the chambers he concluded that the dead man was a person of unusual coolness and confidence, with an accurate knowledge of the position of the heart. Then, for he was cold, Traheron moved rapidly away, his mind empty of all thought except that he would go to a certain wood and then strike over the fields, following a route that would bring him home in the gentleness of evening.

He opened the door. The table was spread for tea. His wife, divining all, said:

'Shall I make tea?'

'Please,' he replied, thinking himself impenetrably masked.

Insomnia[18]

Night after night deliberately we take upon ourselves the utmost possible weakness, because it is the offering most acceptable to sleep. Our thick coverings give us warmth without need of motion. The night air we moderate into a harmless rustling or stroking coolness; or, if it be an obstreperous air, we may shut it out altogether, and with it all sounds. We choose to be alone, and in darkness. We make ourselves so weak, so easy, so content with nothing, that scarce anything but personal danger, and that immediate and certain, could stir us. Thus cunningly we oppose the utmost possible weakness to the assault of sleep.

Sometimes I have a lighted candle and a book at my bedside, but seldom for more than five minutes. The light and the effort of reading, though I may have gone early to bed, are too much for my instinctive weakness, this religious malingering. I find

that I desire to enter without gradation into perfect helpless-
ness, and I exercise a quiet resolution against the strains even of
memory. For once I have lain down, safe, warm, and unanx-
ious, nothing I can remember is worthy for more than a moment
to interrupt. In this weakness there is a kind of power. Still and
relaxed, as it were lacking bones and muscles entirely, I lie in a
composed eagerness for sleep. And most often sleep will stoop
and swallow me up, and I have no more dream or trouble than
a grain swallowed by a bird.

But the mighty weakness that so allures sleep is turned to a
powerless strength during the night. I wake before dawn, and
then, much as I desire sleep, I cannot have it. I am now the prey
of anything but sleep, anything real or unreal that comes to
sight, touch, or hearing, or straight to the brain. It seems that
all night I have heard the poplars shivering across the street in
the strong lamplight, with a high singing note like a flame
instead of a noise of showers; it seems that this shivering and
this light will continue for ever, and for ever shall I lie restless
under their afflictions. I strive, but no longer with unconscious
power, to sink into the weakness that commands or deserves
sleep. Any memory now can discompose me; any face, any
word, any event, out of the past has to be entertained for a
minute or an hour, according to its will, not mine. Those pop-
lar leaves in the bright street are mightier than I or sleep. In
vain I seek the posture and simulate the gesture of an already
favoured victim. I am too weak. I am too strong, yet I cannot
rise and darken the room or go out and contemn sleep. It is a
blessed thing if I am strong enough at last to wear myself out to
sleep.

The other night I awoke just as the robin was beginning to
sing outside in the dark garden. Beyond him the wind made a
moan in the little fir-copse as of a forest in a space magically
enclosed and silent, and in the intervals of his song silence fell
about him like a cloak which the wind could not penetrate. As
well as I knew the triple cry farther off for the crow of the first
cock, I knew this for the robin's song, pausing but unbroken,
though it was unlike any song of robin I had heard in daylight,
standing or walking among trees. Outside, in the dark bush, to

me lying prostrate, patient, unmoving, the song was absolutely monotonous, absolutely expressionless, a chain of little thin notes linked mechanically in a rhythm identical at each repetition. This was not the voluntary personal utterance of a winged sprite that I used to know, but a note touched on the instrument of night by a player unknown to me, save that it was he who delighted in the moaning fir-trees and in my silence. Nothing intelligible to me was expressed by it; since he, the player, alone knew, I call it expressionless.

When the light began to arrive, the song in the enclosed hush, and the sound of the trees beyond it, remained the same. I remained awake, silently and as stilly as possible, cringing for sleep. I was an unwilling note on the instrument; yet I do not know that the robin was less unwilling. I strove to escape out of that harmony of bird, wind, and man. But as fast as I made my mind a faintly heaving, shapeless, grey blank, some form or colour appeared; memory or anticipation was at work.

Gradually I found myself trying to understand this dawn harmony. I vowed to remember it and ponder it in the light of day. To make sure of remembering I tried putting it into rhyme. I was resolved not to omit the date; and so much so that the first line had to be 'The seventh of September', nor could I escape from this necessity. Then September was to be rhymed with. The word 'ember' occurred and stayed; no other would respond to my calling. The third and fourth lines, it seemed, were bound to be something like –

> The sere and the ember
> Of the year and of me.

This gave me no satisfaction, but I was under a very strong compulsion. I could do no more; not a line would add itself to the wretched three; nor did they cease to return again and again to my head. It was fortunate for me as a man, if not as an unborn poet, that I could not forget the lines; for by continual helpless repetition of them I rose yet once more to the weakness that sleep demanded. Gradually I became conscious of nothing but the moan of trees, the monotonous expressionless robin's song, the slightly aching body to which I was, by ties more and more slender, attached. I felt, I knew, I did not think that there would always be an unknown player, always wind and trees, always a robin singing, always a listener listening in the stark dawn: and I knew also that if I were the listener I should not always lie thus in a safe warm bed thinking myself alive . . . And so I fell asleep again on the seventh of September.

Chalk Pits[19]

It is sometimes consoling to remember how much of the pleasantness of English country is due to men, by chance or design. The sowing of various crops, the planting of hedges and building of walls, the trimming of woods to allow trees to grow large and shapely, and so on, are among the designed causes of this pleasantness. Here men have obviously co-operated with Nature. But as great effects are produced when they have seemed at first to insult or ignore her. A new house, for example, however well proportioned, and however wisely chosen the material, is always harsh to the eye and the mind. In a hundred years it little matters what the form or the material; if the house survives, and is inhabited for a century, it has probably made its place. If it is deserted, it makes a place yet more rapidly. There is no building which the country cannot digest and assimilate if left to itself in about twenty years. Cottage or factory or mansion is powerless against frost, wind, rain, grass and ivy, and the entirely assimilated building is always attractive unless the beholder happens to know the reason why it was deserted; and even if he does, his sympathy will very likely not conflict with his sense of beauty, but will aid it in secret – that is what is consoling. London deserted would become a much pleasanter place than Richard Jefferies pictured it in *After London*. The mere thought of the jackdaws who would dwell there is a cheerful one, and they would not be alone. I like to think what mysteries the shafts, the tubes, the tunnels and the vaults would make, and what a place to explore. The railway cuttings, unless very steep-sided, soon become romantic, and near London they are a refuge for many plants and insects.

But among the works of men that rapidly become works of Nature, and can be admired without misanthropy, are the chalk and marl pits. The great ones are pleasing many miles away, both in themselves and through association. On a hill-side they always assume a good shape, like those of a scallop shell or even of a fan. Those on the Downs above Lewes, Maidstone and Midhurst, will be remembered. Against their white walls we can like the limeworks themselves, whether they offer only the ordinary black chimneys as at Buriton, or whether they are majestic in their arched masonry like those which are consuming the Dinas above Llandebie in Carmarthenshire. If there were only one of these fans or scallops of white low down on a bare hill-side it would be as celebrated as the inverted fan of Fujiyama in Japan. They are impressive, I think, chiefly as being, with the exception of glass-houses and sheets of water, the only distinctly luminous objects on the comparatively dark earth. They show up like arched windows or doorways of gigantic proportions lighted from within the hills. Their all but perpendicular walls take long to be grassed over when deserted, even if the rabbits do not seek refuge in them and keep the chalk moving by their narrow terraces. Perhaps that enormous scoop is one that has been so grassed over, on the steep hill-side facing southward near East Meon. It is completely covered with fine grass, and has an almost level green floor, which is used as a playing field. It bears the name of 'The Vineyard', and it has been suggested that it was used by the Romans or Romanized Britons for the cultivation of vines. But this is very much like one of the lesser natural coombes of the chalk country, and except for its name, and possible use, it has no particular interest. The lesser chalk pits are the better. These may be divided roughly into two kinds – first, those which are dug out of more or less level ground, and are shaped like a bowl or funnel, or a series of such; second, those which have been carved out of a slope. Those upon a slope are usually the more charming to the eye. They are met, for example, suddenly where the road bends round a steep bank, and whether the chalk is dazzling or shadowed it is welcome. The white or grey-white wall is over-hung by roots of ash and beech trees, and if it be old by a curtain of traveller's joy or ivy. These overhanging roots and climbers often form a covered way large enough for a man to creep through, and much used by foxes and lesser beasts. At the foot is a waste space of turf. Here grows the wayfaring tree with its pendent clusters of cherry-coloured fruit, or the beam tree, whose leaves fall with their heavy sides uppermost and so lie all through the winter; or perhaps bracken and purple-stemmed angelica, nine feet high and straight, with graceful bracketed frondage all still; or perhaps the sweetest flowers of the chalk, the yellow St John's wort, birdsfoot, agrimony, and hawkweed, the pink bramble and mallow, the mauve marjoram and basil, the purple knapweed, and to these come the Red Admiral and Peacock and Copper butterflies, the bright-winged flies and bees, and the grasshoppers like emerald armoured horsemen – four white butterflies float past hundreds of flowers without heeding them, and then all four try to alight on one. The air is full of the sweetness of wild carrot and parsnip seeds. Sometimes the floor is filled up with a dense Paradise of bramble and blackthorn, and there is a nightingale in it or a blackcap and in the winter a wren.

The hollow pits are not so familiar, because they lie often in the middle of the fields which they used to supply with chalk. They may be so shallow that they have been ploughed over, and now merely serve to break the surface of a great cornfield. Or they may be deep like mines, so that the chalk had to be raised by a windlass; and these are now protected by rails, and used only for depositing carrion. As a rule the bowl-shaped pits have been overgrown by bushes, or where large enough, planted with trees, with beech, oak, ash and holly; and they are surrounded by a hedge to keep out cattle. They have names of their own; often they are dells, such as Stubridge Dell, or Slade Dell. Thus they often form pretty little islands of copse in the midst of arable, and show their myriads of primroses or bluebells through the hazels when the neighbour field is crumbling dry in an east wind. These islands are attractive largely, I think, because they suggest fragments of primaeval forest that have been left untouched by the plough on account of their roughness. I call them islands because that is the impression made on the passer-by. Cross over to them, and they are seen to be more like ponds full of everything but water. There are some small ones brimful of purple rosebay flowers in the midst of the corn. Others are full of all that a goldfinch loves – teasel, musk, thistle and sunshine. One is so broken up by the uneven diggings, the roots of trees, and the riot of brambles that a badger is safe in it with a whole pack of children. Some farms have one little or big dell to almost every field, and to enterprising children there must be large tracts of country which exist chiefly to provide these dells. One or two of the best of them are half-way between the hollow pit and the hillside scoop. One in particular, a vast one, lies under a steep road which bends round it, and has to protect its passengers by posts and rails above the perpendicular. At the upper side it is precipitous, but it has a level floor, and the old entrance below is by a very gradual descent. It is very old, and some of the trees, which are now only butts, must have been two centuries old when they were felled. It is big enough for the Romany Rye to have fought there with the Flaming Tinman. But in Borrow's days it had more trees in it. Now it has about a score of tall ash trees only, ivy covered, and almost branchless, rising up out of it above the level of the road. Except at midsummer, only the tops of the ash trees catch the sunlight. The rest is dark and wild, and somehow cruel. The woodmen looked tiny and dark, as if working for a punishment, when they were felling some of the trees below. That hundred yards or so of road running round the edge of the ancient pit is as fascinating as any other similar length in England. From the rails above you could well watch the Romany Rye and the Flaming Tinman and fair-haired Isopel. But except the woodmen and the horses drawing out the timber, no one visits it. It is too gloomy. This is no vineyard, unless for growing the ruby grape of Proserpine, the nightshade. Though roofed with the sky, it has the effect of a cave, an entrance to the underworld.

Other roadside dells, facing the south or south-west, are not so deserted. The old chalk pits, being too steep and rough to be cultivated, soon grow into places as wild as ancient Britain. They are especially good at a meeting of several roads. They form wayside wastes which are least easily enclosed. These strips are, or were, called slangs, and a waste of a larger kind gave us the curious word Flash. Flash is a village in a wild quarter of Derbyshire, between Buxton and Macclesfield. The people were mostly squatters who used the place as headquarters when they were not travelling to and from the fairs; and the lingo in which they talked to one another was called flash-talk. There is flash-talk still to be heard in some of the wayside chalk pits. There is no better place for a camp than one of these with a good aspect. It gives a man a little of the sense of a room. At the best it has almost four walls, which keep out neither sun nor rain. Some of them are much used by tramps and gipsies and other travellers, until they are enclosed on the ground that these persons are a nuisance or are spoiling the beauty of the country. I think these travellers ought to be protected – say by the Zoological Society. Many of them are happy and they are at least as interesting, though often not as beautiful, as anything at the Zoo. They cost very little, being far too meek to steal much. For the price of a first-rate cigar one of them could be fed for a week, or a family for a bottle of wine. They give endless quiet amusement to civilized men who here behold what they have come from and what some of them would like to return to again. It seems to require some philosophy to sit high on the Downs on a rainy February day, reading half a sheet of a week-old daily paper, on the leeside of a copse which was once a chalk pit. I have seen the man several times, but never observed that anyone was sitting at his feet to learn his wisdom. He had not wife, nor other possessions, nor desire to converse. He was lean, dirty, quite unpicturesque and not strong, but he made the best of a wet February day. Most men would have preferred to be one of the chestnut horses ploughing near, their coats marked as with the hammer-marks on copper.

In summer, he and his kind are more picturesque. The best

group I ever saw – and it was at the entrance to a chalk pit – was three wild women in black rags, with a perambulator and a large black cat. They had hair like hemp, and glittering blue eyes. They were lean but tall and strong. They were quite silent. When I first saw them they had a fire and were cooking – the cat knew what – upon a windy Sunday morning, while the church bells were ringing.

They were not supernatural, I can swear, because one of them asked the time as I left, though it was upon a solitary and remote roadway, and they appeared to have no affairs in this world that could depend upon 'the time'. I laughed at the question, and they seemed surprised, but they were too busy – thinking, shall I say? – to say any more. Two days later the races at — began, but they were not there. On the morning of the races human beings crawled out of all kinds of holes, and the chalk pits supplied one or two. There is, presumably, no horse-racing after death, so that the lot of these devotees is not to be envied, though in this world they seem content. I saw one crawl out of an archway where a considerable stream of water ran in winter. But the chalk pit was better – it seemed to hold, as in a treasury, half the sun of a glorious morning, and across the floor, beside a dead fire, sprawled a middle-aged sports-woman in old black velvet, fast asleep, though the racegoers were streaming past in some haste. Those were the days of the green-finches – little bands flitting and twittering through hedges and over yew trees with clear thin notes, breezy in the breeze – and of linnets scattering now over the brassy ragwort flowers, and millions of poppies in the wheat. Once I met a small bear in one of the tangled dells in this neighbourhood. He was curled up in the sun between bushes of gorse, and his master's head was buried in his fur. If the bear had been alone it might have been a scene in Britain before Caesar's time, but though it was 1904 the bear looked indigenous. This dell is one of those which may be natural or artificial, or perhaps partly both, a small natural coombe having been convenient for excavation in the chalk. It lies at the foot of a wild Down which is climbed, chiefly for the sake of its chalk pits, by a slanting steep road. The dell is a long narrow chamber with a floor rising towards the beginning of the steep slope. The sides of it are worn by the rabbits and support little but gaunt elder bushes. The floor grows a few ash trees and much gorse. The tallest tree is dead, but the coombe is sheltered and the great ash still holds up its many arms in the form of a lyre, high above the rest. It is grey and stiff and without bark. But the jackdaws love it. All through the afternoons of summer they come and go among the hills, and the dead tree is their chief station. It might almost seem a religious place to them. There are always two or three perched on the topmost branches, talking to those arriving or departing. Now and then a turtledove flies up and they do not resent it. As to the bear, it was nothing to them. Their ancestors had seen many such. There are jackdaws in the elms of the neighbouring meadows, but those religious ones upon the dead ash tree seem the most important, and it alone is never deserted.

Saved Time[20]

I dreamed that I walked far along a solitary and unknown road. Nobody met or passed me, and though I looked through many gateways on either hand I saw nobody at work in the vast plains. Nor had I passed or seen anywhere in the land one house, one coil of hearth smoke, or even one ruin, when suddenly at the roadside between two trunks of oak, and under their foliage two small windows gleamed faintly in the shadow. The glass was dark with cobwebs, dead spiders, and dead flies caught in the webs of the dead spiders; nothing could be seen through it but vague forms, yet darker than the darkness within, such as are to be seen under water in a momentary half calm. But there was a door between the two windows, and I entered as if I had been expected, though never had I seen or heard before of a house in the heart of an empty and boundless wilderness, but resembling a low second-hand furniture or marine store in a decayed part of London.

The door would not open wider than just to admit me sideways, so full was the room of its shadowy wares. These were all objects for holding things – cupboards, chests, and nests of drawers of all kinds, delicate cabinets, heavy oak chests, boxes massive or flimsy and of every material and workmanship, some no bigger than children's money-boxes, iron safes, small decorated caskets of ivory, metals, and precious woods, bags and baskets, and resting in numbers or solitary on the larger articles were trinkets with lids, snuff-boxes, and the like. They were clear and dark in a light of underground, the rows and piles that I could see mysteriously suggested one invisible infinity of others. As I trod a haze of dust rained and whispered unceasingly down upon them and from off them. Through this haze, or out of it in some way, like an animal out of its lair, appeared a small old grey man with cobweb hair, whiskers, and eyebrows, and blue eyes that flashed out of the cobwebs and dust whenever they moved. His large long grey hands wriggled and twitched like two rats cleaning themselves. He was all head and hands, and shadowy grey clothing connected him with the carpetless floor of rotten planks on which he made no sound. The dust fell upon him unnoticed and from time to time dribbled from his hair and beard to the ground.

'This,' said I suddenly, 'is a useful kind of box. I should like to open it, if I may, to see whether it would suit me. It is for papers that I shall never look at again, but may serve to light a fire or make a footnote for an historian in my grandchildren's time. If you would brush the dust off . . .'

'Have you the key?' he asked in a voice that made my throat itch into a cough. Did he think me a locksmith, or what? I was annoyed, but said questioningly, 'No.'

'Then I am afraid it cannot be yours.'

'But of course not. I wish to buy it.'

'It is not for sale.'

'It is reserved then for one of the multitude upon this highway?'

'Well, yes. But I hardly expect the owner to come for it now. It has been here some fifty years.'

'You can't sell it?'

'Oh, no! I assure you it would be of no use except to its owner. It is full.'

I rapped it, thickening the haze of dust and glancing at him to see the effect of the hollow sound on his expression. It had not the effect I expected, but he raised his eyes for a moment and said:

'You hear? It is quite full.'

I smiled with a feeling in which amused expectation swamped my contempt for his deceit.

'You have made a mistake. Try one of the others,' he said patiently.

I cast about for something as suitable, and having found an old oak tool-box of not too heavy make, I pointed to it and asked if he would open it. Again he replied simply:

'Have you the key?'

'Naturally not.'

'Most unnaturally not. But if you have not, then the box cannot be opened. I am afraid, sir, you have come under a pretence or a mistake. This box, like all the other receptacles here is owned by someone who alone has the power to open it, if he wishes. They are stored here because it is found that they are seldom wanted. All are full. They contain nothing but time.'

'Time?'

'Yes, time. It is abundant, you perceive. All those boxes, bags, etc., contain time. Down below' – here he pointed to the decayed floor – 'we have more, some of them as much as fifty thousand years old.'

'Then probably you have time to explain,' I said, hardly covering my amazement, and in a moment awed by the reverberation of my words in a cavern which the echoes proclaimed as without end. The planks rippled under me. My eyes wandered over the shop until they stopped at a very small copper box enamelled on the sides with a green pattern as delicate as the grass-blade armour of a grasshopper; the top had the usual grey fur of dust.

'What is here?' I asked.

'That is the time saved by Lucy Goldfinch and Robert Ploughman twenty years ago. They were lovers, and used to walk every Saturday afternoon along the main road for a mile, and then by green lanes three miles more, until they came to a farm where her uncle kept twenty-five cows, and there the old man and his wife gave them tea. After they had been doing this for two years Robert learnt a path going straight from the main road to the farm, thus saving a mile or nearly an hour, for they kissed at the gates. By and by they gave up kissing at the stiles and found that they could walk the whole way in three-quarters of an hour. Soon afterwards they were married. She died long ago, but he probably has her key. Neither of them has ever called here. This,' he continued, touching a plain deal box with iron edges, 'This is another box of his. After they had been married a little while he thought there was no good reason for walking three miles into the town to his work, so they moved into the town. The time thus saved was deposited in this box and it also has not been called for.'

Against Robert Ploughman's box was a solemn chest of oak with panelled sides, and I asked what it was.

'This may have to go back at any time,' said the manager. 'Many times Mr Beam has been expected to send for it, though it is only three or four years old. He was a squire, whose day was full from morning till night with country works and pleasures, mostly the same thing. There was no doubt that he did very much, what with planting, building, and so on, and that he liked doing it. Sometimes he used to turn his horse Fencer up an old road and let him do as he liked, while he himself sat on a gate and read Virgil, at least such parts as he had succeeded in thoroughly understanding at school. But at last the horse died and before he had begun to remember at the thought of the old road that Fencer really was dead, a kind friend gave him a motor car. He could not read Virgil in a motor car nor could he go up the old road, so that it was clear that he saved many hours a week. Those saved in this way are sent down here, but as he has not yet learned what to do with them or had any need of them, here they remain.'

He spoke with the same grey voice, scattering dust from his beard as his lips moved. I glanced here and there. The boxes were without end and I could no longer see the windows and door. The room was vast, and neither walls nor ceiling could be seen through the rows and piles. Most were of similar pattern. They were square, made of yellowish brown tin, or deal, or wicker, of about the size which holds the property of a young general servant. In the midst of some of these monotonous groups were chests or cabinets of more massive or more delicate make. I pointed to one of the groups and asked what they contained. He thrust his finger through the dust on top of the master box which was an iron safe.

'This,' he said, 'holds the savings of a man who invented machines for saving time. In a few years he grew rich and bought the chief house of his native parish. He employed four gardeners. He did not live there, but occasionally paid visits with business friends. The boxes you see round about belong to his less fortunate neighbours in the parish. They also have saved time. For when he went out into the world the women used to bake their own bread, make most of the family clothes, and work in the fields half the year. Now they do none of these things, but they have saved time.'

No ordinary shopman could have refrained from pride in the neat regiment of boxes over which he waved his hands at these words. But he turned with me to a solitary cabinet at the side of another group. It might have been supposed to hold letters or a few hundred cigars, and was scarcely large enough for my purpose.

'It contains,' he said, 'the savings of a young journalist. He was an industrious youth, earning a living without quite knowing why or how. He bit off the ends of many penholders, and often blackened his mouth with ink. He had an old pewter inkstand, once the property of a great-great-grandfather who was a pirate. He used to say that out of this inkstand he got more than ink, but his friends proved that this was not so by emptying it and showing that it was free from sediment. They advised him to buy a fountain pen because it wasted no time and it was impossible to bite the end of it. This he did. He no longer bit his pen or paused with the nib in his inkstand which was now put on his mantelpiece and polished faithfully once a week. He saved a quantity of time as his friends told him; but he did not notice it, for he continued to be industrious and to earn a living just as before. His friends, however, were right, and that box is full of the hours saved by him in ten years. It is not likely that he will come in search of them. He is busy saving more time. There are thousands of similar cabinets, saved by fountain pens, typewriters, cash registers, and the like. We have also some millions ready for holding the hours to be saved by the navigation of the air.'

He became verbose, enumerating tools, processes and machines for time saving. In one parish alone enough time was saved to extend back to William the Conqueror; in some cities it went beyond the landing of Caesar to the Stone Age and even, according to some calculators, to the Eolithic Age – if such an age there ever was. But most of this time was now in the underground chambers that gave so solemn a resonance to my footsteps. To this too mathematical monologue I was indifferent and I strayed here and there until I seemed to recognize a home-made chest of deal. I had made several myself of the same pattern in former years. The proportions and peculiar workmanship marked this one surely as mine. I felt in my pocket for my keys and with some agitation chose one from the bunch. Yes! ... No, not quite. Or ... I could not open it. Yet I could have sworn ... Meantime the manager had come up.

'This is my chest,' said I excitedly.

'Have you the key?' he asked.

'This almost fits.'

'Then you must wait until you have found the right one. People sometimes lose their keys. This chest contains ...'

But what he said was so absurdly true that I raised my hand to strike him. He fled. I followed, thundering after him through the haze of dust and the myriad chests and caskets. I slid, I waded, I leapt, with incredible feats of speed and agility after the silent grey man until he went perpendicularly down. I plunged after him into space, to end, I suppose, among the boxes containing hours saved in the time of Lear; but I awoke before I had touched ground in that tremendous apartment. Forcing myself asleep again I recovered the dream and heard much more from the shopman which it would be tedious or ridiculous to mention.

People Who Live in Glass Houses Shouldn't Throw Stones[21]

Archie Flinders lived at Wallop in a big, dark house, surrounded and hidden by a tall yew hedge. Some boys believed that there was really no house at all inside the hedge. They used to laugh at Archie, saying that he lived behind the hedge. For several reasons he was disliked. He used to tell tales, and lies too. He peeped at things that had nothing at all to do with him. But his chief offence was running from school and lurking in his garden to throw stones at the boys going home. It seemed useless to throw back at one hiding behind those tall, thick yew trees. But one day when a stone had hit Will Reynolds on the head, the other boys decided to throw over the hedge and see what would happen. Each one armed himself with several flints, and at a word from Will all together began the attack. Like the Norman archers at Hastings, they threw high up into the air. There was a moment when they thought that nothing had happened. They feared that the stones had simply fallen on the earth, or whatever there was inside. The crash and clatter following told another tale. Archie was heard screaming: 'They've broken the glass house.' Another volley of stones was thrown immediately, another clash of glass was the result, and another scream from Archie. Laughing, but a little scared, the boys ran away.

When Archie came to school next morning, Will said to him: 'People who live in glass houses shouldn't throw stones.' That night he had a dream. He dreamed that he was living in an enormous palace with rooms and halls too many for him to count. They were full of beautiful things, and all were his. Nevertheless Archie was not happy; for the walls, the floors, and the roof of his palace were made of glass. Nobody else was in the palace; yet he kept looking round, out of the glass walls, up out of the glass roof, and down through the glass floor; he was afraid to do anything lest he should be peeped at, and somebody should tell tales about him. He was afraid to eat. He did nothing but wander up and down the staircases and along the passages, from room to room, searching for a corner where there was no glass. His search was in vain. Miserable and helpless, he looked out through the walls. The palace was surrounded by a yew hedge as high as the hills: he could not see over it, nor could anyone standing on the hill-top see into the enclosure. But though he could see nobody he had a feeling that he was being looked at through the hedge. It was more than he could endure. Downstairs he rushed, and out of the palace into the grounds. Without a pause he picked up a stone and hurled it at the walls. A crash, a hundred clashes, and a long clattering dissolved the palace to a heap like a pyramid, and Archie awoke, saying to himself the words of Will Reynolds, as if they were a line out of a copy-book: 'People who live in glass houses shouldn't throw stones.'

Rain[22]

I lay awake listening to the rain, and at first it was as pleasant to my ear and my mind as it had long been desired; but before I fell asleep it had become a majestic and finally a terrible thing, instead of a sweet sound and symbol. It was accusing and trying me and passing judgment. Long I lay still under the sentence, listening to the rain, and then at last listening to words which seemed to be spoken by a ghostly double beside me. He was muttering: The all-night rain puts out summer like a torch. In the heavy, black rain falling straight from invisible, dark sky to invisible, dark earth the heat of summer is annihilated, the splendour is dead, the summer is gone. The midnight rain buries it away where it has buried all sound but its own. I am alone in the dark still night, and my ear listens to the rain piping in the gutters and roaring softly in the trees of the world. Even so will the rain fall darkly upon the grass over the grave when my ears can hear it no more. I have been glad of the sound of rain, and wildly sad of it in the past, but that is all over as if it had never been; my eye is dull and my heart beating evenly and quietly; I stir neither foot nor hand; I shall not be quieter when I lie under the wet grass and the rain falls, and I of less account than the grass. The summer is gone, and never can it return. There will never be any summer any more, and I am weary of everything. I stay because I am too weak to go. I crawl on because it is easier than to stop. I put my face to the window. There is nothing out there but the blackness and sound of rain. Neither when I shut my eyes can I see anything. I am alone. Once I heard through the rain a bird's questioning watery cry – once only and suddenly. It seemed content, and the solitary note brought up against me the order of nature, all its beauty, exuberance, and everlastingness like an accusation. I am not a part of nature. I am alone. There is nothing else in my world but my dead heart and brain within me and the rain without. Once there was summer, and a great heat and splendour over the earth terrified me and asked me what I could show that was worthy of such an earth. It smote and humiliated me, yet I had eyes to behold it, and I prostrated myself, and by adoration made myself worthy of the splendour. Was I not once blind to the splendour because there was something within me equal to itself? What was it? Love . . . a name! . . . a word! . . . less than the watery question of the bird out in the rain. The rain has drowned the splendour. Everything is drowned and dead, all that was once lovely and alive in the world, all that had once been alive and was memorable though dead is now dung for a future that is infinitely less than the falling dark rain. For a moment the mind's eye and ear pretend to see and hear what the eye and ear themselves once knew with delight. The rain denies. There is nothing to be seen or heard, and there never was. Memory, the last chord of the lute, is broken. The rain has been and will be for ever over the earth. There never was anything but the dark rain. Beauty and strength are as nothing to it. Eyes could not flash in it.

I have been lying dreaming until now, and now I have awakened, and there is still nothing but the rain. I am alone. The unborn is not more weak or more ignorant, and like the unborn

I wait and wait, knowing neither what has been nor what is to come, because of the rain, which is, has been, and must be. The house is still and silent, and those small noises that make me start are only the imagination of the spirit or they are the rain. There is only the rain for it to feed on and to crawl in. The rain swallows it up as the sea does its own foam. I will lie still and stretch out my body and close my eyes. My breath is all that has been spared by the rain, and that comes softly and at long intervals, as if it were trying to hide itself from the rain. I feel that I am so little I have crept away into a corner and been forgotten by the rain. All else has perished except me and the rain. There is no room for anything in the world but the rain. It alone is great and strong. It alone knows joy. It chants monotonous praise of the order of nature, which I have disobeyed or slipped out of. I have done evilly and weakly, and I have left undone. Fool! you never were alive. Lie still. Stretch out yourself like foam on a wave, and think no more of good or evil. There was no good and no evil. There was life and there was death, and you chose. Now there is neither life nor death, but only the rain. Sleep as all things, past, present, and future, lie still and sleep, except the rain, the heavy, black rain falling straight through the air that was once a sea of life. That was a dream only. The truth is that the rain falls for ever and I am melting into it. Black and monotonously sounding is the midnight and solitude of the rain. In a little while or in an age – for it is all one – I shall know the full truth of the words I used to love, I knew not why, in my days of nature, in the days before the rain: 'Blessed are the dead that the rain rains on.'

'All These Things Are Mine'[23]

He had an inexhaustible desire to know about everything that lives on the earth, both near and far. He had learned the songs of many birds, and spoke of them familiarly with admiration and delight. The immensity and variety of Nature, as he found himself, or read of it in the gorgeous records of travellers, were a source of continual satisfaction; he had never dreamed of them before. Everywhere he found beauty, personality, and differences without end. The old simplicity and horror of the world conceived as the abode of evil man and a dissatisfied, incompatible Deity were forgotten. He could speak of God without emotion. After reading a book in which a liberal and gentle soul created a liberal and gentle Deity, and showed the necessity for his own adherence to the religion of his fathers, his only comment was: 'It is a good book ... a good God, but not a very great God after all ... What does that thrush say? We must consider him. But so far they do not seem to know very much about him, except his skeleton and his diet. There must be one God for both of us. We can afford to wait. So can He.' But that was only a casual, light-hearted expression of the creed that was coming to him under the sky. He turned away to look at a blackcap singing every minute high up in golden-green blossom against the blue sky, where the sun and the south-west wind ruled over large, eager grey clouds with edges of gleaming white. The little dead-leaf coloured bird quivered all over; his throat swelled in bubble after bubble; his lifted black head was turned from side to side as he sang; and he moved slowly among the blossom.

The high, quick, dewy notes filled the paralytic with a thin, exquisite pleasure, as if his soul had climbed upon the line of his vision and crept into the singing bird. 'All these things are mine. They are me. And that is not all: I am them. We are one. We are organs and instruments of one another.'

The First Cuckoo[24]

In each spring, as in each man's youth, all things are new, and the finer our feelings the more numerous and powerful the impressions made on them. As life or the year advances new things appear continually, the old are repeated or varied, both by chance and design; multitudinousness, coupled often with decrease of sensibility, reduces the impressions, in number, in power, or in both. Countless are the things which may impress us for ever. It may be the sound of bells pealing, it may be the smell of glue on a toy dissolving in a hot bath. But the majority fade away or can be revived only by poetry or strange chance. Very few endure. Those that do, most men are pleased and even proud to recall over and over again.

Usually it is supposed that the first experience makes the lasting impression, and by a kind of natural superstition a special importance is attached to 'first' experiences, even when of a kind that can be repeated. Instinctively, but not unconsciously, we prepare ourselves in a reverent or enthusiastic manner for the first sight of a house or tree or hill which has a meaning for ourselves only. And so with unexpected recurring things of universal significance, like the appearance of the new moon, or of the faint Pleiades in early autumn. Almost every one is pleased to report the crescent moon low in the west on a fine evening: many probably have an exaltation, however faint or indeterminate, at the sight, which they have no idea what to do with. Thus many times a year we enjoy in a milder, more Epicurean way, something like an imitation of a real first experience. I am not forgetting how much of the thrill may be due to the feeling of a fresh start, combined with that of being an old inhabitant of the earth.

But the first cry of the cuckoo in spring is more to us than the new moon. The first flicker and twitter of the swallow is its only possible rival. The first snowdrop, the first blackbird's song or peewit's love cry, the first hawthorn leaves, are as nothing even to those who regard them, compared with the cuckoo's note, while there are many for whom it is the one powerfully significant natural thing throughout the year, apart from broad gradual changes, such as the greening or the baring of the woods. The old become fearful lest they should not hear it: having heard it, they fear lest it should be for the last time. It has been accepted as the object upon which we concentrate whatever feeling we have towards the beginning of spring. It constitutes a natural, unmistakable festival. We wish to hear it, we are eager and anxious about it, we pause when it reaches us, as if perhaps it might be bringing more than it ever brought yet. Vaguely enough, as a rule, we set much store by this first hearing, and the expectancy does not fail to bring its reward of at least a full and intense impression. And for this purpose the cuckoo's note is perfectly suited. It is loud, clear, brief, and distinct, never in danger of being lost in a chorus of its own or another kind: it has a human and also a ghostly quality which earns it the reputation of sadness or joyousness at different times.

When we hear a bird's note for the first time in spring, it usually happens that conditions are favourable. If rain is falling or wind roaring in tossing branches any noise but a loud or near one may be drowned; also mere cold and cloudiness, if they do not keep us indoors, suffice to put us out of the humour for expecting. Thus only naturalists are likely, as a rule, to hear the 'first' note in conditions which are unfavourable, that is to say, which will not further its effect. Again, if we have minds bent on other things or altogether troubled and self-centred, the chances are against hearing it. Company and conversation, the sounds of men or horses or wheels, have the same effect as rain or wind. Thus we often first hear the cuckoo in the first mild, quiet weather of spring, with minds more or less tranquil. If I hear it so, though I cannot imagine anyone less superstitious, I have a feeling of luck. Nine or ten years ago, I remember hearing the cuckoo sing for the first time when I had started out for the day. The bird was slanting down towards our plum-trees and cuckooing there, so that I could not help running home in the hope that I should be first to tell the news.

When I heard it this April, I could not be wholly absorbed in it, yet something of me was carried away, floating in a kind of bliss over the river between the hills. I had been walking all day in Carmarthenshire in hot, bright weather. But no mossy lane overhung by ash trees, no little valley of ivy-mantled oaks or gorse blossoming, no crooked orchard above the roadside, no bushy, dripping precipices that echoed to the gulls' cry on pale sand and white serpentine water, possessed a cuckoo. One bird

I heard for the first time that morning – a corncrake in a thicket of thorn and sallow by Goose's Bridge. But at the moment I had no wish to hear that wooden comb scraped. It is a sound for the mowing grass, for the height and heat of midsummer. I was, in fact, irritated by hearing this undesired, unseasonable call already, before the cuckoo's note which I had been listening for during a whole, fine week. Then some hours later I was returning by that same road between Laugharne and St Clear's. I did not pass one man, woman, or child, for each of the four practically houseless miles. It is a road that rises and falls in following the direction of the Taf, and keeps usually in sight below it the loops of the river, the rushy levels and the low hills opposite, divided by dark hedges with a few red ploughlands and many green pastures, with a scattering of gorse. The corresponding hills crossed or skirted by my road on this side, were similar. The mile between the hills was silent. It being then after seven and the sun having just fallen crimson upon my right, the air was still and cool, the sky cloudless as it had been all day.

The road was deep in dust, but the marigolds in the ditch preserved their brightness and their coolness. Coming over the shoulder of the hill called Pwll y Pridd, by the farm Morfa Bach, where the primroses were so thick under the young emerald larches, I began to have a strong desire – almost amounting to a conviction – that I should hear the cuckoo. When I was down again at Goose's Bridge, by the brook that descends out of a furzy valley towards the Taf, I heard it, or thought I did. I stopped. Not a sound. I went on stealthily that I might stop as soon as I heard anything. Again I seemed to hear it; again it had gone by the time I was still. The third time I had no doubt. The cuckoo was singing over on the far side of the valley, perhaps three-quarters of a mile away, probably in a gorse bank just above the marsh. For half a minute he sang, changed his perch unseen and sang again, his notes as free from the dust and heat as the cups of the marigolds, and as soft as the pale white-blue sky, and as dim as the valley into whose twilight he was gathered, calling fainter and fainter, as I drew towards home.

From In Pursuit of Spring[25]

THE CHIFFCHAFF

It was here, and at eleven, that I first heard the chiffchaff saying, 'Chiff-chaff, chiff-chaff, chiff-chaff, chiff!' A streamlet darted out of the park towards the Wey, and on the other side of the road, and below it, had to itself a little steep coomb of ash trees. An oak had been felled on the coomb side, and a man was clearing the brushwood round it, but the small bird's double note, almost as regular as the ticking of a clock, though often coming to an end on the first half, sounded very clear in the coomb. He sang as he flitted among the swaying ash tops in that warm, cloudy sun. I thought he sang more shrilly than usual, something distractedly. But I was satisfied. Nothing so convinces me, year after year, that Spring has come and cannot be repulsed, though checked it may be, as this least of songs. In the blasting or dripping weather which may ensue, the chiffchaff is probably unheard; but he is not silenced. I heard him on March 19 when I was fifteen, and I believe not a year has passed without my hearing him within a day or two of that date. I always expect him and always hear him. Not all the blackbirds, thrushes, larks, chaffinches, and robins can hide the note. The silence of July and August does not daunt him. I hear him yearly in September, and well into October – the sole Summer voice remaining save in memory. But for the wind I should have heard him yesterday. I went on more cheerfully, as if each note had been the hammering of a tiny nail into Winter's coffin.

THE OTHER MAN

We took the Frome road as far as Winkfield, where we turned off westward to Farleigh Hungerford. In half a mile we were in Somerset, descending by a steep bank of celandines under beeches that rose up on our right towards the Frome. The river lay clear ahead of us, and to our left. A bushy hill, terraced horizontally, rose beyond it, and Farleigh Hungerford Castle, an ivied front, a hollow-eyed round tower, and a gateway, faced us from the brow. From the bridge, and the ruined cottages and mills collected round it, we walked up to the castle, which is a show place. From here the Other Man would have me turn aside to see Tellisford. This is a hamlet scattered along half a mile of by-road, from a church at the corner down to the Frome. Once there was a ford, but now you cross by a stone footbridge with white wooden handrails. A ruined flock-mill and a ruined ancient house stand next to it on one side; on the other the only house is a farm with a round tower embodied in its front. Away from this farm a beautiful meadow slopes between the river and the woods above. This grass, which becomes level for a few yards nearest the bank, was the best possible place, said the Other Man, for running in the sun after bathing at the weir – we could see its white wall of foam half a mile higher up the river, which was concealed by alders beyond. He said it was a great haunt of nightingales. And there was also a service tree; and, said he, in that tree sang a thrush all through May – it was the best May that ever was – and so well it sang, unlike any other thrush, that it made him think he would gladly live no longer than a thrush if he could do some one thing as right, as crisp and rich, as the song was. 'I suppose you write books,' said I. 'I do,' said he. 'What sort of books do you write?' 'I wrote one all about this valley of the Frome . . . But no one knows that it was the Frome I meant. You look surprised. Nevertheless, I got fifty pounds for it.' 'That is a lot of money for such a book!' 'So my publisher thought.' 'And you are lucky to get money for doing what you like.' 'What I like!' he muttered, pushing his bicycle back uphill, past the goats by the ruin, and up the steps between walls that were lovely with humid moneywort, and saxifrage like filigree, and ivy-leaved toadflax. Apparently the effort loosened his tongue. He rambled on and on about himself, his past, his writing, his digestion; his main point being that he did not like writing. He had been attempting the impossible task of reducing undigested notes about all sorts of details to a grammatical, continuous narrative. He abused notebooks violently. He said that they blinded him to nearly everything that would not go into the form of notes; or, at any rate, he could never afterwards reproduce the great effects of Nature and fill in the interstices merely – which was all they were good for – from the notes. The notes – often of things which he would otherwise have forgotten – had to fill the whole canvas. Whereas, if he had taken none, then only the important, what he truly cared for, would have survived in his memory, arranged not perhaps as they were in Nature, but at least according to the tendencies of his own spirit. 'Good God!' said he.

From Walter Pater[26]

PATER AND STYLE

For the last hundred years ideas and the material of ideas have come to the reading classes mainly through books and bookish conversation. Their ideas are in advance of their experience, their vocabulary in advance of their ideas, and their eyelids 'are a little weary'. They think more of cold than those who have to feel it. They are aware of all the possible vices by the time their blood has chilled and they have understood that they are old. The passions seem to them to belong to a golden age of the past, and it is of their ghosts that they sing. Since everything is an illusion they have no illusions. Not even beauty deceives them. Beauty, says Pater in the preface to *The Renaissance*, is like all other qualities presented to human experience: it is relative. He is, above all men, 'the aesthetic critic', willing – or compelled – to give up the common grey or purple-patched experience for one that clicks incessantly with maybe faint but certainly conscious sensations. He regards everything, in art, nature and human life, 'as powers or forces producing pleasurable sensations'. He writes for those whose education becomes complete in proportion as their susceptibility to these sensations increases in depth and variety. His qualification is that he has a temperament which is 'deeply moved by the presence of beautiful objects'; his end is reached when he has disengaged the virtue by which a thing in art, nature or human life, produced its impression of beauty or pleasure. It is not enough to be capable of leaving his mistress' arms to write a sonnet about her eyebrow. In fact, such a one would hardly be an aesthetic critic at all; it would be better that he should first write the sonnet and then proceed to her arms for verification. The aesthetic critic will hardly have time for the passions except of others. There is an austerity about his life. His virtues and his vices must be fugitive and cloistered. He must beware of the bestial waste of nature, the violent, brief passion and the long languors following.

Pater lived a sober, almost ascetic life at Oxford, varied by tours in continental churches and galleries with his sisters. Yet his was the head upon which all 'the ends of the world are come', 'the animalism of Greece, the lust of Rome, the mysticism of the Middle Age with its spiritual ambition and imaginative loves, the return of the Pagan world, the sins of the Borgias'. Pater liked to think of the sins of the Borgias: they had enriched the pageantry of life by which he lived; and with the help of them and of Swinburne's Faustine and Dolores he made his most famous piece of prose. He did not recommend their sins, or any kind of sin. 'He spoke once with great gravity and seriousness of one whom he had known, whom he thought to be drifting into dangerous courses, and expressed a deep desire to help or warn him, or at all events, to get a warning conveyed to him.' In some frames of mind he may have condemned the sins of the Borgias, as a eugenist would, and he does say that 'the spirit of controversy lays just hold' of wicked popes and the like: he would certainly have condemned them in a contemporary, because they are so inconvenient, causing pain, vulgar laughter, scandal, uncomfortable moments when women or strangers are present, and so on. There is no reason to suppose that he disapproved of the ten commandments or the moral ideals of the middle-class, though he would never have ascended a pulpit to recommend them. He lived a quiet life with books and pictures, and he saw good of one kind or another in everything. A thing might pain or disgust or sadden him, but in his pensive citadel he believed this was better than to feel nothing at all. He was, I suppose, not inclined to throw away time in such general emotions as regret or indignation, especially over the past, nor did he pretend to do so. A great many men like to read about the sins of the Borgias or of the Joneses, to see a little real sin or what they regard as such, and to enjoy some at discreet intervals; but they do not in general name these things among their recreations when talking in the bosom of their family or writing for Who's Who. Even Pater probably suppressed something. He had a conscious, or more likely unconscious ideal of himself which his writing was not allowed to misrepresent. Even so, sin appears on his pages for the most part as a beautiful abstraction: there is no vision portrayed of those temptations of the scholar in his 'dreamy tranquillity', such as visited Abelard's world of shadows. He was still more attracted to the pure, the wholesome, the refined, the delicate, if, at his distance, he distinguished them. In *The House Beautiful*, he says, 'the saints too have their place'. In his mind, as, according to his opinion, in *The Renaissance* generally, there are 'no exclusions'; 'whatsoever things are comely', all are reconciled 'for the elevation and adorning' of his spirit; he recognizes no essential incompatibility between any really beautiful things, between the freshness of a youthful art and the 'subtle and delicate sweetness' of a 'refined and comely decadence'. He hardly distinguishes between life and art: as they reach his mirror they are alike. Thus he speaks of the 'life of refined pleasure and action in the conspicuous places of the world', as if it were a kind of pictorial art by a greater than Bellini or Titian. Yet, again, in an age like that of Pericles or Lorenzo the Magnificent, he sees the fullest beauty, where artists, philosophers, men of action, all communicate in a spirit of 'general elevation and enlightenment'. There is nothing which he cannot enjoy when it is in focus, and only a faintly surviving human weakness enables him to choose one thing rather than another. He is a spectator. His aim is to see; if he is to become something it is by seeing.

It may be said of *The Renaissance* that it suggests a writer who treats life in the spirit of art. The same phrase occurs in his *Diaphaneite* and his *Wordsworth*. That the end of life is contemplation, not action, being, not doing, is, he says, 'the principle of all higher morality'. He connects poetry and art with this principle because they 'by their very sterility are a type of beholding for the joy of beholding'. Thus he thinks they encourage the treatment of life 'in the spirit of art'; and to identify the means and the ends of life is to do this. He calls it 'impassioned contemplation', and poets the experts in it, withdrawing our thoughts from 'the mere machinery of life' to the spectacle of men and nature in their grandeur. To witness this spectacle with appropriate emotions, he says, 'is the aim of all culture'.

It is impossible not to regard this aim, as Pater expressed it, as a kind of higher philately or connoisseurship. He speaks like a collector of the great and beautiful. He collected them from books, and pictures, not from life.

I have no wish to plead for the 'natural eloquence of ordinary conversation, the language in which we address our friends, wives, children, and servants, and which is intended only to express our thoughts, and requires no foreign or elaborate ornament'. It is for most people easier to speak as they write, or more or less as journalists write, than to write as they speak. Nor do I consider the matter settled by Mr Arnold Bennett's *dicta*:

> Style cannot be distinguished from matter. When a writer conceives an idea he conceives it in a form of words. That form of words constitutes his style, and it is absolutely governed by the idea ... When you have thought clearly you have never had any difficulty in saying what you thought, though you may have some difficulty in keeping it to yourself.

This amounts to nothing more than that no man can escape self-expression in the presence of a sufficiently intelligent listener or reader, though it also implies an exclusive acquaintance with very ready speakers and writers. It is certain that there is a kind of unconscious self-expression which no man escapes. Thus Pater expressed something in himself which made John Addington Symonds revolt as from a civet-cat. Some have thought that his style reveals his use of gilt-edged note-paper. Style, even in Pater, is not a 'mere dress' for something which could be otherwise expressed and remain the same. A thing which one or a thousand men would be tempted to express in different ways is not one but many, and only after a full realization of this can we agree with Pater's statement that in all art 'form, in the full signification of the term, is everything, and the mere matter nothing': we can agree and yet wonder how Pater could say also that 'form counts equally with, or for more than, the matter'. Even carelessness or conventionality of language has its value as expression, though if it ends in a pale, muddy, or inharmonious style, the value will be very little in this world. That two men possess walking-sticks of the same kind is not nearly so important as that one twirls and flourishes it, while the other regularly swings it once in every four steps – unless, of course, the observer is a manufacturer, or retailer, or connoisseur, of walking-sticks. Literature is not for connoisseurs. Is there no difference but in length and sound between 'It has not wit enough to keep it sweet' and 'It has not vitality enough to preserve it from putrefaction'? or between 'Under the impression that your peregrinations in this metropolis have not as yet been extensive, and that you might have some difficulty in penetrating the arcana of the Modern Babylon in the direction of the City Road' and the form of that idea which Mr Micawber introduced with the words 'In short'? It is not satisfactory, then, to say that we think with words, or that 'the best words generally attach themselves to our subject, and show themselves by their own light'. John Hawkins spoke with feeling and spoke truly when he ended the account of his third voyage with these words: 'If all the miseries and troublesome affairs of this sorrowful voyage should be perfectly and thoroughly written, there should need a painful man with his pen, and as great a time as he that wrote the lives and deaths of the martyrs.'

Yet some wise men have thought well of the language of the unlearned. Vaugelas, the grammarian, recommended women and the unlearned, rather than the learned, as authorities on words. Pedants are like some old people who know so much about a man's parents and grandparents that they take little note of himself, unless he present some differences, in which case they regret the old and condemn the new. Herrick used scores of words known to him as a University man, and only to be understood by the like to-day: few of these are to be found in those poems which are now thought best even by University men. He would not write in Latin or Volapuk, but he had cravings for better bread than is made with wheat. He was fortunately most often aware that 'the Poet writes under one restriction only, namely, the necessity of giving immediate pleasure to a Human Being possessed of that information which may be expected of him, not as a lawyer, a physician, a mariner, an astronomer, or a natural philosopher, but as a Man'.

Somewhere in *Wilhelm Meister*, Goethe says that a man will not think clearly unless he talks. Mr George Moore, after quoting Numa Roumestan's 'I cannot think unless I talk', says: 'I often find my brain will not work except in collaboration with my tongue: when I am composing a novel I must tell my ideas; and as I talk I formulate and develop my scheme of narrative and character.' Many a man has said or written much as Goldsmith did: 'To feel your subject thoroughly, and to speak without fear, are the only rules of eloquence.' When Coleridge wishes to praise Southey's style, he says: 'It is as if he had been speaking to you all the while.' But he does not say that Southey's writing was the same as his speech: for a mere copy of speech might have a different effect from the spoken words, in the absence of the individual voice and its accompaniment of looks and gestures.

It is the last thing that many writers would think of, to write as they speak: and the more solitary and learned the writer, the less likely is he to attempt so unnatural a thing.

*

What Wordsworth condemns in that sonnet of Gray's beginning

> In vain to me the smiling mornings shine,
> And reddening Phoebus lifts his golden fire . . .

is due to the remoteness of the words, not from speech, but from thought. It is unlikely that Gray was thinking of Phoebus Apollo. Much good poetry is far from the speech of any men now, or perhaps at any recorded time, dwelling on this earth. There would be no poetry if men could speak all that they think and all that they feel. Each great new writer is an astonishment to his own age, if it hears him, by the apparent shrillness and discordancy of the speech he has made in solitude. It has to become vulgarized before common ears will acknowledge the sweetness and wisdom of it. Pater still astonishes men with his falsetto delicacy, but may lift posterity up to him.

The more we know of any man the more singular he will appear, and nothing so well represents his singularity as style. Literature is further divided in outward seeming from speech by what helps to make it in fact more than ever an equivalent of speech. It has to make words of such a spirit, and arrange them in such a manner, that they will do all that a speaker can do by innumerable gestures and their innumerable shades, by tone and pitch of voice, by speed, by pauses, by all that he is and all that he will become.

The most and the greatest of man's powers are as yet little known to him, and are scarcely more under his control than the weather: he cannot keep a shop without trusting somewhat to his unknown powers, nor can he write books except such as are no books. It appears to have been Pater's chief fault, or the cause of his faults, that he trusted those powers too little. The alternative supposition is that he did not carry his self-conscious labours far enough. On almost every page of his writing words are to be seen sticking out, like the raisins that will get burnt on an ill-made cake. It is clear that they have been carefully chosen as the right and effective words, but they stick out because the labour of composition has become so self-conscious and mechanical that cohesion and perfect consistency are impossible. The words have only an isolated value; they are labels; they are shorthand: they are anything but living and social words.

Pater was, in fact, forced against his judgment to use words as bricks, as tin soldiers, instead of flesh and blood and genius. Inability to survey the whole history of every word must force the perfectly self-conscious writer into this position. Only when a word has become necessary to him can a man use it safely; if he try to impress words by force on a sudden occasion, they will either perish of his violence or betray him. No man can decree the value of one word, unless it is his own invention; the value which it will have in his hands has been decreed by his own past, by the past of his race. It is, of course, impossible to study words too deeply, though all men are not born for this study: but Pater's influence has tended to encourage meticulosity in detail and single words, rather than a regard for form in its largest sense. His words and still less his disciples' have not been lived with sufficiently. Unless a man write with his whole nature concentrated upon his subject he is unlikely to take hold of another man. For that man will read, not as a scholar, a philologist, a word-fancier, but as a man with all his race, age, class, and personal experience brought to bear on the matter.

How I Began[27]

Talking prose is natural to most of the species; writing it is now almost as common, if not as natural; having it published when written is the third step which distinguishes an author from the more primitive minority of mankind. No author, I suppose, except Miss Helen Keller, has varied this method of progress. Every one begins by talking, stumbles into writing, and succumbs to print.

The first step is the most interesting and the most difficult to explain and describe. I shall leave it alone. The second step is very interesting, and less difficult to explain and describe, yet I can remember little of it. I can only remark here that the result of teaching a child to read before it can write is that it begins and usually ends by writing like a book, not like a human being. It was my own experience. From the age of one, I could express by words and inflections of the voice all that ever sought expression within me, from feelings of heat, cold, hunger, repletion, indigestion, etc., to subtle preferences of persons and things. But when I came to write the slowness of that unnatural act decimated and disconcerted my natural faculties. I laboriously covered a square foot of note-paper, communicating nothing much beyond the fact that I had begun to hold a pen, and to master English grammar.

That the best of fountain-pens is slow, does not entirely account for the inexpressiveness of that square foot of note-paper. The slowness made it practically impossible to say what I was thinking, even if I had tried. I did not try hard. I do not believe that it was by any means my sole or chief aim to write what I was thinking, or what I should have spoken had my correspondent been in the same room with me. I felt it to be highly important that I should use terms such as I had met in books, seldom if ever in speech. Nor do I remember hearing it said that I could, or should, write as I thought or as I spoke.

Until the age of eight or nine, therefore, all my writing was painful and compulsory, and I knew well that it displayed a poorer creature than the severest critic could judge me. But at that age I was given a small notebook in a cover as much like tortoiseshell as could be made for a penny. In this I wrote down a number of observations of my own accord, though I dare say the notebook had been designed as a trap; if there was a separate bait, I have forgotten it. All that I can remember is that I pronounced the houses of Swindon to be 'like bull-dogs, small but strongly built'. They were of stone, and I was accustomed to brick. Stone seemed to be a grander material. Hence the note. The sententious form was, no doubt, due to a conscious desire to be impressive, that is to say, adult. It was not the last time I experienced this desire, but I shall not trouble you with more instances.

With short intervals, from that time onwards I was a writer

by choice. I began several diaries, carrying on the entries in some of them as far as February. By the time I was fourteen or fifteen, I did more; I kept a more or less daily record of notable events, the finding of birds' nests, the catching of moles or fish, the skinning of a stoat, the reading of Richard Jefferies and the naturalists.

These notes aimed at brevity: they were above syntax and indifferent to dignity. I was not, however, permitted to forget syntax or dignity. I was obliged to write essays on Imperial Federation, the Greek Colonization of Sicily, Holidays, etc., where I gave myself up to an almost purely artistic rendering of such facts as I remembered, and such opinions as I could concoct by the help of memory, fancy and the radical and the free-thinking influence of home. Thus, like nearly every other child, I virtually neglected in my writing the feelings that belonged to my own nature and my own times of life – an irreparable loss, whether great or not. If I wrote about what really pleased or concerned me, like a walk all day or all night in Wiltshire, I had in view not the truth but the eyes of elders, and those elders clothed in the excess and circumstance of elderliness regularly assumed in the presence of children. I was considered to excel in this form of rhetoric. So seriously, too, did I take myself in it, that from the time I was sixteen I found myself hardly letting a week pass without writing one or two descriptions – of a man, or a place, or a walk – in a manner largely founded on Jefferies' *Amateur Poacher*, Kingsley's *Prose Idylls*, and Mr Francis A. Knight's weekly contributions to the *Daily News*, but doubtless with tones supplied also by Shelley and Keats, and later on by Ruskin, De Quincey, Pater, and Sir Thomas Browne. I had quite a number of temptations to print, and at the age of fifteen easily gave way. At seventeen, some of those descriptions were printed in the *Speaker* and the *New Age*, and soon afterwards took the form of a book.

While I was afflicted with serious English composition and English literature, I was reading Scott, Fenimore Cooper, Henty, and the travellers, because I loved them; I was also thinking and talking in a manner which owed little to those dignified exercises, though the day was to come when I spoke very much as I wrote. Presently, also, myself and English, as she is taught in schools, came to a conflict, and gradually to a more and more friendly agreement through the necessity of writing long letters daily to one who was neither a schoolboy nor an elder, the subject of the letters being matters concerning nobody else in the world. Now it was that I had a chance of discarding or of adapting to my own purpose the fine words and infinite variety of constructions which I had formerly admired from afar off and imitated in fairly cold blood. There is no doubt that my masters often lent me dignity and subtlety altogether beyond my needs.

Both in these letters and in papers intended for print, I ravaged the language (to the best of my ability) at least as much for ostentation as for use, though I should not like to have to separate the two. This must always happen where a man has collected all the colours of the rainbow, 'of earthquake and eclipse', on his palette, and has a cottage or a gasometer to paint. A continual negotiation was going on between thought, speech and writing, thought having as a rule the worst of it. Speech was humble and creeping, but wanted too many fine shades and could never come to a satisfactory end. Writing was lordly and regardless. Thought went on in the twilight, and wished the other two might come to terms for ever. But maybe they did not and never will, and perhaps, they never do. In my own case, at any rate, I cannot pronounce, though I have by this time provided an abundance of material for a judgment.

From The Childhood of Edward Thomas[28]

INFANCY

I have only one clear early glimpse of my father – darting out of the house in his slippers and chasing and catching a big boy who had bullied me. He was eloquent, confident, black-haired, brown-eyed, all that my mother was not. By glimpses, I learnt with awe and astonishment that he had once been of my age. He knew, for example, far more about marbles than the best players at school. His talk of 'alley-taws' – above all the way his thumb drove the marble out of the crook of his first finger, the speeding sureness of it – these betokened mastery. Once or twice I spent an hour or so in his office in an old government building. The presence of a washstand in a sitting-room pleased me, but what pleased me still more was the peculiar large brown carraway biscuit which I never got anywhere else. My father at this time gave or was to have given lessons to Lady Somebody, and he mentioned her to me once when we were together in his office. She became connected somehow with the carraway biscuit. With or without her aid, this rarity had a kind of magic and beauty as of a flower or bird only to be found in one wood in all the world. I can hear but never see him telling me for the tenth or hundredth time the story of the Wiltshire moon-rakers hanging in a chain over a bridge to fetch the moon out, which they had mistaken for a green cheese, and the topmost one, whose hold on the parapet began slipping, crying out, 'Hold tight below while I spit on my hands', and many another comic tale or rhyme. My mother I can hardly see save as she is now while I am writing. I cannot see her but I can summon up her presence. She is plainest to me not quite dressed, in white bodice and petticoat, her arms and shoulders rounded and creamy smooth. My affection for her was leavened with lesser likings and with admiration. I liked the scent of her fresh warm skin and supposed it unique. Her straight nose and chin made a profile that for years formed my standard. No hair was so beautiful to me as hers was, light golden brown hair, long and rippling. Her singing at fall of night, especially if we were alone together, soothed and fascinated me, as though it had been divine, at once the mightiest and the softest sound in the world. Usually perhaps there was a servant, but my mother did everything for us in the house, made many of our clothes and mended them, prepared and gave us food, tended us when sick, comforted us when cold, disappointed, or sorrowful. The one terrible thing I witnessed as a small child was my mother suddenly rising from the dining-table with face tortured and crying, 'I am going to die.' My father took her on his knee and soothed her. I had and have no idea what was the matter. For her younger sister I felt a similar affection and admiration, though less, and far less often exercised, for her visits were neither long nor frequent. The grace, smoothness and gentleness of her voice and movements gave me pleasure. My first conscious liking for the female body was at sight of her sitting less than half dressed in a chair, her head bent and one foot on to which she was pulling a stocking lifted from the floor. Years afterwards I used to think of this from time to time to envy the privilege of early childhood. [. . .]

My waking life was divided between home, school and the streets and neighbouring common. Glimpses of the outer world I had few. But I remember General Gordon's death at Khartoum, and, whether from a picture in a newspaper or from imagination, I retain an image of a soldier in a fez and armed with a revolver standing with his back to a portico, facing the enemies who swarmed up the steps below and being struck at by one from the side.

Our street like three or four others parallel to it was in two halves, running straight up the opposite sides of a slight valley, along the bottom of which ran the principal street of mixed shops and private houses. Our house was low down in the half which ran up westwards to Bolingbroke Grove, the eastern boundary of Wandsworth Common. These little semi-detached one-storied pale brick houses in unbroken lines on both sides of the street had each, even then when they were new, something distinguishing them and preventing monotony. The people in them made them different. In addition, some were beginning to be draped in creepers. Some gates stood open, some were shut. One had bushes in the garden, another had flowers, another nothing but dark trodden gravel. The house above ours, in the next pair, was presumably meant for a doctor, and possessed a coach house which looked almost as if it belonged to us. That was our outward distinction. Inside from the front door to the back of the house there was as long a passage as possible, the rooms opening out of it. The staircase ran up to a room with an opaque glass window in the door, a second room, and two others connected by a door. The rooms downstairs I hardly remember at all. But in one of them my great-uncle James Jones lay asleep after dinner, a red handkerchief covering his face and trembling in the blast of his snoring which we called 'driving the pigs to market'. Through the open window of another, one Mayday, Jack-in-the-Green bounded in to beg a penny, showing white teeth, white eyes, black face, but the rest of him covered and rippling with green leaves. The passage was a playground when it was too wet or too dark to be out of doors. Here, when I had at any rate one brother – probably three or four years old when I was five or six – who could run, we two raced up and down the passage to be pounced upon by the servant out of a doorway and swallowed up in her arms with laughter. Upstairs the room with the glass door was at long intervals occupied by a visitor, such as my father's uncle James or my mother's sister, and I think cards were played there. Except relatives I think there were few visitors to the house. Sometimes the old red-faced gent next door, a court usher, came in: and once as he laid his hand on a large sheet of printed matter, perhaps at an election time, he said impressively, 'I am a staunch Liberal, staunch.' Once a young couple had tea with us and everyone laughed at some cheerful remark about the lady's name being about to be changed ... I and at least one brother slept in one of the two connected bedrooms. I had no night fears and few dreams. Several times some shapeless invisible thing threatened me at the end of the bed and I lay in terror, trying vainly to scream for help. On Christmas morning I used to wake up in the dark and smell the oranges and feel my presents, and guess at them and begin an apple and go on to sweets, especially those contained in a cardboard box scented curiously, loaf-shaped, and coloured like a top of a bun, which came from a cousin of my mother's at the Much Birch Vicarage. When I and a brother were recovering from scarlet fever we lay or sat up in our cots, while our father in the other room read aloud the *Cuckoo Clock*. Not a shred of the story is left to me, but I seem to see my father – though I could not see him at the time – sitting in an arm-chair bent over the book. He also read at least the opening chapters of *Great Expectations*, with such effect that, though I have never since looked at them, I have an indelible impression of a churchyard in cold and misty marshland and out among the stones a convict in clanking chains, and a tiny feeble boy with the absurd and as it were enfeebling name of Pip. I do not know whether I read *Robinson Crusoe* or had it read aloud to me. I loved it entirely, and a faint spice of amusement was added to my love by the repetition of 'says I'. Two scenes most impressed me. The first was the picture of men tumbling savages over the sides of a ship by means of brushes like a sweep's dipped in tar. The second was where wolves are pursuing a doomed riderless horse over the snow. But I cannot remember the act of reading this or any other book at home. *Fairy Know-a-bit* by A.L.O.E. was read to me. The fairy in it was created for the purpose of imparting facts about things in everyday use. The facts though not distasteful passed rapidly through my brain, and the fairy, though probably an inartistic invention, fascinated me and attained such a measure of reality for me that I used to fancy it possible for him to appear from between the leaves of some big old books as he did in the story. To my mind the book would have been a certain cookery book with pictures of flesh, fish, and fowl, or dishes. There were, I suspect, invented fairies in another book which had and has a charm impossible for me either to communicate or, I fear, to make credible. It was my first school prize. The words, 'The Key of Knowledge', occurred in its title or they stood out somewhere else. It was illustrated by coloured pictures. But it disappeared, I never had any idea how, before I had read far into it, and I never saw it again. From time to time down to the present day I have recalled the loss, and tried to recover first of all the book, later on the thread of its story, something that would dissipate from its charm the utter darkness of mystery. For example, fifteen years ago in Wiltshire two strangers passed me and I heard one of them, a big public schoolboy, say to the other, a gamekeeper, 'What do you think is the key of knowledge?' and back again came the old loss, the old regret and yearning, faint indeed, but real.

There were times when I fancied that the book had held the key to an otherwise inaccessible wisdom and happiness, and the robbery appeared satanically sinister.[29]

HOLIDAYS

Swindon was a thousand times better. It was delicious to pass Wantage, Challow, Uffington, Shrivenham, to see the 75th, 76th mile marks by the railwayside, to slow down at last to the cry of 'Swindon' and see my grandmother, my uncle or my aunt waiting. My aunt was an attendant in the refreshment bar, and sometimes gave me a cake or sandwich to eat amid the smell of spirits, or took me to the private apartments, talking in a high bright voice and showing me round to various other neat women in black with high bright voices and nothing but smiles and laughs. My uncle was a fitter in the Great Western Railway works and knew everybody. He was tall, easy-going, and had a pipe in his mouth and very likely a dog at his heels. I was proud to be with him as he nodded to the one-legged signalman and the man with a white apron and a long hammer for tapping the wheels of all the carriages.

The look of the town pleased me altogether. I could think no ill of houses built entirely of stone instead of brick, especially as they seemed to exist chiefly to serve as avenues by which I happily approached to my grandmother's. It was for me a blessed place. The stonework, the flowers in the gardens, the Wiltshire accent, the rain if it was raining, the sun if it was shining, the absence of school and schoolmaster and of most ordinary forms of compulsion – everything was paradisal. No room ever was as cosy as my grandmother's kitchen. Its open range was always bright. There was a pair of bellows frequently in use. A brass turnspit hung from under the mantelpiece. The radiant steel trivet was excellent in itself but often bore a load of girdle cakes or buttered toast or more substantial things. An old brown earthenware teapot stood eternally upon the hob. Tea-caddies, brass candlesticks, clay pipes and vases full of spills, stood on the mantelpiece. On its walls hung coloured engravings entitled 'Spring' and 'Summer' and painted in England some time before the Fall, and photographs of me and Mr Gladstone's Cabinets and Mr Gladstone, of Belle Bitton, and of an uncle who had died long before I was born. There were chairs and there was an old mahogany table piano at one side. The smell of 'Westward Ho' tobacco hung about the room. My uncle got us chatting instantly. He seemed grown up, yet a boy, by the way he laughed, whistled and sang a bit of a gay tune. At supper, with our bread and cheese, or cold bacon, or hot faggots, or chitterlings, and pickles, he would now and then give us a little tumbler, or 'tot', of ale.

My grandmother being all important, omnipotent, omnipresent if not omniscient, she stood out less. She marketed, cooked, cleaned, did everything. She made pies with pastry a full inch thick, and many different undulant fruit tarts on plates. Above all, she made doughy cakes, of dough, all spice and many raisins, which were as much better than other cakes as Swindon was better than other towns, and always as much better than other so-called doughy cakes. She knew, too, where to get butter which taught me how divine a thing butter can be made. On the other hand, she was a Conservative and a churchwoman. Without her, these holidays would have been impossible, and she gave me countless pleasures. But if I loved her it was largely because of these things, not instinctively or because she loved me. She was marvellously kind and necessary but we were never close together; and, when there was any quarrel, contempt mingled with my hate of her inheritance from semi-rural Wales of George the Fourth's time. She was bigoted, worldly, crafty, narrow-minded, and ungenerous, as I very early began to feel. She read her Bible and sang hymns to herself, sometimes in Welsh. She also sang Welsh songs that were not hymns, in particular one that an old beggar used to sing at Tredegar when she was a girl, something about a son whom the mother was begging not to be married. When she wanted to warn me against going fishing some miles off with a strange man she hinted that he might be Jack the Ripper.

She first took me to church. Clad in those uncomfortable clothes, I walked beside her, who looked more uncomfortable in her layers of black. I felt that everyone enjoyed being stiff, solemn, black, except myself. On entering the church she bent forward to pray, dragging me down with her to blur my sight for a similar period. I rose with an added awkwardness in gazing at the grim emotionless multitude of hats, bonnets, and bare heads. It was an inexplicable conspiracy for an hour's self-torture. The service was a dreary discomfort in which the hymns were green isles. When all was over, we crept with a shuffle, a pause, a shuffle, a pause, out to the tombstones and the astonishing fresh light. I was introduced to other women and discussed. I was always being told how like my mother I was and how tall for my age. My grandmother took me to several old Welshwomen, and they all said, 'He's a regular —.' They used to remark how well my father was doing, my grandfather who had long been dead having only been a fitter. To hide something from me, they spoke in Welsh. Sometimes I was more elaborately shown off. Behind a shop smelling of bacon, butter and acid sweets, I stood up before a stout woman smelling a little strongly of the same, to recite 'The Charge of the Light Brigade'. My reward was a penny or a screw of sweets. The only visit of this kind which I enjoyed was to a farmhouse a mile away, though I can only recall the walk, the various gates, the best parlour with a Bible in the window between the lace curtains, and the glass of warm milk. Between her and my uncle who kept the house going I saw much bickering. Spending most of his evenings out at club or public-house, he neglected the garden and I dare say other things. I dimly knew that he was usually courting a farmer's daughter somewhere a few miles out, not always the same one. Sometimes when I was walking with him the girl appeared and joined us and at twilight I returned alone.

The little ivy-covered house, therefore, though I enjoyed the meals and evenings there, was above all a convenient centre for games and rambles. In my earlier visits the rambles of any length were on a Sunday with my uncle. He and I and usually my next brother who was two years younger would set out after a late breakfast. The Club was the first stop. It seemed to be full of grown men in a good temper and very much like schoolboys over their ale, their pipes of shag or 'Westward Ho', their *Reynolds News*. My uncle would tell them a little about us. They chaffed us. The men talked or whispered. Then before we were really impatient my uncle drained his glass and we got on to the canal-side and out of the town, not without greetings or a word or two from men lounging in their back-gardens over their vegetables, their fowls and pigeons. We kept to the canal for a mile or two, and sometimes another man joined us. The roach played in the deep green streams among the reeds, many of them bigger than any fish we had ever caught, here and there a monster. Better still my uncle would discover a long thin jack close inshore, as if anchored. If it did not shoot out with a kick and a swirl of water my uncle probably aimed at it with a stone. One great jack excited us by leaping again and again out of the water, at times so near the bank that we made sure he was ours. But the chief Sunday sport was with water rats. We were fascinated as men yelled encouragements, threats, advice, or praises, and a terrier swam down a rat in spite of its divings. When no dog was handy a rat surprised in mid-stream was a good mark for a stone, a snake's head a more difficult one. The moorhens in the reeds had no more mercy from them, but more often than not escaped. A dead dog was a good deal better than nothing. Not that we were unhappy without something for a mark. We threw flat stones to make ducks and drakes along the sunny water, or sheltering from rain under one of the low stone bridges plunged heavy stones with all our might down into the black depth.

Alongside the canal were many narrow copses of oak with underwood of ash and willow, the resorts of lovers and gamblers. The pleasantest thing I ever did in them at that time was to peel rings off the bark of a willow stick, in imitation of a carter's brass-ringed whip. My uncle taught us. He could also fashion a whistle by slipping the bark whole off a section of willow, but I never could. Or he made a 'cat' or 'catty' by tapering both ends of a round stick six inches long. Hit at one end by a downward blow from a longer stick the cat rose spinning up into the air and had then to be slashed horizontally as far as possible. My uncle could play tipcat better than any boy. In these copses or in the hedges or roadside trees, as we went along, he pointed out the nests.

And then at one o'clock after another visit to the Club, home to a dinner of lamb, green peas, and mint-sauce, followed by rhubarb tart and custard.

A Third-Class Carriage[30]

When the five silent travellers saw the colonel coming into their compartment, all but the little girl looked about in alarm to make sure that it was a mere third-class carriage. His expression, which actually meant a doubt, whether it was not perhaps a fourth-class carriage, had deceived them; and one by one – some with hypocritical, delaying mock-unconsciousness, others with faint meaning looks – they began to look straight before them again, except while they cast casual eyes on the groups waving or turning away from the departing train. Even then every one looked round suddenly because the colonel knocked the ashes out of his pipe with four sharp strokes on the seat. He himself was looking neither to the right nor to the left. But he was not, therefore, looking up or down or in front of him; he was restraining his eyes from exercise, well knowing that nothing worthy of them was within range. The country outside was ordinary downland, the people beside him were but human beings.

Having knocked out the ashes, he used his eyes. He was admiring the pipe – without animation, even sternly – but undoubtedly admiring what he and the nature of things had made of the briar in 1910 and 1911. It had been choice from the beginning, not too big, not too small, neither too long nor too short, neither heavy nor slim; absolutely straight, in no way fanciful, not pretentious; the grain of the wood uniform – a freckled or 'bird's-eye' grain – all over. In his eyes it was faultless, yet not austerely perfect; for it won his affection as well as his admiration by its 'cobby' quality, inclining to be shorter and thicker than the perfect one which he had never yet possessed save in dreams. A woman who by unprompted intelligence saw the merit of this favourite could have done anything with the colonel; but no woman ever did, though when instructed by him they all assented in undiscriminating warmth produced by indifference to the pipe and veneration for its master. As for the men, he had chosen his friends too well for there to be one among them who could not appreciate the beauty of the pipe, the exquisitely trained understanding of the colonel.

He was not merely its purchaser; in fact, it was not yet paid for. The two years of expectant respect, developing into esteem, cordial admiration, complacent satisfaction, had not been a period of indolent possession. Never once had he failed in alert regard for the little briar, never overheated it, never omitted to let it rest when smoked out, never dropped it or left it about among the profane, never put into it any but the tobacco which now, after many years, he thought the best, the only, mixture. Its dark chestnut with an amber overgleam was reward enough.

As he filled the pipe he allowed his eyes to alight on it with a kindliness well on this side of discretion, yet unmistakable once the narrow but subtle range of his emotional displays had been gauged. He showed no haste as he kept his pale, short second finger working by a fine blend of instinct and of culture; his whole body and spirit had for the time being committed themselves to that second fingertip. After having folded the old but well-cared-for pouch, removed the last speck of tobacco from his hands, and restored the pipe to his teeth, he lit a wooden match slowly and unerringly, and sucked with decreasing force until the weed was deeply, evenly afire. The hand holding the match, the muscles of the face working, the eyes blinking slightly, the neck bending – all seemed made by divine providence for the pipe.

When the match was thrown out of the window, and the first perfect smoke-cloud floated about the compartment, only the eye that sees not and the nose that smells not could deny that it was worth while. The dry, bittersweet aroma – the perfumed soul of brindled tawniness – was entirely worthy of the pipe. No wonder that the man had consecrated himself to this service. To preserve and advance that gleam on the briar, to keep burning that Arabian sweetness, was hardly less than a vestal ministry.

There was not a sound in the carriage except the colonel's husky, mellow breathing. His grey face wrinkled by its office, his stiff white moustache of hairs like quills, his quiet eyes, his black billycock hat, his unoccupied recumbent hands, the white waterproof on which they lay, his spotless brown shoes matching the pipe, were parts of the delicate engine fashioning this aroma. Certainly they performed no other labour. His limbs moved not; his eyes did not see the men and women or the child, or the basketful of wild roses in her lap, which she looked at when she was not staring out at the long, straight-backed green hill in full sunlight, the junipers dappling the steep slope, and whatever was visible to her amongst them. His brain subdued itself lest by its working it should modify the joys of palate and nostrils.

At the next station a pink youth in a white waterproof, brown shoes, and hollycock hat, carrying golf-clubs and a suitcase, entered the carriage. The colonel noted the fact, and continued smoking. Not long afterwards the train stopped at the edge of a wood where a thrush was singing, calling out very loud, clear things in his language over and over again. In this pause the other passengers were temporarily not content to look at the colonel and speculate on the cost of his tobacco, his white waterproof, and his teeth and gold plate, on how his wife was dressed, whether any of his daughters had run away from him, why he travelled third-class; they looked out of the window and even spoke shyly about the thrush, the reason of the stop, their destination. Suddenly, when all was silent, the little girl held up her roses towards the colonel saying:

'Smell.'

The colonel, who was beginning to realize that he was more than half-way through his pipe, made an indescribable joyless gesture designed to persuade the child that he was really delighted with the suggestion, although he said nothing, and did nothing else to prove it. No relative or friend was with her, so again she said:

'Smell. I mean it, really.'

Fortunately, at this moment the colonel's eyes fell on the pink youth, and he said:

'Is Borely much of a place, sir?'

Every one was listening.

'No, sir; I don't think so. The railway works are there, but nothing else, I believe.'

'I thought so,' said the colonel, replacing his pipe in his mouth and his mind in its repose. Every one was satisfied. The train whistled, frightening the thrush, and moved on again. Until it came to the end of the journey the only sound in the carriage was the colonel knocking out the ashes of his pipe with a sigh.

Tipperary[31]

To the tune of 'It's a long, long way to Tipperary' I have just travelled through England, from Swindon to Newcastle-on-Tyne, listening to people, in railway carriages, trams, taverns, and public places, talking about the war and the effects of it. They were people, for the most part, who worked with their hands, and had as little to do with the pen as with the sword. The period was from August 29th to September 10th,* when everybody in town and village, excepting, as a rule, the station-master, was discussing the transport of Russian troops down the country – 'if they were not Russians, then they were Canadians or else Indians', as a man said in Birmingham. I shall write down, as nearly as possible, what I saw and heard, hoping not to offend too much those who had ready-made notions as to how an Imperial people should or would behave in time of war, of such a war, and while the uncertainty was very dark. For their sakes I regret that men should everywhere be joking when our soldiers were fighting and our poets writing hard. Though

* 1914.

not magnificent, it is war. At Coventry a fat man stepped stately off a weighing machine. Seventeen stone, accumulated in peace. A lean man with a duck's-bill nose at once attacked him. 'You're the sort of man that stays behind, while a lot of fine young fellows go to fight for their country. I suppose you stay to take care of the ladies. When the Kaiser reaches Coventry he'll see a lot like you. You ought to be ashamed of yourself. You will be.'

Every one had his joke. The porter who dropped something and caused another to jump, covered up his fault by exclaiming, 'Here comes the Germans.' Precisely the same remark was made when small boys let off crackers after dark. The hostess with the false hair, being asked if her husband had gone to the war, and how she liked the idea of his being in Paris, replied with a titter that she did not fear – 'the gay girls have all left Paris'. More serious, but not more satisfactory, were the thousands of young men streaming away from the football ground at Sheffield on a Saturday afternoon. Yet even at a football match recruiting can be done and the hat sent round. Some professionals were paying five per cent of their wages to the Relief Fund, as men in a number of factories were contributing 2d. or 3d. a week. And a man in blue overalls said to me in Birmingham, 'If a man doesn't fight, he will do better to go to a football match than to drink in a pub or stay indoors moping.' On the other hand, everyone seemed to acknowledge that the war was the great thing; at the free library a hundred shuffling coughers were studying war to one that concentrated on Aston Villa.

The most cheerful man I met was reading *The British Weekly*, and continually saying rotund and benignant things. 'The Irish,' he would pronounce, 'have responded manfully. In fact, this unfortunate business has bound people together more than anything else could have done.' A young Northumbrian recruit was the most wretched. He had walked twenty-six miles to enlist. 'I wish to God I was back again in the village,' he said, 'though it is a cock-eyed little place. Since I came here I haven't had a wash or a brush or changed my clothes. If I were you I would sit farther off. I have had a cement floor for a bed, and some of them singing till three in the morning. We have to be out at six. The food's all right, but it's worse than a dog's life. I wish I could get back, and I will too.' Here a recruit of slightly longer standing, and already wearing a uniform, cut in with, 'I wish I had your chance, I'd be off. We have been moved fifteen times since July.' 'You'll be all right in a day or two,' said a decent, wooden-legged man, flicking away this fly from the jam of patriotism.

Most men fell short of the recruit in wretchedness and the reader of *The British Weekly* in benignity. Unless the Kaiser was mentioned they used, as a rule, the moderate language of sober hope or philosophic doubt. The one act of violence I witnessed was an oldish man, with a head like a German Christ, knocking down a sot who persisted in saying, 'You look like a — German.' More typical was the man I overheard at Ardwick, talking of the black and white pig he was fattening for Christmas, regardless of the fact that the Kaiser had God 'magnificently supporting him'.

Wherever I went I was told that employers – 'the best firms' – were dismissing men, the younger unmarried men, in order to drive them to enlist. 'Not exactly to drive them,' said one, 'but to encourage.' Nobody complained. They suggested that the 'Government' had put the employers up to it, or that 'It don't seem hardly fair', or 'It comes near conscription, and only those that don't care will give up good wages and leave their wives to charity.' One old man at Sheffield remarked that it used to be, 'Oh, you're too old' for a job; now it's 'You're too young.' It was added that the men's places were to be kept open for them; they were to receive part of their wages; if rejected by the doctor, they would be taken back. 'They *have* to like it,' said one man. These were not the only men who had lost their work. The jewellery-makers of Birmingham, for example, young or old, could not expect to be employed in war-time. Collieries near Newcastle that used to supply Germany were naturally idle, and many of the lads from these pits enlisted. Factories that supplied Russia were not busy either, and Russian debts looked like bad debts. Some trades were profiting by the war. Leicester was so busy making boots for the English and French armies that it had to refuse an order from the Greek army. Harness-makers had as much work as they could do at Walsall.

The factories for explosives at Elswick the same. Publicans were flourishing though still ambitious; one public-house at Manchester had these 'Imperial Ballads' printed on a placard:

> What plucks your courage up each day;
> What washes all your cares away?
> What word do you most often say?
> Why, Imperial!

the reference being to a drink of that name. But these successes were extraordinary. Already it was said at Newcastle that shop-assistants were serving for longer hours at reduced pay. Men in motor-car works were on short time. A photographer at Manchester had to resort to this advertisement:

> Gone to the front!
> A beautiful enlargement of any photo of our
> brave comrades may be had at a discount of
> 25 per cent.

Where relief was being given, a queue of women stood along a wall in the sun.

For the women the sun was too hot, but not for the corn, the clover-hay, the apples, of this great summer, nor for the recruits sleeping out. The sun gilded and regilded the gingerbread. Everybody that could, made an effort to rise to the occasion of the weather. The parks and the public gardens were thronged. The public-houses overflowed, often with but a single soldier as an excuse. Bands played in the streets – at Newcastle bagpipes – to quicken recruiting. A crowd listened to a band at Birmingham outside the theatre before going into hear Mr Lewis Waller recite 'Kipling and Shakespeare', and the first remark to break the ensuing silence was, 'It's by far the best band in Birmingham, by far.' Street meetings having no connection with the war were held. Men in the Bull Ring at Birmingham one afternoon argued furiously on faith and works, quoting Scripture amid eager onlookers. At the top of Oldham Street, Manchester, two knots of men on a Sunday evening debated what would or would not happen under Socialism, while one in the centre of a looser knot shouted, 'Oh, my friends, God wants all of you.' The war, in fact, was the one subject that was not debated in public. A man breaking this rule was branded a Socialist. For instance, near the statue of James Watt at Birmingham a man had got into an argument about the provision for soldiers' wives. Moistening dry lips with dry tongue, he declared that the working class made fifty times the sacrifice of the upper class. He met nothing but opposition, and perhaps only persevered because he was wedged tight among his enemies and could not for ever keep his eyes downcast. At length a vigorous elderly man in a grey suit stepped in with fists clenched, said he was a working man himself, and laid it down that every one's business was to fight, to sink class, and to avoid quarrelling. His wife, smiling behind him, told the heretic that he ought to be ashamed. Someone chipped in, saying that as a matter of fact many wives were better off with their one-and-twopence than when the men were working. 'God help them before!' ejaculated the solitary man. Then another said he was going himself, and would go if his wife was penniless. 'Hear, hear!' said several; and others muttered, 'These here Socialists.' Of course, class feeling did exist. A workman in Birmingham hoped that not too many of the well-to-do would go to the front, because they were needed to give employment and to control it. The rich and the working class, said a Coventry man, were doing their duty, but not the middle class – he called it the 'second class' – 'these young fellows who are neither man nor girl, and think about their socks all day'.

The war was not debated, but every one was bound to turn into it as into a main road of conversation, bound also to turn out of it. It could not be avoided. The newspapers issued edition after edition without reason. Pavement artists were strong on admirals, generals, and ships. Portraits of General French and Admiral Jellicoe adorned the entrances to picture palaces. Someone had chalked on a pavement at Manchester: 'See no sports. Fight the good fight.' Young men going to work by train began talking about the Russians. One interjected that he *was* glad to receive his salary in full at the end of the month. Another looked up from his paper saying, 'Kitchener's getting his second hundred thousand.' A Socialist was quoted as having said that 'we might as well be exploited by Germans as by British'. Gradually they drifted into stories about public men, into indecent stories about anybody, until running into a fog at Birmingham one exclaimed: 'It's a bombardment. We must be careful what we do and say to-day. It's a warning.' Older men going out to the Peak for Sunday, zigzagged from fishing yarns to 'uncreditable' tales told by a German in the Secret Service, on to the moorland appetite that makes you eat three-quarters of a pound of ham at a meal, and back again to 'I haven't had a day off except Sunday since the war began.' 'You durstn't.' The street roar of Newcastle or Sheffield was compounded of hoofs, boots, wheels, gongs, a thousand voices interwoven and one shouting, 'Fourth edition', one whispering, 'If Turkey . . .'

Conversations definitely on the subject of the war, fed on the abstract diet which the Press provided, were much of a muchness. A man began reading: 'This bloke says the rapidity of the German advance on Paris fairly stupefied the French', or he reminded his friend that 'this war has often been predicted in this very place'. A man interrupted his game of dominoes to say: 'I thought before now we were going to cut the German communications.' A man stands silent for a long time among his mates, and suddenly blurts out: 'What I want to know is, are these bombs' (he means mines) 'made of iron?' A favourite opening was, 'There's some great move coming.' The end of a conversation about the retreat was: 'The English have always been cool, calm, and collected.'

All kinds of abstract legends were current, as that the Germans were cowards, that the Kaiser was mad; but not many concrete ones. There was the Russian legend. Then there was a tale earlier in the war that British wounded were arriving at Grimsby, and the town was like a shambles. One man actually in Grimsby, answering an inquiry on the telephone, said that this was so; but another was able to deny it on good evidence.

One of the legends was that England was careless and slack. In the levelling of this charge I think there was a certain fondness as well as indignation. Men liked to think that we could play bowls and win a battle in the same day. 'England is too good-hearted,' said a man at Swindon. He came into the bar asking for 'Down where the waterlilies grow' on the gramophone, and, being disappointed, he sighed and began to speak of his 'month of misery'; for he had three sons and five nephews, or, as he sometimes put it, five sons and three nephews, at the front. 'The English are too good-hearted. Here, look'ee. If any damned foreigner comes into this bar we give him a penny as soon as if he was an Englishman. Now I thinks and studies a lot. You recollect the manoeuvres at Faringdon? Well, there was all nations there, Germans, Italians, Russians, French, Egyptians, and I don't know what – fifteen nations. Do you think they wasn't taking notes? Of course they were. And the Kaiser – the mad bull – didn't he come over and kiss King Edward, and wouldn't he as soon have knocked him down?' There was a man at Birmingham who began by talking about the Russians and Ostend, two millions of them, he believed. Oh, yes, they had certainly come down through England by night. He thought the Russians would repay the Germans for their atrocities. Nor do I think he minded. Yet he drew satisfaction from the faith that the English themselves would not retaliate. No, he said, the English are 'easy'. A Sheffield man who was advocating the bloodiest treatment for the Kaiser said that, 'If English soldiers fired at the Red Cross, Lord Kitchener would blow their brains out, he would.' Men were bloody-minded, to judge by their talk. They would have had no patience with the gentle person who had his favourite horse shot to save it from the battlefield. More intelligible to them would have been the gentleman of Cromwell's time who sent orders to have the sucking foals slaughtered that the mares might become chargers.

Such men had a strong, simple idea of a perfidious barbaric Germany. 'They have been preparing for this war ever since old Queen Vic died, and before that. I'd turn all the Germans out of England, same as they would turn us out.' 'I wouldn't; I would shoot the lot of them.' 'These nationalized Germans – you don't know what they are up to. Double-faced, they're all double-faced. They're savages, killing children and old men. I'd like to get at the Kaiser. I wouldn't kill him. I'd just turn him loose . . .' 'I wouldn't. If I could get at him, I'd . . . and choke him with them.' Thus spoke two workmen in Coventry. An old woman at Swindon – one of thousands – wanted to 'get at the Kaiser'. Everywhere men were drinking health – with a wink and 'You know what I mean' – to the Kaiser or the 'King of Proosher'. A very sober workman of fifty in Newcastle who was working short time simply did not know what epithets to give the man, and had to relapse on 'that tinker' (with much expression). Almost the only judicious reference to him that I heard was: 'Either the Kaiser is mad or he has found a new explosive.' People varied a little more in their attitude towards the German nation. 'They have got to be swept out of Europe,' said a man at Sheffield. A gentle old man was going to Harrogate with 'nerves run down' and 'distorted views', and he had got it into his head that he had eaten a German sausage. The man with *The British Weekly* was consoling him: 'Oh, you may depend upon it, it did not come from Germany. There's nothing coming from there now. They make a great quantity at Leeds. They don't call it German sausage either.' A Tyneside Scot, after pronouncing the Kaiser mad to make war on 'all nations', said: 'The Germans are a rotten lot. They won't stand and fight like any other nation. They keep moving all the time.' Others regarded the German army as a sort of ridiculous bully and coward, with this one grace, that it would probably shoot the Kaiser. A few praised German strategy and organization. One youth at Manchester even ventured to think 'they must be a fine race of soldiers'. A man at Sheffield held up a pair of German nail-scissors, lamenting that now he could not buy anything so neat at fourpence-halfpenny. A man at Manchester was asking: 'Where shall we get our gas mantles?' It was a Coventry man who went so far as to say that the German people were as good as ourselves and not so very different. 'They don't want war. It's not the Kaiser either. It's the aristocracy. Still, the Kaiser must not come here, like other deposed monarchs.'

This man, like every one else, was sure of victory. Some expected Paris to fall, but . . . They only laughed at any doubter. Most held the opinion that in retiring on Paris the Allies were leading the enemy into a trap. They did not stomach the idea of English soldiers retiring and retiring, and they imagined it must be deliberate. Open boasting had gone out of fashion, unless the man is a boaster who says on a black day that an Englishman is equal to five Germans. Patriotism took subtler forms. It was reported that one of the new Territorials weighed nineteen stone. 'Oh, but he will soon lose four or five stone, don't you fear. It's a healthy life, a grand life.' 'What I most rejoice at,' said a man at Swindon, 'is that we did not want the war.' Scores said something like it. It was 'the greatest war of all time', said all sorts of people. In Sheffield a solitary pessimist was content to think it the ruin of Europe, a great sudden movement in 'evolution'. The dirtiest man in Sheffield, with the most rasping voice, talking among his mates on a Sunday afternoon about rights of way, dukes, corporations, trespassing, and poaching, jerked out the remark: 'The capitalist is forking out now to save his own property.' A printer in the same town said: 'We are not soldiers or politicians; we are workmen. We have our trades, it is not for us to fight. That is another trade: let the soldiers fight. That is what I used to say; but it won't do now. All I can say is that I don't feel like fighting, myself. There is a great deal of loyalty everywhere, and I hope we shall win.'

Peace was not much talked about. A man at Swindon was figuring a reconstruction of Europe after the war. 'Why,' he asked, 'why shouldn't all the countries be bound together like the United States? There are a lot of nationalities over there, and they agree very well, I fancy.' Probably many were using the same phrases as the Birmingham chess-player: 'The pity of it, when you think of all the education in England and Germany. We don't go out into the street and fight if we have a difference. It sets a bad example to the nation.' 'It's man's nature to fight.' 'It isn't mine.' 'Your move.'

Only one eloquent militarist did I hear, a Manchester Irishman. He, too, declared it man's nature to fight. From Cain and Abel, having demolished and labelled as un-Christian the suggestion that we were descended from monkeys, he branched out to the animals. 'It's the same everywhere,' he said. 'They must hit out. Until they have hit out, they don't know themselves. To hit out is a man's very life and nature, the best he can do, his greatest pleasure, what he was made for. Most of us have to obey the law, if we can. But the soldier is a hired law-breaker and murderer, and we must let him enjoy himself sometimes. Don't you go pitying the poor soldier. Poor soldier! This is the time he has been waiting for. He is in a passion, and nothing hurts him. Sudden death is a glorious thing.'

This was not a soldier. He was a workman, a looker-on, one of the thousand loitering workers and unemployed who stare at the hundred recruits between the statues of Watt and Edward the Seventh at Birmingham, and in squares or by-streets all over the country. The soldier has another style. A crippled pensioner at Birmingham said simply that if he was fit they would not have to call him twice; then he gossiped of the Burmah war, of catching and killing your own mutton before eating it, of an immortally tough bullock, of having a foot cut off by a Dacoit, of how far better off to-day's soldier is with his bacon and jam and tea for breakfast. A soldier's father at Swindon just said his son was glad to go, but wished it had been with Buller. These were men who would not be hurt till they were struck, and I do not know how much then. The Irishman was not one to squander himself on a battlefield; his duty to his country was to preserve his tongue without having to hold it. But he was a patriot.

Probably there are two kinds of patriot; one that can talk or write, and one that cannot; though I suspect that even the talkers and writers often come down in the end to 'I do not understand. I love.' It must happen more than once or twice that a man who can say why he ought to fight for his country fails to enlist. The very phrase, 'to fight for one's country', is a shade too poetical and conscious for any but non-combatants. A man enlists for some inexplicable reason which he may translate into simple, conventional terms. If he has thought a good deal about it, he has made a jump at some point, beyond the reach of his thought. The articulate and the inarticulate are united in the ranks at this moment by the power to make that jump and come to the extreme decision. I heard a mother trying to persuade – pretending she was trying to persuade – a young man against enlisting. She said: 'I would not risk my life for anybody. It isn't yours, for one thing. Think of Mary. I would sooner go to America . . .' She found a hundred things to say, few of them quite genuine, since it was her desire to overpower him, not to express herself. In argument he was overpowered. His reasons he could not give. Nevertheless, if he passed the doctor he was going; if the doctor rejected him, he rather hoped some girl would taunt him – she would have to produce a champion to justify her. Had the eleven or twelve thousand recruits from Birmingham written down their reasons, I dare say they would not have been worth much more than the pen, ink, and paper. That is, assuming they included no poets, and I do not see that they were more likely to prove poets than the men, women, and children who made haste to send in their verses to the papers. Out of the crowd at Newcastle the dissatisfied one spoke best. If any at Coventry or elsewhere were kept waiting so long outside the recruiting office that they changed their minds and went away, they might speak better still. Some men of spirit may have kept back to spite their interfering persuaders. Why, the lowest slut in the town, fetching her beer at eleven-thirty, would look after a procession of recruits and say: 'So they ought to. Lord! look what a lot of fellows hang about the corners. They ought to fight for their country.'

There was really no monotony of type among these recruits, though the great majority wore dark clothes and caps, had pale faces tending to leanness, and stood somewhere about five foot seven. It was only the beginning, some thought, of a wide awakening to a sense of the danger and the responsibility. Clean and dirty – some of them, that is, straight from the factory – of all ages and features, they were pouring in. Some might be loafers, far more were workers. I heard that of one batch of two hundred and fifty at Newcastle, not one was leaving less than two pounds a week. Here and there a tanned farm labourer with lighter-coloured, often brownish, clothes, chequered the pale-faced dark company. The streets never lacked a body of them or a tail disappearing. Their tents, their squads drilling this way and that, occupied the great bare Town Moor above Newcastle. The town was like a vast fair where men were changing hands instead of cattle. The ordinary racket of tram-car and crowd was drowned by brass instruments, bagpipes, drums and tin boxes beaten by small boys, men in fifties and in hundreds rounding a corner to the tune of 'It's a long, long way to Tipperary'. Thousands stood to watch them. With crowds on the kerbstones, with other crowds going up and down and across, with men squatting forward on the pavement, it was best to have no object but to go in and out. The recruits were the constant, not the only attraction. The newest ones march-ing assumed as military a stiff uprightness as possible. The older ones in uniform were slacker. Some stood at corners talk-ing to girls; others went in and out of 'pubs' attended by civilians; more and more slouched, or staggered, or were heavy-eyed with alcohol. Everyone was talking, but the only words intelligible were 'Four o'clock winner' and 'It's a long, long way to Tipperary'. At nightfall the boys who beat the drums and tins began to carry around an effigy and to sing 'The Kai-ser, the Kaiser', or

> And when we go to war
> We'll put him in a jar,
> And he'll never see his daddy any more.

Companies of recruits were still appearing. Perhaps their faces were drawn and shining with drink, fatigue, and excitement, but they remained cheerful even when a young officer with a dry, lean face and no expression said 'Good night' without expression and rode off. His was the one expressionless, dead calm face in the city, the one that seemed to have business of its own, until I crossed the river and saw the women on the door-steps of the steep slum, the children on pavement and in gutter. They were not excited by the fever in Clayton Street and Mar-ket Street, any more than by St Mary's bells banging away high above slum and river, or by the preacher at the top of Church Street bellowing about 'the blessed blood of Jesus Christ'. In an almost empty tavern a quiet old man was treating a lad in a new uniform, and giving him advice: 'Eat as much as you can, and have a contented mind.' It was a fine warm evening. But what could the great crowd do to spend its excitement? As a crowd, nothing. In a short time it was doubled. For at nine o'clock the public-houses had to be emptied and shut. The burly bell of St Nicholas tolled nine over thousands with nothing to do. Those who had not taken time by the forelock and drunk as much as they would normally have done by eleven, stood about aimlessly. A man took his stand in Bigg Market and sang for money. It was not what people wanted. Several youths got together at a short distance and tried to bawl down the singer. Even that was not what people wanted. Even the temperance man was only half pleased when he reflected that what he had long agitated for in vain had been done by one stroke of the military pen. There was nothing to be done but to go to bed and wait for the morning papers.

It's a Long, Long Way[32]

'All the other nations are coming in, Canada, India, and ... They wouldn't let England be beat. Oh, no, sir. England will win, right enough, you'll see. Oh, yes, sir.' An old Gloucestershire labourer was speaking, who had fought under Roberts. He had been at Kandahar, over his boots in blood. East and West, he had had glimpses of many nations; his geography was but the battered remnant of a few infant lessons in Crimean days. When he tried to enumerate 'all the other nations' he had to stop at 'Canada, India'. Russia was in his mind, but as an enemy: he spoke of the Russians when he meant the Germans.

I should like to be able to draw a map of the world as it appears to him. It would be easy enough to make one very picturesque, more than medieval, with strange gaps, and removals and bringings near; but it would be all wrong, because he does not see the world as reduced to a flat, coloured surface; all he

knows is earth, sea, burning sun, India, China, Gloucester, the
Malvern Hills, the Severn. Those who can do something with
maps go as far astray. One woman who had been expecting
friends from Canada was inclined to think they could not reach
England, because the North Sea was closed by mines.

I should like to know what the old soldier meant by
'England', if it was anything more than some sort of a giant
with Gloucestershire for its eyes, its beating heart, for every-
thing that raised it above a personification. His was a very little
England. The core and vital principle was less still, a few thou-
sand acres of corn, meadow, orchard, and copse, a few farms
and cottages; and he laughed heartily over a farmer's artfulness
who had hid away some horses wanted by the War Office.
If England was against Germany, the parish was against
Germany, England, and all the world. Some of his neighbours,
not so fearless, went even greater lengths in their parochialism.
They had made up their minds about invasion. They not only
imagined themselves suffering like Belgian peasants, but being
specially attacked in the Forest of Dean by German aeroplanes.
Napoleon, a hundred years ago, was expected to sail up the
Severn and destroy the Forest: now it was feared that the
Germans were coming.

The scale of the war baffles country people as it does war
correspondents. They take hold of some simple fact and make
what they can of it. A woman coming from the town stops
you to tell the news – she adds that it is official – that twenty
thousand Germans have been killed and another cruiser sunk.
The two things have already combined; she does not know
whether those twenty thousand were killed on land or sea.
Then the arrangements of 'all the other nations' took them
aback at the start, and probably still does. It seems a new-
fangled notion to have our troops in France fighting for, not
against, the French. Perhaps this is considered an heretical
innovation by a Liberal Government. The farmer's wife says
'France' with a haughty coolness towards the lady of that name:
she had not anticipated such a travelling companion. So when
she is really disturbed and is entertaining the idea that it is the
Kaiser's 'hambition to eat his Christmas dinner in London', she

says: 'If the Germans try to beat us, the United States will join us.' Very slowly they are readjusting the old multiplication table, which said:

One Englishman = three Frenchmen.

Before the war the word 'Frenchman' had stood for something as distinct and venerable as the Bank of England or the Derby. The word 'German', in spite of 'The King of Prussia' and 'General Blucher' here and there on a signboard, meant little or nothing. It was almost in vain that the newspapers had been erecting a German Colossus to terrify us. Neither the country people nor their newspapers had read Mr Charles M. Doughty's 'Cliffs'. They had not listened to the spying Prussian aeroplanists on the East Coast saying of Turkey:

> We've barely gotten her goodwill, till now.
> Yet having that, it is a Key of State.
> Be as be may, it costs no more to us
> Than promises; and that's only paper-breath.
> To us all's one, Muslem or Galilean;
> So there's but profit or *Welt-politik* in it . . .;

or, worse still, attacking our national songs:

> Ignoble taunting songs, which they call *komisch*;
> Jigging malicious street banality;
> Whereat all fleer like hounds and show their teeth;
> But hounds should howl to hear them in our parts.

Nobody knew how old shepherd Hobbe, Crimean veteran, had set upon the spies with his crook, crying:

> Knives and mailed-fist been cowards' terms with us,
> For murder-tools of them low foreign seafolk,
> On England's quays. Belike ye're some of them,
> Would kick an honest man below the belt:
> That bayonet wounded soldiers on the ground . . .

On the East Coast, of course, by this time they know what a German is. They have begun to scent a new reality in the old proverbial prophecy:

> When England's took,
> 'Twill be at Weybourne Nook.

One fisherman who quoted it was being advised, if the Germans landed, to leave fighting to the soldiers, and not endanger the women and children by private efforts.

'Ef I see a Jarman coming up that gangway,' said he, pointing to the cliff, 'do ee know what I'd do? I'd shoot 'm.'

'But—'

'I'd *shoot* 'm.'

Away from the coast the German is not of necessity a devil and a bogy pure and simple. One morning, as I was leaving a lodging at Brecon, and had my hand on the latch, the woman of the house drew me back to know what my opinion of the war was, what was really happening in France, with all these men going out. She also feared invasion. 'I am an active woman,' said she, 'busy all day with my head and hands. What should I do if they cut off my hands?' I told her I did not believe it was part of the German plan to cut off the hands of women, that it was all exaggerated to blacken the enemy. 'That's what I tell my husband,' she said; 'if it was true it would be such a stupid thing to do, to cut off working people's hands. Now, last summer, I had some Germans in this house, and they were nice, polite people, you couldn't wish for better. And look what our own people will do, in times of peace, too.' She was trying hard to retain the idea that there were Germans and Germans.

This woman would not have taken kindly to spying on possible spies. Nor, I think, would many other country people. But once it got about, in a certain part of Gloucestershire, that a Dutchman had been staying in one house, that an American family lived in another, that a party (including a Russian boy) had arrived by motor-car at a third in the middle of the night, all sorts of people joined in the hunt – the policeman, the retired clergyman, acting on the principle that 'you never know what these naturalized Americans are', and the illiterate anonymous senders of reports that we sat up late at night. People in a country road, nowadays, look hard and sometimes wisely at the stranger passing them. The cottager, however, does not easily regard himself as the policeman's assistant. It is the villa resident that tracks out your alien schoolmaster like a sleuth-hound, and bestirs himself with the police long before the law does. The cottage woman in the Hampshire hop-garden was far less savage than the townswoman. She never saw a newspaper. News came along somehow like fine days, and she knew that far-off battles were being fought, and men dying night and day, in foreign places. When she was told precisely that the Germans had lost several thousands the day before, she said: 'Well, what I say is, God bless every mother's son of them.' Another, more sophisticated, hearing of Germans slaughtered by the bayonet, went so far as to suppose that they also have 'human feelings as we have'.

It may be my misfortune, but I have not heard any abuse of the Kaiser or the Germans, worth mentioning, from country people. Stories of mutilations have reached them. They have met somebody in Petersfield market who saw a soldier in hospital at Guildford, mutilated in the style of William Rufus. Only, they make a short story of it. I was travelling with a drunken hussar to Woking. He had fought at Omdurman, but was in a condition to forget the date. Lying back in a corner seat, he talked to nobody in particular, with a grin for everybody, that is to say, for those sitting in the other three corners. Most of the time he had it his own way, complaining of slow trains, arguing against compulsory abstinence, threatening Lloyd George, trying to figure out the date of Omdurman. Later on, two women entered, and sat facing one another in the two middle seats, one a small, middle-aged woman, bright and demure, with a kind of pretty plainness, the other a buxom wife of thirty. The soldier grinned at them with the sarcasm: 'Don't you sit near me.'

'Oh, I'm not afraid of you,' said the young one, smiling.

'I'm not afraid of you, either,' said the middle-aged one, who was on his side of the carriage. She looked at her knees with a twinkle, but as demure as ever, while she added: 'But I know some one who is.'

'Who's that?' the soldier asked, almost eagerly.

'The Kayser,' she said, still looking at her knees, but as bright as she was demure.

'Ah,' he said, 'the Kayser won't let me get near him.'

'I wish he would,' she concluded.

Outside the towns they see little of the papers; they are not quick at using insubstantial words; they catch few newspaper phrases of the grand style to stand between them and facts. More natural to them, if anything, would be words like Mr Doughty's, in 'The Clouds':

> That Love of Country, which constraineth us,
> Doth every virtue comprehend. Teach us
> The very fowls, which under heaven flit,
> And field and forest beasts, after their kinds.
> Those tender each, that little round of Earth,
> Where they were fostered. And should Englishmen not
> Their island Britain love, above the World?

Mr Hardy makes the soldiers sing: 'We see well what we are doing.' But those who are left behind in the hamlets do not know what to make of big things, or how to put them into words. One boy I talked with, whose brother had joined the Royal Horse Artillery the day after war broke out, said chiefly that his brother was now quite fond of a wild horse, and that he looked much better in uniform than in civilian clothes. He added that they had paid four pounds a sack, all but three shillings, for wheat to sow, which was a great price. If they can make anything of the sinking of an English ship, at least their conversation profits little by it. On the Sunday morning when the loss of the *Hermes* was published, I was at an inn where I had formerly met sailors. Opposite Colonel —'s house, down the street, hung a list of sailors and soldiers from the village, and a frame on which the Colonel posted up telegrams. But the landlord laid down the paper on the counter, saying: 'A cruiser sunk in the Straits of Dover', and not a man commented. After

a pause, the conversation turned to a job that an old man pres-
ent had just got, of driving a milk-cart at fifteen shillings a
week. Not that the war was wholly neglected. One of them
mentioned a certain recruit. 'He looks a regular Tom Thumb,'
said the spokesman; 'you'd think he'd seen ten years' service.
But it's all uniform. It will give the Germans encouragement to
see him coming along. Now, at Longmoor Camp, some of the
German prisoners are fine-set-up chaps, with something in
front and behind, not like this little Tommy Thumb.' After this
they wandered, as they often do, to speaking of old days, when
they were working on the church out at —, when old — kept
the 'New Inn', and there was a baker's shop where the smithy
is now, and —, who is superintendent of police down at the
opposite corner of the county, was policeman – he was one for
a bit of fun; he would do *anything* that was right.

If the soldiers see, they do not say, what they are doing. One
day I had two lads for travelling companions, one a bright,
pale, thin boy, with round shoulders, whom I should never
have taken for a soldier. But as the train ran between some oak
woodland, he waved towards a copse, and said to the other
lad: 'That's where I was keeper before I enlisted.' No more; and
the other said nothing. Only an old soldier in the carriage
asked: 'Terriers?' 'No,' he answered, 'Regular Army. Twelve
years. Seven with the colours. Go to Reading on Thursday.'
Their farewells are brief. On the night when the hooter at
Swindon announced the war at a quarter to eight by hooting
ten times, I heard a soldier struggling through his farewells.
They were continually being renewed for the sake of a young
sister who would burst out crying at the last moment. Just as he
said: 'Well, good-bye, Aunt. Good-bye, all', she screamed, and
he had to say: 'I'm not going away for ever, don't you fret.
Now, don't carry on like that. I shall come back again.'

In two hours spent at an inn one Sunday with a company of
labourers and a young fellow from the village, now a 'Flying
Corpse' man, I heard only one reference to the war. 'Regular
Winchester Fair weather,' said one, coming in out of the rain,
and soon they were guessing the weight and price of some
steers across the road, and the one who was glibbest recalled

his master being offered thirty-two p'n ten for a beast and refusing it, and then getting twenty-nine and a crown at Winchester market. Most of the time they were recalling old days; how they did a job at —, and slept at the 'Rack and Manger', taking up a gallon of beer to the bedroom, and the landlord's wife kept them company, and in the morning the landlord drove to a farm for eggs, and they had eggs and bacon. They talked of bacon lofts, open fireplaces, fire-dogs, logs that burned for two days after Christmas, mushrooms that grow with the moon – always at night, as you can see by noting one at nightfall like a button that will be as big round as a tumbler in the morning – and 'waste as the moon wast-es', and mead – 'I'll get you a bottle. I know where there is some, and I think it's three year old.' One man mentioned Sparsholt. 'Which Sparsholt?' asked a stranger, who knew the neighbourhood as well as any. 'T'other side of Winchester.' 'I know. That's the place to hide from Germans.' They laughed. It was the one reference. Yet the paper was lying on the table. Later on, a youth entered, and bent over the song printed on the outer page, but said not a word. The 'Flying Corpse' man was content to treat his old friends. At half-past two, the one nearest him said: 'Let's come and see about that pig.' 'Are you going to kill a pig?' asked the youth. 'Going to eat a bit of one.' The 'Flying Corpse' man put a bottle of stout in each pocket, and all left. The afternoon turned fine, and as I approached the town, the girls, in their best dresses, were walking among the dead leaves, but not a young man with them.

This lack of eloquence does not mean a stupid waiting for a drop in the price of bacon. One day I fell into a company talking very radically, and chiefly because they had some thousands of recruits encamping near them and did not like their ways. Some of these recruits had enlisted for 'hunger', some for fun, not all to serve their country. So said the landlord, an old soldier. 'I wouldn't enlist for anything,' said a man with his cheese waiting on his knife-tip, 'not unless I was made. I would if it was a fair war. But it's not, it's murder. Waterloo was a fair war, but this isn't.' 'That's right,' said the postman; 'a man's only got seventy years to live, and ninety per cent don't get beyond fifty. I reckon we want a little peace. Twentieth century, too.' It was not the postman, but another, that was complaining how a number of postmen had gone out, and their places had been taken by a few boys in civilian dress who did twice as much work for half the pay, and on their own cycles: 'It's the same everywhere. The man who does most work gets least pay. Nobody's worse paid than the men doing all the work out in France now.' This man, unlike the landlord, was down on the gentry, did not think they were doing their share. He told a story of a lady stopping a youth in a cart to ask him why he was not fighting. Why, he asked, hadn't she sent out her two sons from college? She couldn't spare them, she answered. At his conclusion, 'My mother can't spare me', the company laughed violently.

In one place I thought I had stumbled on treason. A truculent recruit in the private bar and a drunken old artilleryman were arguing over a dozen heads and tankards.

'We're not fighting for Lord Kitchener,' the artilleryman said slowly. 'We're not fighting for King George. We're fighting for our country.'

'Quite right,' said somebody.

'Who is Lord Kitchener?' asked the artilleryman, swelling.

'He's a good man,' retorted the recruit.

'So he is,' the other had to say, 'but why does he stop a man from having a pint of beer?'

'It's the twenty-fifth pint he's against.'

This was a purely intellectual duel, a very uncommon one. The countryman fights with no such grand motive on his tongue as a journalist could write down. Even the little boys know that, and are not so mighty serious as to be ashamed of laughing when the gawky Territorial shambles down the street in his scarlet tunic for the first time. But the trumpet, a little later, stings them to another mood. The recruits are drilling on the shore in mist, opening and closing, in ghostly silence. For their feet make no sound on the sand, and the calm sea, sucking at the rocks, drowns the shout of the sergeant and all other noise but a dog barking at the waves. The boys watch in silence.

*This England*³³

It was a part of the country I had never known before, and I
had no connections with it. Once only, during infancy, I had
stayed here at a vicarage, and though I have been told things
about it which it gives me, almost as if they were memories, a
certain pleasure to recall, no genuine memory survives from the
visit. All I can say is that the name, Hereford, had somehow
won in my mind a very distinct meaning; it stood out among
county names as the most delicately rustic of them all, with a
touch of nobility given it long ago, I think, by Shakespeare's
'Harry of Hereford, Lancaster, and Derby'. But now I was here
for the third time since the year began. In April here I had heard,
among apple trees in flower, not the first cuckoo, but the first
abundance of day-long-calling cuckoos; here, the first nightin-
gale's song, though too far-off and intermittently, twitched
away by gusty night winds; here I found the earliest may-
blossom which by May Day, while I still lingered, began to
dapple the hedges thickly, and no rain fell, yet the land was
sweet. Here I had the consummation of Midsummer, the wea-
ther radiant and fresh, yet hot and rainless, the white and the
pink wild roses, the growing bracken, the last and best of the
songs, blackbird's, blackcap's. Now it was August, and again
no rain fell for many days; the harvest was a good one, and
after standing long in the sun it was gathered in and put up in
ricks in the sun, to the contentment of men and rooks. All day
the rooks in the wheat-fields were cawing a deep sweet caw, in
alternating choirs or all together, almost like sheep bleating,
contentedly, on until late evening. The sun shone, always warm,
from skies sometimes cloudless, sometimes inscribed with a
fine white scatter a mile high, sometimes displaying the full
pomp of white moving mountains, sometimes almost entirely
shrouded in dull sulphurous threats, but vain ones.

Three meadows away lived a friend, and once or twice or
three times a day I used to cross the meadows, the gate, and the
two stiles. The first was a concave meadow, in April strewn

with daffodils. There, day and night, pastured a bay colt and a black mare, thirty years old, but gay enough to have slipped away two years back and got herself made the mother of this 'stolen' foal. The path led across the middle of the meadow, through a gate, and alongside one of the hedges of the next, which sloped down rather steeply to the remnant of a brook, and was grazed by half a dozen cows. At the bottom a hedge followed the line of the brook and a stile took me through it, with a deep drop, to a plank and a puddle, and so to the last field, a rough one. This rose up as steeply and was the night's lodging of four cart horses. The path, having gradually approached a hedge on the left, went alongside it, under the horse-chestnut tree leaning out of it, and in sight of the house, until it reached the far hedge and the road. There, at another stile, the path ceased. The little house of whitened bricks and black timbers lay a few yards up the road, a vegetable garden in front with a weeping ash and a bay-tree, a walnut in a yard of cobbles and grass behind, a yew on the roadside, an orchard on the other.

How easy it was to spend a morning or afternoon in walking over to this house, stopping to talk to whoever was about for a few minutes, and then strolling with my friend, nearly regardless of footpaths, in a long loop, so as to end either at his house or my lodging. It was mostly orchard and grass, gently up and down, seldom steep for more than a few yards. Some of the meadows had a group or a line of elms; one an ash rising out of an islet of dense brambles; many had several great old apple or pear trees. The pears were small brown perry pears, as thick as haws, the apples chiefly cider apples, innumerable, rosy and uneatable, though once or twice we did pick up a wasp's remnant, with slightly greasy skin of palest yellow, that tasted delicious. There was one brook to cross, shallow and leaden, with high hollow bare banks. More than one meadow was trenched, apparently by a dried watercourse, showing flags, rushes, and a train of willows.

If talk dwindled in the traversing of a big field, the pause at gate or stile braced it again. Often we prolonged the pause, whether we actually sat or not, and we talked – of flowers, childhood, Shakespeare, women, England, the war – or we looked at a far horizon, which some dip or gap occasionally disclosed. Again and again we saw, instead of solid things, dark or bright, never more than half a mile off, the complete broad dome of a high hill six miles distant, a beautiful hill itself, but especially seen thus, always unexpectedly, through gaps in this narrow country, as through a window. Moreover, we knew that from the summit, between the few old Scots firs and the young ones of the plantation, we could command the Severn and the Cotswolds on the one hand, and on the other the Wye, the Forest of Dean, the island hills of North Monmouthshire, dark and massive, the remote Black Mountains pale and cloud-like, far beyond them in Wales. Not that we often needed to escape from this narrow country, or that, if we did, we had to look so far. For example, the cloud and haze of a hot day would change all. As we sat on a gate, the elms in a near hedge grew sombre, though clear. Past them rose a field like a low pitched roof dotted over with black stooks of beans and the elms at the top of that rise looked black and ponderous. Those in farther hedges were dimmer and less heavy, some were as puffs of smoke, while just below the long straight ridge of the horizon, a mile or two away, the trees were no more than the shadows of smoke.

Lombardy poplars rose out from among the elms, near and far, in twos and threes, in longer or shorter lines, and at one point grouping themselves like the pinnacles of a cathedral. Most farmhouses in the neighbourhood, and even pairs of cottages, possessed a couple or more. If we got astray we could steer by this or that high-perched cluster, in which, perhaps, one tree having lost a branch now on one side, now on the other, resembled a grass stalk with flowers alternating up it. When night came on, any farmhouse group might be transmuted out of all knowledge, partly with the aid of its Lombardy poplars. There was also one tree without a house which looked magnificent at that hour. It stood alone, except for a much lesser tree, as it were, kneeling at its feet, on the long swooping curve of a great meadow against the sky; and when the curve and the two trees upon it were clear black under a pale sky and the first stars, they made a kind of naturally melodramatic

'C'est l'empereur' scene, such as must be as common as paint-
ers in a cypress country.

Whatever road or lane we took, once in every quarter of a
mile we came to a farm-house. Only there by the two trees we
tasted austere inhuman solitude as a luxury. Yet a man had
planted the trees fifty or sixty years back. (Who was it, I won-
der, set the fashion or distributed the seedlings?) It was really
not less human a scene than that other one I liked at nightfall.
Wildly dark clouds broke through the pallid sky above the
elms, shadowy elms towering up ten times their diurnal height;
and under the trees stood a thatched cottage, sending up a thin
blue smoke against the foliage, and casting a faint light out
from one square window and open door. It was cheerful and
mysterious too. No man of any nation accustomed to houses
but must have longed for his home at the sight, or have suffered
for lacking one, or have dreamed that this was it.

Then one evening the new moon made a difference. It was
the end of a wet day; at least, it had begun wet, had turned
warm and muggy, and at last fine but still cloudy. The sky was
banded with rough masses in the north-west, but the moon, a
stout orange crescent, hung free of cloud near the horizon. At
one stroke, I thought, like many other people, what things that
same new moon sees eastward about the Meuse in France. Of
those who could see it there, not blinded by smoke, pain, or
excitement, how many saw it and heeded? I was deluged, in a
second stroke, by another thought, or something that over-
powered thought. All I can tell is, it seemed to me that either I
had never loved England, or I had loved it foolishly, aestheti-
cally, like a slave, not having realized that it was not mine unless
I were willing and prepared to die rather than leave it as Bel-
gian women and old men and children had left their country.
Something I had omitted. Something, I felt, had to be done
before I could look again composedly at English landscape, at
the elms and poplars about the houses, at the purple-headed
wood-betony with two pairs of dark leaves on a stiff stem, who
stood sentinel among the grasses or bracken by hedge-side or
wood's-edge. What he stood sentinel for I did not know, any
more than what I had got to do.

POEMS

Up in the Wind[34]

'I could wring the old thing's neck that put it here!
A public-house! it may be public for birds,
Squirrels, and suchlike, ghosts of charcoal-burners
And highwaymen.' The wild girl laughed. 'But I
Hate it since I came back from Kennington.
I gave up a good place.' Her cockney accent
Made her and the house seem wilder by calling up –
Only to be subdued at once by wildness –
The idea of London, there in that forest parlour,
Low and small among the towering beeches,
And the one bulging butt that's like a font.

Her eyes flashed up; she shook her hair away
From eyes and mouth, as if to shriek again;
Then sighed back to her scrubbing. While I drank
I might have mused of coaches and highwaymen,
Charcoal-burners and life that loves the wild.
For who now used these roads except myself,
A market waggon every other Wednesday,
A solitary tramp, some very fresh one
Ignorant of these eleven houseless miles,
A motorist from a distance slowing down
To taste whatever luxury he can
In having North Downs clear behind, South clear before,
And being midway between two railway lines,
Far out of sight or sound of them? There are
Some houses – down the by-lanes; and a few
Are visible – when their damsons are in bloom.
But the land is wild, and there's a spirit of wildness
Much older, crying when the stone-curlew yodels
His sea and mountain cry, high up in Spring.
He nests in fields where still the gorse is free as
When all was open and common. Common 'tis named

And calls itself, because the bracken and gorse
Still hold the hedge where plough and scythe have
    chased them.
Once on a time 'tis plain that 'The White Horse'
Stood merely on the border of waste
Where horse and cart picked its own course afresh.
On all sides then, as now, paths ran to the inn;
And now a farm-track takes you from a gate.

Two roads cross, and not a house in sight
Except the 'White Horse' in this clump of beeches.
It hides from either road, a field's breadth back;
And it's the trees you see, and not the house,
Both near and far, when the clump's the highest thing
And homely too upon a far horizon
To one that knows there is an inn within.

''Twould have been different,' the wild girl shrieked,
    'suppose
That widow had married another blacksmith and
Kept on the business. This parlour was the smithy.
If she had done, there might never have been an inn;
And I, in that case, might never have been born.
Years ago, when this was all a wood
And the smith had charcoal-burners for company,
A man from a beech-country in the shires
Came with an engine and a little boy
(To feed the engine) to cut up timber here.
It all happened years ago. The smith
Had died, his widow had set up an alehouse –
I could wring the old thing's neck for thinking of it.
Well, I suppose they fell in love, the widow
And my great-uncle that sawed up the timber:
Leastways they married. The little boy stayed on.
He was my father.' She thought she'd scrub again –
'I draw the ale and he grows fat' she muttered –
But only studied the hollows in the bricks
And chose among her thoughts in stirring silence.

The clock ticked, and the big saucepan lid
Heaved as the cabbage bubbled, and the girl
Questioned the fire and spoke: 'My father, he
Took to the land. A mile of it is worth
A guinea; for by that time all trees
Except these few about the house were gone:
That's all that's left of the forest unless you count
The bottoms of the charcoal-burners' fires –
We plough one up at times. Did you ever see
Our signboard?' No. The post and empty frame
I knew. Without them I should not have guessed
The low grey house and its one stack under trees
Was a public-house and not a hermitage.
'But can that empty frame be any use?
Now I should like to see a good white horse
Swing there, a really beautiful white horse,
Galloping one side, being painted on the other.'
'But would you like to hear it swing all night
And all day? All I ever had to thank
The wind for was for blowing the sign down.
Time after time it blew down and I could sleep.
At last they fixed it, and it took a thief
To move it, and we've never had another:
It's lying at the bottom of the pond.
But no one's moved the wood from off the hill
There at the back, although it makes a noise
When the wind blows, as if a train were running
The other side, a train that never stops
Or ends. And the linen crackles on the line
Like a woodfire rising.' 'But if you had the sign
You might draw company. What about Kennington?'
She bent down to her scrubbing with 'Not me:
Not back to Kennington. Here I was born,
And I've a notion on these windy nights
Here I shall die. Perhaps I want to die here.
I reckon I shall stay. But I do wish
The road was nearer and the wind farther off,
Or once now and then quite still, though when I die

I'd have it blowing that I might go with it
Somewhere distant, where there are trees no more
And I could wake and not know where I was
Nor even wonder if they would roar again.
Look at those calves.'

                              Between the open door
And the trees two calves were wading in the pond,
Grazing the water here and there and thinking,
Sipping and thinking, both happily, neither long.
The water wrinkled, but they sipped and thought,
As careless of the wind as it of us.
'Look at those calves. Hark at the trees again.'

March[35]

Now I know that Spring will come again,
Perhaps tomorrow: however late I've patience
After this night following on such a day.

While still my temples ached from the cold burning
Of hail and wind, and still the primroses
Torn by the hail were covered up in it,
The sun filled earth and heaven with a great light
And a tenderness, almost warmth, where the hail dripped,
As if the mighty sun wept tears of joy.
But 'twas too late for warmth. The sunset piled
Mountains on mountains of snow and ice in the west:
Somewhere among their folds the wind was lost,
And yet 'twas cold, and though I knew that Spring
Would come again, I knew it had not come,
That it was lost too in those mountains chill.

What did the thrushes know? Rain, snow, sleet, hail,
Had kept them quiet as the primroses.
They had but an hour to sing. On boughs they sang,
On gates, on ground; they sang while they changed perches

And while they fought, if they remembered to fight:
So earnest were they to pack into that hour
Their unwilling hoard of song before the moon
Grew brighter than the clouds. Then 'twas no time
For singing merely. So they could keep off silence
And night, they cared not what they sang or screamed;
Whether 'twas hoarse or sweet or fierce or soft;
And to me all was sweet: they could do no wrong.
Something they knew – I also, while they sang
And after. Not till night had half its stars
And never a cloud, was I aware of silence
Rich with all that riot of songs, a silence
Saying that Spring returns, perhaps tomorrow.

Old Man[36]

Old Man, or Lad's-love, – in the name there's nothing
To one that knows not Lad's-love, or Old Man,
The hoar-green feathery herb, almost a tree,
Growing with rosemary and lavender.
Even to one that knows it well, the names
Half decorate, half perplex, the thing it is:
At least, what that is clings not to the names
In spite of time. And yet I like the names.

The herb itself I like not, but for certain
I love it, as some day the child will love it
Who plucks a feather from the door-side bush
Whenever she goes in or out of the house.
Often she waits there, snipping the tips and shrivelling
The shreds at last on to the path, perhaps
Thinking, perhaps of nothing, till she sniffs
Her fingers and runs off. The bush is still
But half as tall as she, though it is as old;
So well she clips it. Not a word she says;
And I can only wonder how much hereafter
She will remember, with that bitter scent,

Of garden rows, and ancient damson trees
Topping a hedge, a bent path to a door,
A low thick bush beside the door, and me
Fobidding her to pick.

        As for myself,
Where first I met the bitter scent is lost.
I, too, often shrivel the grey shreds,
Sniff them and think and sniff again and try
Once more to think what it is I am remembering,
Always in vain. I cannot like the scent,
Yet I would rather give up others more sweet,
With no meaning, than this bitter one.

I have mislaid the key. I sniff the spray
And think of nothing; I see and I hear nothing;
Yet seem, too, to be listening, lying in wait
For what I should, yet never can, remember:
No garden appears, no path, no hoar-green bush
Of Lad's-love, or Old Man, no child beside,
Neither father nor mother, nor any playmate;
Only an avenue, dark, nameless, without end.

The Sign-Post[37]

The dim sea glints chill. The white sun is shy,
And the skeleton weeds and the never-dry,
Rough, long grasses keep white with frost
At the hilltop by the finger-post;
The smoke of the traveller's-joy is puffed
Over hawthorn berry and hazel tuft.

I read the sign. Which way shall I go?
A voice says: You would not have doubted so
At twenty. Another voice gentle with scorn
Says: At twenty you wished you had never been born.

One hazel lost a leaf of gold
From a tuft at the tip, when the first voice told
The other he wished to know what 'twould be
To be sixty by this same post. 'You shall see,'
He laughed – and I had to join his laughter –
'You shall see; but either before or after,
Whatever happens, it must befall,
A mouthful of earth to remedy all
Regrets and wishes shall freely be given;
And if there be a flaw in that heaven
'Twill be freedom to wish, and your wish may be
To be here or anywhere talking to me,
No matter what the weather, on earth,
At any age between death and birth, –
To see what day or night can be,
The sun and the frost, the land and the sea,
Summer, Autumn, Winter, Spring, –
With a poor man of any sort, down to a king,
Standing upright out in the air
Wondering where he shall journey, O where?'

The Other[38]

The forest ended. Glad I was
To feel the light, and hear the hum
Of bees, and smell the drying grass
And the sweet mint, because I had come
To an end of forest, and because
Here was both road and inn, the sum
Of what's not forest. But 'twas here
They asked me if I did not pass
Yesterday this way. 'Not you? Queer.'
'Who then? and slept here?' I felt fear.

I learnt his road and, ere they were
Sure I was I, left the dark wood
Behind, kestrel and woodpecker,

The inn in the sun, the happy mood
When first I tasted sunlight there.
I travelled fast, in hopes I should
Outrun that other. What to do
When caught, I planned not. I pursued
To prove the likeness, and, if true,
To watch until myself I knew.

I tried the inns that evening
Of a long gabled high-street grey,
Of courts and outskirts, travelling
An eager but a weary way,
In vain. He was not there. Nothing
Told me that ever till that day
Had one like me entered those doors,
Save once. That time I dared: 'You may
Recall' – but never-foamless shores
Make better friends than those dull boors.

Many and many a day like this
Aimed at the unseen moving goal
And nothing found but remedies
For all desire. These made not whole;
They sowed a new desire, to kiss
Desire's self beyond control,
Desire of desire. And yet
Life stayed on within my soul.
One night in sheltering from the wet
I quite forgot I could forget.

A customer, then the landlady
Stared at me. With a kind of smile
They hesitated awkwardly:
Their silence gave me time for guile.
Had anyone called there like me,
I asked. It was quite plain the wile
Succeeded. For they poured out all.

And that was naught. Less than a mile
Beyond the inn, I could recall
He was like me in general.

He had pleased them, but I less.
I was more eager than before
To find him out and to confess,
To bore him and to let him bore.
I could not wait: children might guess
I had a purpose, something more
That made an answer indiscreet.
One girl's caution made me sore,
Too indignant even to greet
That other had we chanced to meet.

I sought then in solitude.
The wind had fallen with the night; as still
The roads lay as the ploughland rude,
Dark and naked, on the hill.
Had there been ever any feud
'Twixt earth and sky, a mighty will
Closed it; the crocketed dark trees,
A dark house, dark impossible
Cloud-towers, one star, one lamp, one peace
Held on an everlasting lease:

And all was earth's, or all was sky's;
No difference endured between
The two. A dog barked on a hidden rise;
A marshbird whistled high unseen;
The latest waking blackbird's cries
Perished upon the silence keen.
The last light filled a narrow firth
Among the clouds. I stood serene,
And with a solemn quiet mirth,
An old inhabitant of earth.

Once the name I gave to hours
Like this was melancholy, when
It was not happiness and powers
Coming like exiles home again,
And weaknesses quitting their bowers,
Smiled and enjoyed, far off from men,
Moments of everlastingness.
And fortunate my search was then
While what I sought, nevertheless,
That I was seeking, I did not guess.

That time was brief: once more at inn
And upon road I sought my man
Till once amid a tap-room's din
Loudly he asked for me, began
To speak, as if it had been a sin,
Of how I thought and dreamed and ran
After him thus, day after day:
He lived as one under a ban
For this: what had I got to say?
I said nothing. I slipped away.

And now I dare not follow after
Too close. I try to keep in sight,
Dreading his frown and worse his laughter.
I steal out of the wood to light;
I see the swift shoot from the rafter
By the inn door: ere I alight
I wait and hear the starlings wheeze
And nibble like ducks: I wait his flight.
He goes. I follow: no release
Until he ceases. Then I also shall cease.

After Rain

The rain of a night and a day and a night
Stops at the light
Of this pale choked day. The peering sun
Sees what has been done.
The road under the trees has a border new
Of purple hue
Inside the border of bright thin grass:
For all that has
Been left by November of leaves is torn
From hazel and thorn
And the greater trees. Throughout the copse
No dead leaf drops
On grey grass, green moss, burnt-orange fern,
At the wind's return:
The leaflets out of the ash-tree shed
Are thinly spread
In the road, like little black fish, inlaid,
As if they played.
What hangs from the myriad branches down there
So hard and bare
Is twelve yellow apples lovely to see
On one crab-tree.
And on each twig of every tree in the dell
Uncountable
Crystals both dark and bright of the rain
That begins again.

Birds' Nests

The summer nests uncovered by autumn wind,
Some torn, others dislodged, all dark,
Everyone sees them: low or high in tree,
Or hedge, or single bush, they hang like a mark.

Since there's no need of eyes to see them with
I cannot help a little shame
That I missed most, even at eye's level, till
The leaves blew off and made the seeing no game.

'Tis a light pang. I like to see the nests
Still in their places, now first known,
At home and by far roads. Boys knew them not,
Whatever jays and squirrels may have done.

And most I like the winter nests deep-hid
That leaves and berries fell into:
Once a dormouse dined there on hazelnuts,
And grass and goose-grass seeds found soil and grew.

The Manor Farm[39]

The rock-like mud unfroze a little and rills
Ran and sparkled down each side of the road
Under the catkins wagging in the hedge.
But earth would have her sleep out, spite of the sun;
Nor did I value that thin gilding beam
More than a pretty February thing
Till I came down to the old Manor Farm,
And church and yew-tree opposite, in age
Its equals and in size. The church and yew
And farmhouse slept in a Sunday silentness.
The air raised not a straw. The steep farm roof,
With tiles duskily glowing, entertained
The midday sun; and up and down the roof
White pigeons nestled. There was no sound but one.
Three cart-horses were looking over a gate
Drowsily through their forelocks, swishing their tails
Against a fly, a solitary fly.

The Winter's cheek flushed as if he had drained
Spring, Summer, and Autumn at a draught
And smiled quietly. But 'twas not Winter –
Rather a season of bliss unchangeable
Awakened from farm and church where it had lain
Safe under tile and thatch for ages since
This England, Old already, was called Merry.

The Combe[40]

The Combe was ever dark, ancient and dark.
Its mouth is stopped with bramble, thorn, and briar;
And no one scrambles over the sliding chalk
By beech and yew and perishing juniper
Down the half precipices of its sides, with roots
And rabbit holes for steps. The sun of Winter,
The moon of Summer, and all the singing birds
Except the missel-thrush that loves juniper,
Are quite shut out. But far more ancient and dark
The Combe looks since they killed the badger there,
Dug him out and gave him to the hounds,
That most ancient Briton of English beasts.

The New Year[41]

He was the one man I met up in the woods
That stormy New Year's morning; and at first sight,
Fifty yards off, I could not tell how much
Of the strange tripod was a man. His body,
Bowed horizontal, was supported equally
By legs at one end, by a rake at the other:
Thus he rested, far less like a man than
His wheel-barrow in profile was like a pig.
But when I saw it was an old man bent,

At the same moment came into my mind
The games at which boys bend thus, *High-cocolorum*,
Or *Fly-the-garter*, and *Leap-frog*. At the sound
Of footsteps he began to straighten himself;
His head rolled under his cape like a tortoise's;
He took an unlit pipe out of his mouth
Politely ere I wished him 'A Happy New Year',
And with his head cast upward sideways muttered –
So far as I could hear through the trees' roar –
'Happy New Year, and may it come fastish, too',
While I strode by and he turned to raking leaves.

The Source

All day the air triumphs with its two voices
Of wind and rain
As loud as if in anger it rejoices,
Drowning the sound of earth
That gulps and gulps in choked endeavour vain
To swallow the rain.

Half the night, too, only the wild air speaks
With wind and rain,
Till forth the dumb source of the river breaks
And drowns the rain and wind,
Bellows like a giant bathing in mighty mirth
The triumph of earth.

The Penny Whistle

The new moon hangs like an ivory bugle
In the naked frosty blue;
And the ghylls of the forest, already blackened
By Winter, are blackened anew.

The brooks that cut up and increase the forest,
As if they had never known
The sun, are roaring with black hollow voices
Betwixt rage and a moan.

But still the caravan-hut by the hollies
Like a kingfisher gleams between:
Round the mossed old hearths of the charcoal-burners
First primroses ask to be seen.

The charcoal-burners are black, but their linen
Blows white on the line;
And white the letter the girl is reading
Under that crescent fine;

And her brother who hides apart in a thicket,
Slowly and surely playing
On a whistle an old nursery melody
Says far more than I am saying.

A Private

This ploughman dead in battle slept out of doors
Many a frozen night, and merrily
Answered staid drinkers, good bedmen, and all bores:
'At Mrs Greenland's Hawthorn Bush,' said he,
'I slept.' None knew which bush. Above the town,
Beyond 'The Drover', a hundred spot the down
In Wiltshire. And where now at last he sleeps
More sound in France – that, too, he secret keeps.

Snow

In the gloom of whiteness,
In the great silence of snow,
A child was sighing

And bitterly saying: 'Oh,
They have killed a white bird up there on her nest,
The down is fluttering from her breast!'
And still it fell through that dusky brightness
On the child crying for the bird of the snow.

Adlestrop

Yes. I remember Adlestrop –
The name, because one afternoon
Of heat the express-train drew up there
Unwontedly. It was late June.

The steam hissed. Someone cleared his throat.
No one left and no one came
On the bare platform. What I saw
Was Adlestrop – only the name

And willows, willow-herb, and grass,
And meadowsweet, and haycocks dry,
No whit less still and lonely fair
Than the high cloudlets in the sky.

And for that minute a blackbird sang
Close by, and round him, mistier,
Farther and farther, all the birds
Of Oxfordshire and Gloucestershire.

Tears

It seems I have no tears left. They should have fallen –
Their ghosts, if tears have ghosts, did fall – that day
When twenty hounds streamed by me, not yet combed out
But still all equals in their rage of gladness
Upon the scent, made one, like a great dragon
In Blooming Meadow that bends towards the sun

And once bore hops: and on that other day
When I stepped out from the double-shadowed Tower
Into an April morning, stirring and sweet
And warm. Strange solitude was there and silence.
A mightier charm than any in the Tower
Possessed the courtyard. They were changing guard,
Soldiers in line, young English countrymen,
Fair-haired and ruddy, in white tunics. Drums
And fifes were playing 'The British Grenadiers'.
The men, the music piercing that solitude
And silence, told me truths I had not dreamed,
And have forgotten since their beauty passed.

Over the Hills

Often and often it came back again
To mind, the day I passed the horizon ridge
To a new country, the path I had to find
By half-gaps that were stiles once in the hedge,
The pack of scarlet clouds running across
The harvest evening that seemed endless then
And after, and the inn where all were kind,
All were strangers. I did not know my loss
Till one day twelve months later suddenly
I leaned upon my spade and saw it all,
Though far beyond the sky-line. It became
Almost a habit through the year for me
To lean and see it and think to do the same
Again for two days and a night. Recall
Was vain: no more could the restless brook
Ever turn back and climb the waterfall
To the lake that rests and stirs not in its nook,
As in the hollow of the collar-bone
Under the mountain's head of rush and stone.

The Cuckoo

That's the cuckoo, you say. I cannot hear it.
When last I heard it I cannot recall; but I know
Too well the year when first I failed to hear it –
It was drowned by my man groaning out to his
    sheep 'Ho! Ho!'

Ten times with an angry voice he shouted
'Ho! Ho!' but not in anger, for that was his way.
He died that Summer, and that is how I remember
The cuckoo calling, the children listening, and me
    saying, 'Nay.'

And now, as you said, 'There it is', I was hearing
Not the cuckoo at all, but my man's 'Ho! Ho!' instead.
And I think that even if I could lose my deafness
The cuckoo's note would be drowned by the voice of my dead.

Swedes

They have taken the gable from the roof of clay
On the long swede pile. They have let in the sun
To the white and gold and purple of curled fronds
Unsunned. It is a sight more tender-gorgeous
At the wood-corner where Winter moans and drips
Than when, in the Valley of the Tombs of Kings,
A boy crawls down into a Pharaoh's tomb
And, first of Christian men, beholds the mummy,
God and monkey, chariot and throne and vase,
Blue pottery, alabaster, and gold.

But dreamless long-dead Amen-hotep lies.
This is a dream of Winter, sweet as Spring.

The Unknown Bird

Three lovely notes he whistled, too soft to be heard
If others sang; but others never sang
In the great beech-wood all that May and June.
No one saw him: I alone could hear him
Though many listened. Was it but four years
Ago? or five? He never came again.

Oftenest when I heard him I was alone,
Nor could I ever make another hear.
La-la-la! he called, seeming far-off –
As if a cock crowed past the edge of the world,
As if the bird or I were in a dream.
Yet that he travelled through the trees and sometimes
Neared me, was plain, though somehow distant still
He sounded. All the proof is – I told men
What I had heard.

                                 I never knew a voice,
Man, beast, or bird, better than this. I told
The naturalists; but neither had they heard
Anything like the notes that did so haunt me,
I had them clear by heart and have them still.
Four years, or five, have made no difference. Then
As now that La-la-la! was bodiless sweet:
Sad more than joyful it was, if I must say
That it was one or other, but if sad
'Twas sad only with joy too, too far off
For me to taste it. But I cannot tell
If truly never anything but fair
The days were when he sang, as now they seem.
This surely I know, that I who listened then,
Happy sometimes, sometimes suffering
A heavy body and a heavy heart,
Now straightway, if I think of it, become
Light as that bird wandering beyond my shore.

The Mill-Pond

The sun blazed while the thunder yet
Added a boom:
A wagtail flickered bright over
The mill-pond's gloom:

Less than the cooing in the alder
Isles of the pool
Sounded the thunder through that plunge
Of waters cool.

Scared starlings on the aspen tip
Past the black mill
Outchattered the stream and the next roar
Far on the hill.

As my feet dangling teased the foam
That slid below
A girl came out. 'Take care!' she said –
Ages ago.

She startled me, standing quite close
Dressed all in white:
Ages ago I was angry till
She passed from sight.

Then the storm burst, and as I crouched
To shelter, how
Beautiful and kind, too, she seemed,
As she does now!

[Man and Dog][42]

' 'Twill take some getting.' 'Sir, I think 'twill so.'
The old man stared up at the mistletoe
That hung too high in the poplar's crest for plunder
Of any climber, though not for kissing under:
Then he went on against the north-east wind –
Straight but lame, leaning on a staff new-skinned,
Carrying a brolly, flag-basket, and old coat, –
Towards Alton, ten miles off. And he had not
Done less from Chilgrove where he pulled up docks.
'Twere best, if he had had 'a money-box',
To have waited there till the sheep cleared a field
For what a half-week's flint-picking would yield.
His mind was running on the work he had done
Since he left Christchurch in the New Forest, one
Spring in the 'seventies, – navvying on dock and line
From Southampton to Newcastle-on-Tyne, –
In 'seventy-four a year of soldiering
With the Berkshires, – hoeing and harvesting
In half the shires where corn and couch will grow.
His sons, three sons, were fighting, but the hoe
And reap-hook he liked, or anything to do with trees.
He fell once from a poplar tall as these:
The Flying Man they called him in hospital.
'If I flew now, to another world I'd fall.'
He laughed and whistled to the small brown bitch
With spots of blue that hunted in the ditch.
Her foxy Welsh grandfather must have paired
Beneath him. He kept sheep in Wales and scared
Strangers, I will warrant, with his pearl eye
And trick of shrinking off as he were shy,
Then following close in silence for – for what?
'No rabbit, never fear, she ever got,
Yet always hunts. To-day she nearly had one:
She would and she wouldn't. 'Twas like that. The bad one!
She's not much use, but still she's company,

Though I'm not. She goes everywhere with me.
So Alton I must reach tonight somehow:
I'll get no shakedown with that bedfellow
From farmers. Many a man sleeps worse tonight
Than I shall.' 'In the trenches.' 'Yes, that's right.
But they'll be out of that – I hope they be –
This weather, marching after the enemy.'
'And so I hope. Good luck.' And there I nodded
'Good-night. You keep straight on.' Stiffly he plodded;
And at his heels the crisp leaves scurried fast,
And the leaf-coloured robin watched. They passed,
The robin till next day, the man for good,
Together in the twilight of the wood.

Beauty

What does it mean? Tired, angry, and ill at ease,
No man, woman, or child alive could please
Me now. And yet I almost dare to laugh
Because I sit and frame an epitaph –
'Here lies all that no one loved of him
And that loved no one.' Then in a trice that whim
Has wearied. But, though I am like a river
At fall of evening while it seems that never
Has the sun lighted it or warmed it, while
Cross breezes cut the surface to a file,
This heart, some fraction of me, happily
Floats through the window even now to a tree
Down in the misting, dim-lit, quiet vale,
Not like a pewit that returns to wail
For something it has lost, but like a dove
That slants unswerving to its home and love.
There I find my rest, and through the dusk air
Flies what yet lives in me. Beauty is there.

[*The Gypsy*]

A fortnight before Christmas Gypsies were everywhere:
Vans were drawn up on wastes, women trailed to the fair.
'My gentleman,' said one, 'you've got a lucky face.'
'And you've a luckier,' I thought, 'if such a grace
And impudence in rags are lucky.' 'Give a penny
For the poor baby's sake.' 'Indeed I have not any
Unless you can give change for a sovereign, my dear.'
'Then just half a pipeful of tobacco can you spare?'
I gave it. With that much victory she laughed content.
I should have given more, but off and away she went
With her baby and her pink sham flowers to rejoin
The rest before I could translate to its proper coin
Gratitude for her grace. And I paid nothing then,
As I pay nothing now with the dipping of my pen
For her brother's music when he drummed the tambourine
And stamped his feet, which made the workmen passing grin,
While his mouth-organ changed to a rascally Bacchanal dance
'Over the hills and far away.' This and his glance
Outlasted all the fair, farmer, and auctioneer,
Cheap-jack, balloon-man, drover with crooked stick,
        and steer,
Pig, turkey, goose, and duck, Christmas corpses to be.
Not even the kneeling ox had eyes like the Romany.
That night he peopled for me the hollow wooded land,
More dark and wild than stormiest heavens, that I searched and
        scanned
Like a ghost new-arrived. The gradations of the dark
Were like an underworld of death, but for the spark
In the Gypsy boy's black eyes as he played and stamped
        his tune,
'Over the hills and far away', and a crescent moon.

[Ambition]

Unless it was that day I never knew
Ambition. After a night of frost, before
The March sun brightened and the South-west blew,
Jackdaws began to shout and float and soar
Already, and one was racing straight and high
Alone, shouting like a black warrior
Challenges and menaces to the wide sky.
With loud long laughter then a woodpecker
Ridiculed the sadness of the owl's last cry.
And through the valley where all the folk astir
Made only plumes of pearly smoke to tower
Over dark trees and white meadows happier
Than was Elysium in that happy hour,
A train that roared along raised after it
And carried with it a motionless white bower
Of purest cloud, from end to end close-knit,
So fair it touched the roar with silence. Time
Was powerless while that lasted. I could sit
And think I had made the loveliness of prime,
Breathed its life into it and were its lord,
And no mind lived save this 'twixt clouds and rime.
Omnipotent I was, nor even deplored
That I did nothing. But the end fell like a bell:
The bower was scattered; far off the train roared.
But if this was ambition I cannot tell.
What 'twas ambition for I know not well.

House and Man

One hour: as dim he and his house now look
As a reflection in a rippling brook,
While I remember him; but first, his house.
Empty it sounded. It was dark with forest boughs
That brushed the walls and made the mossy tiles

Part of the squirrels' track. In all those miles
Of forest silence and forest murmur, only
One house – 'Lonely!' he said, 'I wish it were lonely' –
Which the trees looked upon from every side,
And that was his.

               He waved good-bye to hide
A sigh that he converted to a laugh.
He seemed to hang rather than stand there, half
Ghost-like, half like a beggar's rag, clean wrung
And useless on the brier where it has hung
Long years a-washing by sun and wind and rain.

But why I call back man and house again
Is that now on a beech-tree's tip I see
As then I saw – I at the gate, and he
In the house darkness, – a magpie veering about,
A magpie like a weathercock in doubt.

Parting[43]

The Past is a strange land, most strange.
Wind blows not there, nor does rain fall:
If they do, they cannot hurt at all.
Men of all kinds as equals range

The soundless fields and streets of it.
Pleasure and pain there have no sting,
The perished self not suffering
That lacks all blood and nerve and wit,

And is in shadow-land a shade.
Remembered joy and misery
Bring joy to the joyous equally;
Both sadden the sad. So memory made

Parting today a double pain:
First because it was parting; next
Because the ill it ended vexed
And mocked me from the Past again,

Not as what had been remedied
Had I gone on, – not that, oh no!
But as itself no longer woe;
Sighs, angry word and look and deed

Being faded: rather a kind of bliss,
For there spiritualized it lay
In the perpetual yesterday
That naught can stir or strain like this.

First Known when Lost

I never had noticed it until
'Twas gone, – the narrow copse
Where now the woodman lops
The last of the willows with his bill

It was not more than a hedge overgrown.
One meadow's breadth away
I passed it day by day.
Now the soil is bare as a bone,

And black betwixt two meadows green,
Though fresh-cut faggot ends
Of hazel made some amends
With a gleam as if flowers they had been.

Strange it could have hidden so near!
And now I see as I look
That the small winding brook,
A tributary's tributary, rises there.

May 23

There never was a finer day,
And never will be while May is May, –
The third, and not the last of its kind;
But though fair and clear the two behind
Seemed pursued by tempests overpast;
And the morrow with fear that it could not last
Was spoiled. Today ere the stones were warm
Five minutes of thunderstorm
Dashed it with rain, as if to secure,
By one tear, its beauty the luck to endure.

At midday then along the lane
Old Jack Noman appeared again,
Jaunty and old, crooked and tall,
And stopped and grinned at me over the wall,
With a cowslip bunch in his button-hole
And one in his cap. Who could say if his roll
Came from flints in the road, the weather, or ale?
He was welcome as the nightingale.
Not an hour of the sun had been wasted on Jack.
'I've got my Indian complexion back,'
Said he. He was tanned like a harvester,
Like his short clay pipe, like the leaf and bur
That clung to his coat from last night's bed,
Like the ploughland crumbling red.
Fairer flowers were none on the earth
Than his cowslips wet with the dew of their birth,
Or fresher leaves than the cress in his basket.
'Where did they come from, Jack?' 'Don't ask it,
And you'll be told no lies.' 'Very well:
Then I can't buy.' 'I don't want to sell.
Take them and these flowers, too, free.
Perhaps you have something to give me?
Wait till next time. The better the day . . .
The Lord couldn't make a better, I say;

If he could, he never has done.'
So off went Jack with his roll-walk-run,
Leaving his cresses from Oakshott rill
And his cowslips from Wheatham hill.

'Twas the first day that the midges bit;
But though they bit me, I was glad of it:
Of the dust in my face, too, I was glad.
Spring could do nothing to make me sad.
Bluebells hid all the ruts in the copse,
The elm seeds lay in the road like hops,
That fine day, May the twenty-third,
The day Jack Noman disappeared.

The Barn

They should never have built a barn there, at all –
Drip, drip, drip! – under that elm tree,
Though then it was young. Now it is old
But good, not like the barn and me.

Tomorrow they cut it down. They will leave
The barn, as I shall be left, maybe.
What holds it up? 'Twould not pay to pull down.
Well, this place has no other antiquity.

No abbey or castle looks so old
As this that Job Knight built in '54.
Built to keep corn for rats and men.
Now there's fowls in the roof, pigs on the floor.

What thatch survives is dung for the grass,
The best grass on the farm. A pity the roof
Will not bear a mower to mow it. But
Only fowls have foothold enough.

Starlings used to sit there with bubbling throats
Making a spiky beard as they chattered
And whistled and kissed, with heads in air,
Till they thought of something else that mattered.

But now they cannot find a place,
Among all those holes, for a nest any more.
It's the turn of lesser things, I suppose.
Once I fancied 'twas starlings they built it for.

Home

Not the end: but there's nothing more.
Sweet Summer and Winter rude
I have loved, and friendship and love,
The crowd and solitude:

But I know them: I weary not;
But all that they mean I know.
I would go back again home
Now. Yet how should I go?

This is my grief. That land,
My home, I have never seen;
No traveller tells of it,
However far he has been.

And could I discover it,
I fear my happiness there,
Or my pain, might be dreams of return
Here, to these things that were.

Remembering ills, though slight
Yet irremediable,
Brings a worse, an impurer pang
Than remembering what was well.

No: I cannot go back,
And would not if I could.
Until blindness come, I must wait
And blink at what is not good.

The Owl

Downhill I came, hungry, and yet not starved;
Cold, yet had heat within me that was proof
Against the North wind; tired, yet so that rest
Had seemed the sweetest thing under a roof.

Then at the inn I had food, fire, and rest,
Knowing how hungry, cold, and tired was I.
All of the night was quite barred out except
An owl's cry, a most melancholy cry

Shaken out long and clear upon the hill,
No merry note, nor cause of merriment,
But one telling me plain what I escaped
And others could not, that night, as in I went.

And salted was my food, and my repose,
Salted and sobered, too, by the bird's voice
Speaking for all who lay under the stars,
Soldiers and poor, unable to rejoice.

The Child on the Cliff

Mother, the root of this little yellow flower
Among the stones has the taste of quinine.
Things are strange to-day on the cliff. The sun shines so bright,
And the grasshopper works at his sewing-machine
So hard. Here's one on my hand, mother, look;
I lie so still. There's one on your book.

But I have something to tell more strange. So leave
Your book to the grasshopper, mother dear, –
Like a green knight in a dazzling market-place, –
And listen now. Can you hear what I hear
Far out? Now and then the foam there curls
And stretches a white arm out like a girl's.

Fishes and gulls ring no bells. There cannot be
A chapel or church between here and Devon,
With fishes or gulls ringing its bell, – hark! –
Somewhere under the sea or up in heaven.
'It's the bell, my son, out in the bay
On the buoy. It does sound sweet to-day.'

Sweeter I never heard, mother, no, not in all Wales.
I should like to be lying under that foam,
Dead, but able to hear the sound of the bell,
And certain that you would often come
And rest, listening happily.
I should be happy if that could be.

Good-Night

The skylarks are far behind that sang over the down;
I can hear no more those suburb nightingales;
Thrushes and blackbirds sing in the gardens of the town
In vain: the noise of man, beast, and machine prevails.

But the call of children in the unfamiliar streets
That echo with a familiar twilight echoing,
Sweet as the voice of nightingale or lark, completes
A magic of strange welcome, so that I seem a king

Among man, beast, machine, bird, child, and the ghost
That in the echo lives and with the echo dies.
The friendless town is friendly; homeless, I am not lost;
Though I know none of these doors, and meet but
        strangers' eyes.

Never again, perhaps, after tomorrow, shall
I see these homely streets, these church windows alight,
Not a man or woman or child among them all:
But it is All Friends' Night, a traveller's good-night.

But These Things Also

But these things also are Spring's –
On banks by the roadside the grass
Long-dead that is greyer now
Than all the Winter it was;

The shell of a little snail bleached
In the grass; chip of flint, and mite
Of chalk; and the small birds' dung
In splashes of purest white:

All the white things a man mistakes
For earliest violets
Who seeks through Winter's ruins
Something to pay Winter's debts,

While the North blows, and starling flocks
By chattering on and on
Keep their spirits up in the mist,
And Spring's here, Winter's not gone.

The New House[44]

Now first, as I shut the door,
    I was alone
In the new house; and the wind
    Began to moan.

Old at once was the house,
    And I was old;
My ears were teased with the dread
    Of what was foretold,

Nights of storm, days of mist, without end;
    Sad days when the sun
Shone in vain: old griefs and griefs
    Not yet begun.

All was foretold me; naught
    Could I foresee;
But I learned how the wind would sound
    After these things should be.

Sowing

It was a perfect day
For sowing; just
As sweet and dry was the ground
As tobacco-dust.

I tasted deep the hour
Between the far
Owl's chuckling first soft cry
And the first star.

A long stretched hour it was;
Nothing undone
Remained; the early seeds
All safely sown.

And now, hark at the rain,
Windless and light,
Half a kiss, half a tear,
Saying good-night.

*March the 3rd**

Here again (she said) is March the third
And twelve hours' singing for the bird
'Twixt dawn and dusk, from half-past six
To half-past six, never unheard.

'Tis Sunday, and the church-bells end
When the birds do. I think they blend
Now better than they will when passed
Is this unnamed, unmarked godsend.

Or do all mark, and none dares say,
How it may shift and long delay,
Somewhere before the first of Spring,
But never fails, this singing day?

And when it falls on Sunday, bells
Are a wild natural voice that dwells
On hillsides; but the birds' songs have
The holiness gone from the bells.

This day unpromised is more dear
Than all the named days of the year
When seasonable sweets come in,
Because we know how lucky we are.

The Path

Running along a bank, a parapet
That saves from the precipitous wood below
The level road, there is a path. It serves
Children for looking down the long smooth steep,
Between the legs of beech and yew, to where
A fallen tree checks the sight: while men and women

* The author's birthday.

Content themselves with the road and what they see
Over the bank, and what the children tell.
The path, winding like silver, trickles on,
Bordered and even invaded by thinnest moss
That tries to cover roots and crumbling chalk
With gold, olive, and emerald, but in vain.
The children wear it. They have flattened the bank
On top, and silvered it between the moss
With the current of their feet, year after year.
But the road is houseless, and leads not to school.
To see a child is rare there, and the eye
Has but the road, the wood that overhangs
And underyawns it, and the path that looks
As if it led on to some legendary
Or fancied place where men have wished to go
And stay; till, sudden, it ends where the wood ends.

[*The Wasp Trap*]

This moonlight makes
The lovely lovelier
Than ever before lakes
And meadows were.

And yet they are not,
Though this their hour is, more
Lovely than things that were not
Lovely before.

Nothing on earth,
And in the heavens no star,
For pure brightness is worth
More than that jar,

For wasps meant, now
A star – long may it swing
From the dead apple-bough,
So glistening.

Wind and Mist[45]

They met inside the gateway that gives the view,
A hollow land as vast as heaven. 'It is
A pleasant day, sir.' 'A very pleasant day.'
'And what a view here! If you like angled fields
Of grass and grain bounded by oak and thorn,
Here is a league. Had we with Germany
To play upon this board it could not be
More dear than April has made it with a smile.
The fields beyond that league close in together
And merge, even as our days into the past,
Into one wood that has a shining pane
Of water. Then the hills of the horizon –
That is how I should make hills had I to show
One who would never see them what hills were like.'
'Yes. Sixty miles of South Downs at one glance.
Sometimes a man feels proud of them, as if
He had just created them with one mighty thought.'
'That house, though modern, could not be better planned
For its position. I never liked a new
House better. Could you tell me who lives in it?'
'No one.' 'Ah – and I was peopling all
Those windows on the south with happy eyes,
The terrace under them with happy feet;
Girls—' 'Sir, I know. I know. I have seen that house
Through mist look lovely as a castle in Spain,
And airier. I have thought: " 'Twere happy there
To live." And I have laughed at that
Because I lived there then.' 'Extraordinary.'
'Yes, with my furniture and family
Still in it, I, knowing every nook of it
And loving none, and in fact hating it.'

'Dear me! How could that be? But pardon me.'
'No offence. Doubtless the house was not to blame,
But the eye watching from those windows saw,
Many a day, day after day, mist – mist
Like chaos surging back – and felt itself
Alone in all the world, marooned alone.
We lived in clouds, on a cliff's edge almost
(You see), and if clouds went, the visible earth
Lay too far off beneath and like a cloud.
I did not know it was the earth I loved
Until I tried to live there in the clouds
'You had a garden and the earth turned to cloud.'
Of flint and clay, too.' 'True; that was real enough.
The flint was the one crop that never failed.
The clay first broke my heart, and then my back;
And the back heals not. There were other things
Real, too. In that room at the gable a child
Was born while the wind chilled a summer dawn:
Never looked grey mind on a greyer one
Than when the child's cry broke above the groans.'
'I hope they were both spared.' 'They were. Oh yes!
But flint and clay and childbirth were too real
For this cloudcastle. I had forgot the wind.
Pray do not let me get on to the wind.
You would not understand about the wind.
It is my subject, and compared with me
Those who have always lived on the firm ground
Are quite unreal in this matter of the wind.
There were whole days and nights when the wind and I
Between us shared the world, and the wind ruled
And I obeyed it and forgot the mist.
My past and the past of the world were in the wind.
Now you may say that though you understand
And feel for me, and so on, you yourself
Would find it different. You are all like that
If once you stand here free from wind and mist:
I might as well be talking to wind and mist.
You would believe the house-agent's young man

Who gives no heed to anything I say.
Good morning. But one word. I want to admit
That I would try the house once more, if I could;
As I should like to try being young again.'

A Gentleman

'He has robbed two clubs. The judge at Salisbury
Can't give him more than he undoubtedly
Deserves. The scoundrel! Look at his photograph!
A lady-killer! Hanging's too good by half
For such as he.' So said the stranger, one
With crimes yet undiscovered or undone.
But at the inn the Gipsy dame began:
'Now he was what I call a gentleman.
He went along with Carrie, and when she
Had a baby he paid up so readily
His half a crown. Just like him. A crown'd have been
More like him. For I never knew him mean.
Oh! but he was such a nice gentleman. Oh!
Last time we met he said if me and Joe
Was anywhere near we must be sure and call.
He put his arms around our Amos all
As if he were his own son. I pray God
Save him from justice! Nicer man never trod.'

Lob[46]

At hawthorn-time in Wiltshire travelling
In search of something chance would never bring,
An old man's face, by life and weather cut
And coloured, – rough, brown, sweet as any nut, –
A land face, sea-blue-eyed, – hung in my mind
When I had left him many a mile behind.
All he said was: 'Nobody can't stop 'ee. It's

A footpath, right enough. You see those bits
Of mounds – that's where they opened up the barrows
Sixty years since, while I was scaring sparrows.
They thought as there was something to find there,
But couldn't find it, by digging, anywhere.'

To turn back then and seek him, where was the use?
There were three Manningfords, – Abbots, Bohun, and Bruce:
And whether Alton, not Manningford, it was,
My memory could not decide, because
There was both Alton Barnes and Alton Priors.
All had their churches, graveyards, farms and byres,
Lurking to one side up the paths and lanes,
Seldom well seen except by aeroplanes;
And when bells rang, or pigs squealed, or cocks crowed,
Then only heard. Ages ago the road
Approached. The people stood and looked and turned.
Nor asked it to come nearer, nor yet learned
To move out there and dwell in all men's dust.
And yet withal they shot the weathercock, just
Because 'twas he crowed out of tune, they said:
So now the copper weathercock is dead.
If they had reaped their dandelions and sold
Them fairly, they could have afforded gold.

Many years passed, and I went back again
Among those villages, and looked for men
Who might have known my ancient. He himself
Had long been dead or laid upon the shelf,
I thought. One man I asked about him roared
At my description: ''Tis old Bottlesford
He means, Bill.' But another said: 'Of course,
It was Jack Button up at the White Horse.
He's dead, sir, these three years.' This lasted till
A girl proposed Walker of Walker's Hill,
'Old Adam Walker. Adam's Point you'll see
Marked on the maps.'

'That was her roguery,'
The next man said. He was a squire's son
Who loved wild bird and beast, and dog and gun
For killing them. He had loved them from his birth,
One with another, as he loved the earth.
'The man may be like Button, or Walker, or
Like Bottlesford, that you want, but far more
He sounds like one I saw when I was a child.
I could almost swear to him. The man was wild
And wandered. His home was where he was free.
Everybody has met one such man as he.
Does he keep clear old paths that no one uses
But once a life-time when he loves or muses?
He is English as this gate, these flowers, this mire.
And when at eight years old Lob-lie-by-the-fire
Came in my books, this was the man I saw.
He has been in England as long as dove and daw,
Calling the wild cherry tree the merry tree,
The rose campion Bridget-in-her-bravery;
And in a tender mood he, as I guess,
Christened one flower Live-in-idleness,
And while he walked from Exeter to Leeds
One April called all cuckoo-flowers Milkmaids.
From him old herbal Gerard learnt, as a boy,
To name wild clematis the Traveller's-joy.
Our blackbirds sang no English till his ear
Told him they called his Jan Toy "Pretty dear".
(She was Jan Toy the Lucky, who, having lost
A shilling, and found a penny loaf, rejoiced.)
For reasons of his own to him the wren
Is Jenny Pooter. Before all other men
'Twas he first called the Hog's Back the Hog's Back.
That Mother Dunch's Buttocks[47] should not lack
Their name was his care. He too could explain
Totteridge and Totterdown and Juggler's Lane:
He knows, if anyone. Why Tumbling Bay,
Inland in Kent, is called so, he might say.

'But little he says compared with what he does.
If ever a sage troubles him he will buzz
Like a beehive to conclude the tedious fray:
And the sage, who knows all languages, runs away.
Yet Lob has thirteen hundred names for a fool,
And though he never could spare time for school
To unteach what the fox so well expressed,
On biting the cock's head off, – Quietness is best, –
He can talk quite as well as anyone
After his thinking is forgot and done.
He first of all told someone else's wife,
For a farthing she'd skin a flint and spoil a knife
Worth sixpence skinning it. She heard him speak:
"She had a face as long as a wet week"
Said he, telling the tale in after years.
With blue smock and with gold rings in his ears,
Sometimes he is a pedlar, not too poor
To keep his wit. This is tall Tom that bore
The logs in, and with Shakespeare in the hall
Once talked, when icicles hung by the wall.
As Herne the Hunter[48] he has known hard times.
On sleepless nights he made up weather rhymes
Which others spoilt. And, Hob being then his name,
He kept the hog that thought the butcher came
To bring his breakfast. "You thought wrong," said Hob.
When there were kings in Kent this very Lob,
Whose sheep grew fat and he himself grew merry,
Wedded the king's daughter of Canterbury;
For he alone, unlike squire, lord, and king,
Watched a night by her without slumbering;
He kept both waking. When he was but a lad
He won a rich man's heiress, deaf, dumb, and sad,
By rousing her to laugh at him. He carried
His donkey on his back. So they were married.
And while he was a little cobbler's boy
He tricked the giant coming to destroy
Shrewsbury by flood. "And how far is it yet?"
The giant asked in passing. "I forget;

But see these shoes I've worn out on the road
And we're not there yet." He emptied out his load
Of shoes for mending. The giant let fall from his spade
The earth for damming Severn, and thus made
The Wrekin hill; and little Ercall hill
Rose where the giant scraped his boots.[49] While still
So young, our Jack was chief of Gotham's[50] sages.
But long before he could have been wise, ages
Earlier than this, while he grew thick and strong
And ate his bacon, or, at times, sang a song
And merely smelt it, as Jack the giant-killer
He made a name. He too ground up the miller,
The Yorkshireman who ground men's bones for flour.

'Do you believe Jack dead before his hour?
Or that his name is Walker, or Bottlesford,
Or Button, a mere clown, or squire, or lord?
The man you saw, – Lob-lie-by-the-fire, Jack Cade,
Jack Smith, Jack Moon, poor Jack of every trade,
Young Jack, or old Jack, or Jack What-d'ye-call,
Jack-in-the-hedge, or Robin-run-by-the-wall,
Robin Hood, Ragged Robin, lazy Bob,
One of the lords of No Man's Land, good Lob, –
Although he was seen dying at Waterloo,
Hastings, Agincourt, and Sedgemoor too,
Lives yet. He never will admit he is dead
Till millers cease to grind men's bones for bread,
Not till our weathercock crows once again
And I remove my house out of the lane
On to the road.' With this he disappeared
In hazel and thorn tangled with old-man's-beard.
But one glimpse of his back, as there he stood,
Choosing his way, proved him of old Jack's blood,
Young Jack perhaps, and now a Wiltshireman
As he has oft been since his days began.

Digging

To-day I think
Only with scents, – scents dead leaves yield,
And bracken, and wild carrot's seed,
And the square mustard field;

Odours that rise
When the spade wounds the root of tree,
Rose, currant, raspberry, or goutweed,
Rhubarb or celery;

The smoke's smell, too,
Flowing from where a bonfire burns
The dead, the waste, the dangerous,
And all to sweetness turns.

It is enough
To smell, to crumble the dark earth,
While the robin sings over again
Sad songs of Autumn mirth.

Lovers

The two men in the road were taken aback.
The lovers came out shading their eyes from the sun,
And never was white so white, or black so black,
As her cheeks and hair. 'There are more things than one
A man might turn into a wood for, Jack,'
Said George; Jack whispered: 'He has not got a gun.
It's a bit too much of a good thing, I say.
They are going the other road, look. And see her run.' –
She ran. – 'What a thing it is, this picking may!'

In Memoriam [Easter, 1915]

The flowers left thick at nightfall in the wood
This Eastertide call into mind the men,
Now far from home, who, with their sweethearts, should
Have gathered them and will do never again.

Head and Bottle

The downs will lose the sun, white alyssum
Lose the bees' hum;
But head and bottle tilted back in the cart
Will never part
Till I am cold as midnight and all my hours
Are beeless flowers.
He neither sees, nor hears, nor smells, nor thinks,
But only drinks,
Quiet in the yard where tree trunks do not lie
More quietly.

Home

Often I had gone this way before:
But now it seemed I never could be
And never had been anywhere else;
'Twas home; one nationality
We had, I and the birds that sang,
One memory.

They welcomed me. I had come back
That eve somehow from somewhere far:
The April mist, the chill, the calm,

Meant the same thing familiar
And pleasant to us, and strange too,
Yet with no bar.

The thrush on the oaktop in the lane
Sang his last song, or last but one;
And as he ended, on the elm
Another had but just begun
His last; they knew no more than I
The day was done.

Then past his dark white cottage front
A labourer went along, his tread
Slow, half with weariness, half with ease;
And, through the silence, from his shed
The sound of sawing rounded all
That silence said.

[*Health*]

Four miles at a leap, over the dark hollow land,
To the frosted steep of the down and its junipers black,
Travels my eye with equal ease and delight:
And scarce could my body leap four yards.

This is the best and the worst of it –
Never to know,
Yet to imagine gloriously, pure health.

Today, had I suddenly health,
I could not satisfy the desire of my heart
Unless health abated it,
So beautiful is the air in its softness and clearness, while
       Spring
Promises all and fails in nothing as yet;
And what blue and what white is I never knew
Before I saw this sky blessing the land.

For had I health I could not ride or run or fly
So far or so rapidly over the land
As I desire: I should reach Wiltshire tired;
I should have changed my mind before I could be in Wales.
I could not love; I could not command love.
Beauty would still be far off
However many hills I climbed over;
Peace would still be farther.
Maybe I should not count it anything
To leap these four miles with the eye;
And either I should not be filled almost to bursting with desire,
Or with my power desire would still keep pace.

Yet I am not satisfied
Even with knowing I never could be satisfied.
With health and all the power that lies
In maiden beauty, poet and warrior,
In Caesar, Shakespeare, Alcibiades,
Mazeppa, Leonardo, Michelangelo,
In any maiden whose smile is lovelier
Than sunlight upon dew,
I could not be as the wagtail running up and down
The warm tiles of the roof slope, twittering
Happily and sweetly as if the sun itself
Extracted the song
As the hand makes sparks from the fur of a cat:

I could not be as the sun.
Nor should I be content to be
As little as the bird or as mighty as the sun.
For the bird knows not of the sun,
And the sun regards not the bird.
But I am almost proud to love both bird and sun,
Though scarce this Spring could my body leap four yards.

[*She Dotes*]

She dotes on what the wild birds say
Or hint or mock at, night and day, –
Thrush, blackbird, all that sing in May,
    And songless plover,
Hawk, heron, owl, and woodpecker.
They never say a word to her
    About her lover.

She laughs at them for childishness,
She cries at them for carelessness
Who see her going loverless
    Yet sing and chatter
Just as when he was not a ghost,
Nor ever ask her what she has lost
    Or what is the matter.

Yet she has fancied blackbirds hide
A secret, and that thrushes chide
Because she thinks death can divide
    Her from her lover:
And she has slept, trying to translate
The word the cuckoo cries to his mate
    Over and over.

Song

At poet's tears,
Sweeter than any smiles but hers,
She laughs; I sigh;
And yet I could not live if she should die.

And when in June
Once more the cuckoo spoils his tune,
She laughs at sighs;
And yet she says she loves me till she dies.

Melancholy

The rain and wind, the rain and wind, raved endlessly.
On me the Summer storm, and fever, and melancholy
Wrought magic, so that if I feared the solitude
Far more I feared all company: too sharp, too rude,
Had been the wisest or the dearest human voice.
What I desired I knew not, but whate'er my choice
Vain it must be, I knew. Yet naught did my despair
But sweeten the strange sweetness, while through the wild air
All day long I heard a distant cuckoo calling
And, soft as dulcimers, sounds of near water falling,
And, softer, and remote as if in history,
Rumours of what had touched my friends, my foes, or me.

To-Night

Harry, you know at night
The larks in Castle Alley
Sing from the attic's height
As if the electric light
Were the true sun above a summer valley:
Whistle, don't knock, to-night.

I shall come early, Kate:
And we in Castle Alley
Will sit close out of sight
Alone, and ask no light
Of lamp or sun above a summer valley:
To-night I can stay late.

The Glory

The glory of the beauty of the morning, –
The cuckoo crying over the untouched dew;
The blackbird that has found it, and the dove
That tempts me on to something sweeter than love;
White clouds ranged even and fair as new-mown hay;
The heat, the stir, the sublime vacancy
Of sky and meadow and forest and my own heart: –
The glory invites me, yet it leaves me scorning
All I can ever do, all I can be,
Beside the lovely of motion, shape, and hue,
The happiness I fancy fit to dwell
In beauty's presence. Shall I now this day
Begin to seek as far as heaven, as hell,
Wisdom or strength to match this beauty, start
And tread the pale dust pitted with small dark drops,
In hope to find whatever it is I seek,
Hearkening to short-lived happy-seeming things
That we know naught of, in the hazel copse?
Or must I be content with discontent
As larks and swallows are perhaps with wings?
And shall I ask at the day's end once more
What beauty is, and what I can have meant
By happiness? And shall I let all go,
Glad, weary, or both? Or shall I perhaps know
That I was happy oft and oft before,
Awhile forgetting how I am fast pent,
How dreary-swift, with naught to travel to,
Is Time? I cannot bite the day to the core.

July

Naught moves but clouds, and in the glassy lake
Their doubles and the shadow of my boat.
The boat itself stirs only when I break

This drowse of heat and solitude afloat
To prove if what I see be bird or mote,
Or learn if yet the shore woods be awake.

Long hours since dawn grew, – spread, – and passed on high
And deep below, – I have watched the cool reeds hung
Over images more cool in imaged sky:
Nothing there was worth thinking of so long;
All that the ring-doves say, far leaves among,
Brims my mind with content thus still to lie.

The Chalk Pit[51]

'Is this the road that climbs above and bends
Round what was once a chalk pit: now it is
By accident an amphitheatre.
Some ash trees standing ankle-deep in briar
And bramble act the parts, and neither speak
Nor stir.' 'But see: they have fallen, every one,
And briar and bramble have grown over them.'
'That is the place. As usual no one is here.
Hardly can I imagine the drop of the axe,
And the smack that is like an echo, sounding here.'
'I do not understand.' 'Why, what I mean is
That I have seen the place two or three times
At most, and that its emptiness and silence
And stillness haunt me, as if just before
It was not empty, silent, still, but full
Of life of some kind, perhaps tragical.
Has anything unusual happened here?'
'Not that I know of. It is called the Dell.
They have not dug chalk here for a century.
That was the ash trees' age. But I will ask.'
'No. Do not. I prefer to make a tale,
Or better leave it like the end of a play,
Actors and audience and lights all gone;
For so it looks now. In my memory

Again and again I see it, strangely dark,
And vacant of a life but just withdrawn.
We have not seen the woodman with the axe.
Some ghost has left it now as we two came.'
'And yet you doubted if this were the road?'
'Well, sometimes I have thought of it and failed
To place it. No. And I am not quite sure,
Even now, this is it. For another place,
Real or painted, may have combined with it.
Or I myself a long way back in time . . .'
'Why, as to that, I used to meet a man –
I had forgotten, – searching for birds' nests
Along the road and in the chalk pit too.
The wren's hole was an eye that looked at him
For recognition. Every nest he knew.
He got a stiff neck, by looking this side or that,
Spring after spring, he told me, with his laugh, –
A sort of laugh. He was a visitor,
A man of forty, – smoked and strolled about.
At orts and crosses Pleasure and Pain had played
On his brown features; – I think both had lost; –
Mild and yet wild too. You may know the kind.
And once or twice a woman shared his walks,
A girl of twenty with a brown boy's face,
And hair brown as a thrush or as a nut,
Thick eyebrows, glinting eyes—' 'You have said enough.
A pair, – free thought, free love, – I know the breed:
I shall not mix my fancies up with them.'
'You please yourself. I should prefer the truth
Or nothing. Here, in fact, is nothing at all
Except a silent place that once rang loud,
And trees and us – imperfect friends, we men
And trees since time began; and nevertheless
Between us still we breed a mystery.'

Fifty Faggots

There they stand, on their ends, the fifty faggots
That once were underwood of hazel and ash
In Jenny Pinks's Copse. Now, by the hedge
Close packed, they make a thicket fancy alone
Can creep through with the mouse and wren. Next Spring
A blackbird or a robin will nest there,
Accustomed to them, thinking they will remain
Whatever is for ever to a bird:
This Spring it is too late; the swift has come.
'Twas a hot day for carrying them up:
Better they will never warm me, though they must
Light several Winters' fires. Before they are done
The war will have ended, many other things
Have ended, maybe, that I can no more
Foresee or more control than robin and wren.

Sedge-Warblers

This beauty made me dream there was a time
Long past and irrecoverable, a clime
Where any brook so radiant racing clear
Through buttercup and kingcup bright as brass
But gentle, nourishing the meadow grass
That leans and scurries in the wind, would bear
Another beauty, divine and feminine,
Child to the sun, a nymph whose soul unstained
Could love all day, and never hate or tire,
A lover of mortal or immortal kin.

And yet, rid of this dream, ere I had drained
Its poison, quieted was my desire
So that I only looked into the water,
Clearer than any goddess or man's daughter,

And hearkened while it combed the dark green hair
And shook the millions of the blossoms white
Of water-crowfoot, and curdled to one sheet
The flowers fallen from the chestnuts in the park
Far off. And sedge-warblers, clinging so light
To willow twigs, sang longer than the lark,
Quick, shrill, or grating, a song to match the heat
Of the strong sun, nor less the water's cool,
Gushing through narrows, swirling in the pool.
Their song that lacks all words, all melody,
All sweetness almost, was dearer then to me
Than sweetest voice that sings in tune sweet words.
This was the best of May – the small brown birds
Wisely reiterating endlessly
What no man learnt yet, in or out of school.

[I Built Myself a House of Glass[52]]

I built myself a house of glass:
It took me years to make it:
And I was proud. But now, alas!
Would God someone would break it.

But it looks too magnificent.
No neighbour casts a stone
From where he dwells, in tenement
Or palace of glass, alone.

Words[53]

Out of us all
That make rhymes,
Will you choose
Sometimes –
As the winds use
A crack in a wall

Or a drain,
Their joy or their pain
To whistle through –
Choose me,
You English words?

I know you:
You are light as dreams,
Tough as oak,
Precious as gold,
As poppies and corn,
Or an old cloak:
Sweet as our birds
To the ear,
As the burnet rose
In the heat
Of Midsummer:
Strange as the races
Of dead and unborn:
Strange and sweet
Equally,
And familiar,
To the eye,
As the dearest faces
That a man knows,
And as lost homes are:
But though older far
Than oldest yew, –
As our hills are, old, –
Worn new
Again and again:
Young as our streams
After rain:
And as dear
As the earth which you prove
That we love.

Make me content
With some sweetness
From Wales
Whose nightingales
Have no wings, –
From Wiltshire and Kent
And Herefordshire,
And the villages there, –
From the names, and the things
No less.

Let me sometimes dance
With you,
Or climb
Or stand perchance
In ecstasy,
Fixed and free
In a rhyme,
As poets do.

The Word

There are so many things I have forgot,
That once were much to me, or that were not,
All lost, as is a childless woman's child
And its child's children, in the undefiled
Abyss of what will never be again.
I have forgot, too, names of the mighty men
That fought and lost or won in the old wars,
Of kings and fiends and gods, and most of the stars.
Some things I have forgot that I forget.
But lesser things there are, remembered yet,
Than all the others. One name that I have not –
Though 'tis an empty thingless name – forgot
Never can die because Spring after Spring
Some thrushes learn to say it as they sing.
There is always one at midday saying it clear

And tart – the name, only the name I hear.
While perhaps I am thinking of the elder scent
That is like food; or while I am content
With the wild rose scent that is like memory,
This name suddenly is cried out to me
From somewhere in the bushes by a bird
Over and over again, a pure thrush word.

Under the Wood

When these old woods were young
The thrushes' ancestors
As sweetly sung
In the old years.

There was no garden here,
Apples nor mistletoe;
No children dear
Ran to and fro.

New then was this thatched cot,
But the keeper was old,
And he had not
Much lead or gold.

Most silent beech and yew:
As he went round about
The woods to view
Seldom he shot.

But now that he is gone
Out of most memories,
Still lingers on,
A stoat of his,

But one, shrivelled and green,
And with no scent at all,
And barely seen
On this shed wall.

Haymaking[54]

After night's thunder far away had rolled
The fiery day had a kernel sweet of cold,
And in the perfect blue the clouds uncurled,
Like the first gods before they made the world
And misery, swimming the stormless sea
In beauty and in divine gaiety.
The smooth white empty road was lightly strewn
With leaves – the holly's Autumn falls in June –
And fir cones standing up stiff in the heat.
The mill-foot water tumbled white and lit
With tossing crystals, happier than any crowd
Of children pouring out of school aloud.
And in the little thickets where a sleeper
For ever might lie lost, the nettle-creeper
And garden warbler sang unceasingly;
While over them shrill shrieked in his fierce glee
The swift with wings and tail as sharp and narrow
As if the bow had flown off with the arrow.
Only the scent of woodbine and hay new-mown
Travelled the road. In the field sloping down,
Park-like, to where its willows showed the brook,
Haymakers rested. The tosser lay forsook
Out in the sun; and the long waggon stood
Without its team: it seemed it never would
Move from the shadow of that single yew.
The team, as still, until their task was due,
Beside the labourers enjoyed the shade
That three squat oaks mid-field together made
Upon a circle of grass and weed uncut,
And on the hollow, once a chalk pit, but

Now brimmed with nut and elder-flower so clean.
The men leaned on their rakes, about to begin,
But still. And all were silent. All was old,
This morning time, with a great age untold,
Older than Clare and Cobbett, Morland and Crome,
Than, at the field's far edge, the farmer's home,
A white house crouched at the foot of a great tree.
Under the heavens that know not what years be
The men, the beasts, the trees, the implements
Uttered even what they will in times far hence –
All of us gone out of the reach of change –
Immortal in a picture of an old grange.

The Brook

Seated once by a brook, watching a child
Chiefly that paddled, I was thus beguiled.
Mellow the blackbird sang and sharp the thrush
Not far off in the oak and hazel brush,
Unseen. There was a scent like honeycomb
From mugwort dull. And down upon the dome
Of the stone the cart-horse kicks against so oft
A butterfly alighted. From aloft
He took the heat of the sun, and from below.
On the hot stone he perched contented so,
As if never a cart would pass again
That way; as if I were the last of men
And he the first of insects to have earth
And sun together and to know their worth.
I was divided between him and the gleam,
The motion, and the voices, of the stream,
The waters running frizzled over gravel,
That never vanish and for ever travel.
A grey flycatcher silent on a fence
And I sat as if we had been there since
The horseman and the horse lying beneath
The fir-tree-covered barrow on the heath,

The horseman and the horse with silver shoes,
Galloped the downs last. All that I could lose
I lost. And then the child's voice raised the dead.
'No one's been here before' was what she said
And what I felt, yet never should have found
A word for, while I gathered sight and sound.

Aspens[55]

All day and night, save winter, every weather,
Above the inn, the smithy, and the shop,
The aspens at the cross-roads talk together
Of rain, until their last leaves fall from the top.

Out of the blacksmith's cavern comes the ringing
Of hammer, shoe, and anvil; out of the inn
The clink, the hum, the roar, the random singing –
The sounds that for these fifty years have been.

The whisper of the aspens is not drowned,
And over lightless pane and footless road,
Empty as sky, with every other sound
Not ceasing, calls their ghosts from their abode,

A silent smithy, a silent inn, nor fails
In the bare moonlight or the thick-furred gloom,
In tempest or the night of nightingales,
To turn the cross-roads to a ghostly room.

And it would be the same were no house near.
Over all sorts of weather, men, and times,
Aspens must shake their leaves and men may hear
But need not listen, more than to my rhymes.

Whatever wind blows, while they and I have leaves
We cannot other than an aspen be
That ceaselessly, unreasonably grieves,
Or so men think who like a different tree.

The Mill-Water

Only the sound remains
Of the old mill;
Gone is the wheel;
On the prone roof and walls the nettle reigns.

Water that toils no more
Dangles white locks
And, falling, mocks
The music of the mill-wheel's busy roar.

Pretty to see, by day
Its sound is naught
Compared with thought
And talk and noise of labour and of play.

Night makes the difference.
In calm moonlight,
Gloom infinite,
The sound comes surging in upon the sense:

Solitude, company, –
When it is night, –
Grief or delight
By it must haunted or concluded be.

Often the silentness
Has but this one
Companion;
Wherever one creeps in the other is:

Sometimes a thought is drowned
By it, sometimes
Out of it climbs;
All thoughts begin or end upon this sound,

Only the idle foam
Of water falling
Changelessly calling,
Where once men had a work-place and a home.

For These [Prayer][56]

An acre of land between the shore and the hills,
Upon a ledge that shows my kingdoms three,
The lovely visible earth and sky and sea
Where what the curlew needs not, the farmer tills:

A house that shall love me as I love it,
Well-hedged, and honoured by a few ash trees
That linnets, greenfinches, and goldfinches
Shall often visit and make love in and flit:

A garden I need never go beyond,
Broken but neat, whose sunflowers every one
Are fit to be the sign of the Rising Sun:
A spring, a brook's bend, or at least a pond:

For these I ask not, but, neither too late
Nor yet too early, for what men call content,
And also that something may be sent
To be contented with, I ask of fate.

Digging[57]

What matter makes my spade for tears or mirth,
Letting down two clay pipes into the earth?
The one I smoked, the other a soldier
Of Blenheim, Ramillies, and Malplaquet
Perhaps. The dead man's immortality
Lies represented lightly with my own,
A yard or two nearer the living air
Than bones of ancients who, amazed to see
Almighty God erect the mastodon,
Once laughed, or wept, in this same light of day.

Two Houses

Between a sunny bank and the sun
The farmhouse smiles
On the riverside plat:
No other one
So pleasant to look at
And remember, for many miles,
So velvet-hushed and cool under the warm tiles.

Not far from the road it lies, yet caught
Far out of reach
Of the road's dust
And the dusty thought
Of passers-by, though each
Stops, and turns, and must
Look down at it like a wasp at the muslined peach.

But another house stood there long before:
And as if above graves
Still the turf heaves
Above its stones:

Dark hangs the sycamore,
Shadowing kennel and bones
And the black dog that shakes his chain and moans.

And when he barks, over the river
Flashing fast,
Dark echoes reply,
And the hollow past
Half yields the dead that never
More than half hidden lie:
And out they creep and back again for ever.

Cock-Crow

Out of the wood of thoughts that grows by night
To be cut down by the sharp axe of light, –
Out of the night, two cocks together crow,
Cleaving the darkness with a silver blow:
And bright before my eyes twin trumpeters stand,
Heralds of splendour, one at either hand,
Each facing each as in a coat of arms:
The milkers lace their boots up at the farms.

October

The green elm with the one great bough of gold
Lets leaves into the grass slip, one by one, –
The short hill grass, the mushrooms small, milk-white,
Harebell and scabious and tormentil,
That blackberry and gorse, in dew and sun,
Bow down to; and the wind travels too light
To shake the fallen birch leaves from the fern;
The gossamers wander at their own will.
At heavier steps than birds' the squirrels scold.

The rich scene has grown fresh again and new
As Spring and to the touch is not more cool
Than it is warm to the gaze; and now I might
As happy be as earth is beautiful,
Were I some other or with earth could turn
In alternation of violet and rose,
Harebell and snowdrop, at their season due,
And gorse that has no time not to be gay.
But if this be not happiness, – who knows?
Some day I shall think this a happy day,
And this mood by the name of melancholy
Shall no more blackened and obscured be.

There's Nothing Like the Sun

There's nothing like the sun as the year dies,
Kind as it can be, this world being made so,
To stones and men and beasts and birds and flies,
To all things that it touches except snow,
Whether on mountain side or street of town.
The south wall warms me: November has begun,
Yet never shone the sun as fair as now
While the sweet last-left damsons from the bough
With spangles of the morning's storm drop down
Because the starling shakes it, whistling what
Once swallows sang. But I have not forgot
That there is nothing, too, like March's sun,
Like April's, or July's, or June's, or May's,
Or January's, or February's, great days:
August, September, October, and December
Have equal days, all different from November.
No day of any month but I have said –
Or, if I could live long enough, should say –
'There's nothing like the sun that shines to-day.'
There's nothing like the sun till we are dead.

The Thrush

When Winter's ahead,
What can you read in November
That you read in April
When Winter's dead?

I hear the thrush, and I see
Him alone at the end of the lane
Near the bare poplar's tip,
Singing continuously.

Is it more that you know
Than that, even as in April,
So in November,
Winter is gone that must go?

Or is all your lore
Not to call November November,
And April April,
And Winter Winter – no more?

But I know the months all,
And their sweet names, April,
May and June and October,
As you call and call

I must remember
What died in April
And consider what will be born
Of a fair November;

And April I love for what
It was born of, and November
For what it will die in,
What they are and what they are not,

While you love what is kind,
What you can sing in
And love and forget in
All that's ahead and behind.

Liberty

The last light has gone out of the world, except
This moonlight lying on the grass like frost
Beyond the brink of the tall elm's shadow.
It is as if everything else had slept
Many an age, unforgotten and lost –
The men that were, the things done, long ago,
All I have thought; and but the moon and I
Live yet and here stand idle over a grave
Where all is buried. Both have liberty
To dream what we could do if we were free
To do some thing we had desired long,
The moon and I. There's none less free than who
Does nothing and has nothing else to do,
Being free only for what is not to his mind,
And nothing is to his mind. If every hour
Like this one passing that I have spent among
The wiser others when I have forgot
To wonder whether I was free or not,
Were piled before me, and not lost behind,
And I could take and carry them away
I should be rich; or if I had the power
To wipe out every one and not again
Regret, I should be rich to be so poor.
And yet I still am half in love with pain,
With what is imperfect, with both tears and mirth,
With things that have an end, with life and earth,
And this moon that leaves me dark within the door.

[*This is No Case of Petty Right or Wrong*]⁵⁸

This is no case of petty right or wrong
That politicians or philosophers
Can judge. I hate not Germans, nor grow hot
With love of Englishmen, to please newspapers.
Beside my hate for one fat patriot
My hatred of the Kaiser is love true: –
A kind of god he is, banging a gong.
But I have not to choose between the two,
Or between justice and injustice. Dinned
With war and argument I read no more
Than in the storm smoking along the wind
Athwart the wood. Two witches' cauldrons roar.
From one the weather shall rise clear and gay;
Out of the other an England beautiful
And like her mother that died yesterday.
Little I know or care if, being dull,
I shall miss something that historians
Can rake out of the ashes when perchance
The phoenix broods serene above their ken.
But with the best and meanest Englishmen
I am one in crying, God save England, lest
We lose what never slaves and cattle blessed.
The ages made her that made us from dust:
She is all we know and live by, and we trust
She is good and must endure, loving her so:
And as we love ourselves we hate her foe.

*Rain*⁵⁹

Rain, midnight rain, nothing but the wild rain
On this bleak hut, and solitude, and me
Remembering again that I shall die
And neither hear the rain nor give it thanks

For washing me cleaner than I have been
Since I was born into this solitude.
Blessed are the dead that the rain rains upon:
But here I pray that none whom once I loved
Is dying tonight, or lying still awake
Solitary, listening to the rain,
Either in pain or thus in sympathy
Helpless among the living and the dead,
Like a cold water among broken reeds,
Myriads of broken reeds all still and stiff,
Like me who have no love which this wild rain
Has not dissolved except the love of death,
If love it be for what is perfect and
Cannot, the tempest tells me, disappoint.

The Clouds that are so Light [60]

As the clouds that are so light,
Beautiful, swift, and bright,
Cast shadows on field and park
Of the earth that is so dark,

And even so now, light one!
Beautiful, swift and bright one!
You let fall on a heart that was dark,
Unillumined, a deeper mark.

But clouds would have, without earth
To shadow, far less worth:
Away from your shadow on me
Your beauty less would be,

And if it still be treasured
An age hence, it shall be measured
By this small dark spot
Without which it were not.

Roads[61]

I love roads:
The goddesses that dwell
Far along invisible
Are my favourite gods.

Roads go on
While we forget, and are
Forgotten like a star
That shoots and is gone.

On this earth 'tis sure
We men have not made
Anything that doth fade
So soon, so long endure:

The hill road wet with rain
In the sun would not gleam
Like a winding stream
If we trod it not again.

They are lonely
While we sleep, lonelier
For lack of the traveller
Who is now a dream only.

From dawn's twilight
And all the clouds like sheep
On the mountains of sleep
They wind into the night.

The next turn may reveal
Heaven: upon the crest
The close pine clump, at rest
And black, may Hell conceal.

Often footsore, never
Yet of the road I weary,
Though long and steep and dreary,
As it winds on for ever.

Helen of the roads,
The mountain ways of Wales
And the Mabinogion tales
Is one of the true gods,

Abiding in the trees,
The threes and fours so wise,
The larger companies,
That by the roadside be,

And beneath the rafter
Else uninhabited
Excepting by the dead;
And it is her laughter

At morn and night I hear
When the thrush cock sings
Bright irrelevant things,
And when the chanticleer

Calls back to their own night
Troops that make loneliness
With their light footsteps' press,
As Helen's own are light.

Now all roads lead to France
And heavy is the tread
Of the living; but the dead
Returning lightly dance:

Whatever the road bring
To me or take from me,
They keep me company
With their pattering,

Crowding the solitude
Of the loops over the downs,
Hushing the roar of towns
And their brief multitude.

The Ash Grove

Half of the grove stood dead, and those that yet lived made
Little more than the dead ones made of shade.
If they led to a house, long before they had seen its fall:
But they welcomed me; I was glad without cause and
      delayed.

Scarce a hundred paces under the trees was the interval –
Paces each sweeter than sweetest miles – but nothing at all,
Not even the spirits of memory and fear with restless wing,
Could climb down in to molest me over the wall

That I passed through at either end without noticing.
And now an ash grove far from those hills can bring
The same tranquillity in which I wander a ghost
With a ghostly gladness, as if I heard a girl sing

The song of the Ash Grove soft as love uncrossed,
And then in a crowd or in distance it were lost,
But the moment unveiled something unwilling to die
And I had what most I desired, without search or desert
      or cost.

February Afternoon [*Sonnet 2*]

Men heard this roar of parleying starlings, saw,
 A thousand years ago even as now,
 Black rooks with white gulls following the plough
So that the first are last until a caw
Commands that last are first again, – a law
 Which was of old when one, like me, dreamed how
 A thousand years might dust lie on his brow
Yet thus would birds do between hedge and shaw.

Time swims before me, making as a day
A thousand years, while the broad ploughland oak
Roars mill-like and men strike and bear the stroke
Of war as ever, audacious or resigned,
And God still sits aloft in the array
That we have wrought him, stone-deaf and stone-blind.

P.H.T.[62]

I may come near loving you
When you are dead
And there is nothing to do
And much to be said.

To repent that day will be
Impossible
For you and vain for me
The truth to tell.

I shall be sorry for
Your impotence:
You can do and undo no more
When you go hence,

Cannot even forgive
The funeral.
But not so long as you live
Can I love you at all.

[*These Things that Poets Said*]

These things that poets said
Of love seemed true to me
When I loved and I fed
On love and poetry equally.

But now I wish I knew
If theirs were love indeed,
Or if mine were the true
And theirs some other lovely weed:

For certainly not thus,
Then or thereafter, I
Loved ever. Between us
Decide, good Love, before I die.

Only, that once I loved
By this one argument
Is very plainly proved:
I, loving not, am different.

No One So Much As You[63]

No one so much as you
Loves this my clay,
Or would lament as you
Its dying day.

You know me through and through
Though I have not told,
And though with what you know
You are not bold.

None ever was so fair
As I thought you:
Not a word can I bear
Spoken against you.

All that I ever did
For you seemed coarse
Compared with what I hid
Nor put in force.

My eyes scarce dare meet you
Lest they should prove
I but respond to you
And do not love.

We look and understand,
We cannot speak
Except in trifles and
Words the most weak.

For I at most accept
Your love, regretting
That is all: I have kept
Only a fretting

That I could not return
All that you gave
And could not ever burn
With the love you have,

Till sometimes it did seem
Better it were
Never to see you more
Than linger here

With only gratitude
Instead of love –
A pine in solitude
Cradling a dove.

The Unknown

She is most fair,
And when they see her pass
The poets' ladies
Look no more in the glass
But after her.

On a bleak moor
Running under the moon
She lures a poet,
Once proud or happy, soon
Far from his door.

Beside a train,
Because they saw her go,
Or failed to see her,
Travellers and watchers know
Another pain.

The simple lack
Of her is more to me
Than others' presence,
Whether life splendid be
Or utter black.

I have not seen,
I have no news of her;
I can tell only
She is not here, but there
She might have been.

She is to be kissed
Only perhaps by me:
She may be seeking
Me and no other: she
May not exist.

Celandine[64]

Thinking of her had saddened me at first,
Until I saw the sun on the celandines lie
Redoubled, and she stood up like a flame,
A living thing, not what before I nursed,
The shadow I was growing to love almost,
The phantom, not the creature with bright eye
That I had thought never to see, once lost.

She found the celandines of February
Always before us all. Her nature and name
Were like those flowers, and now immediately
For a short swift eternity back she came,
Beautiful, happy, simply as when she wore
Her brightest bloom among the winter hues
Of all the world; and I was happy too,
Seeing the blossoms and the maiden who
Had seen them with me Februarys before,
Bending to them as in and out she trod
And laughed, with locks sweeping the mossy sod.

But this was a dream: the flowers were not true,
Until I stooped to pluck from the grass there
One of five petals and I smelt the juice
Which made me sigh, remembering she was no more,
Gone like a never perfectly recalled air.

'Home'[65]

Fair was the morning, fair our tempers, and
We had seen nothing fairer than that land,
Though strange, and the untrodden snow that made
Wild of the tame, casting out all that was
Not wild and rustic and old; and we were glad.

Fair too was afternoon, and first to pass
Were we that league of snow, next the north wind.
There was nothing to return for, except need,
And yet we sang nor ever stopped for speed,
As we did often with the start behind.
Faster still strode we when we came in sight
Of the cold roofs where we must spend the night.
Happy we had not been there, nor could be,
Though we had tasted sleep and food and fellowship
Together long.

'How quick', to someone's lip
The words came, 'will the beaten horse run home!'

The word 'home' raised a smile in us all three,
And one repeated it, smiling just so
That all knew what he meant and none would say.
Between three counties far apart that lay
We were divided and looked strangely each
At the other, and we knew we were not friends
But fellows in a union that ends
With the necessity for it, as it ought.

Never a word was spoken, not a thought
Was thought, of what the look meant with the word
'Home' as we walked and watched the sunset blurred.
And then to me the word, only the word,
'Homesick', as it were playfully occurred:
No more. If I should ever more admit
Than the mere word I could not endure it
For a day longer: this captivity
Must somehow come to an end, else I should be
Another man, as often now I seem,
Or this life be only an evil dream.

Thaw

Over the land freckled with snow half-thawed
The speculating rooks at their nests cawed
And saw from elm-tops, delicate as flower of grass,
What we below could not see, winter pass.

Household Poems [1 Bronwen][66]

If I should ever by chance grow rich
I'll buy Codham, Cockridden, and Childerditch,
Roses, Pyrgo, and Lapwater,
And let them all to my elder daughter.
The rent I shall ask of her will be only
Each year's first violets, white and lonely,
The first primroses and orchises –
She must find them before I do, that is.
But if she finds a blossom on furze
Without rent they shall all for ever be hers,
Whenever I am sufficiently rich:

Codham, Cockridden, and Childerditch,
Roses, Pyrgo and Lapwater, –
I shall give them all to my elder daughter.

[2 *Morfyn*][67]

If I were to own this countryside
As far as a man in a day could ride,
And the Tyes were mine for giving or letting, –
Wingle Tye and Margaretting
Tye, – and Skreens, Gooshays, and Cockerells,
Shellow, Rochetts, Bandish, and Pickerells,
Martins, Lambkins, and Lillyputs,
Their copses, ponds, roads, and ruts,
Fields where plough-horses steam and plovers
Fling and whimper, hedges that lovers
Love, and orchards, shrubberies, walls
Where the sun untroubled by north wind falls,
And single trees where the thrush sings well
His proverbs untranslatable,
I would give them all to my son
If he would let me any one
For a song, a blackbird's song, at dawn.
He should have no more, till on my lawn
Never a one was left, because I
Had shot them to put them into a pie, –
His Essex blackbirds, every one,
And I was left old and alone.

Then unless I could pay, for rent, a song
As sweet as a blackbird's, and as long –
No more – he should have the house, not I
Margaretting or Wingle Tye,
Or it might be Skreens, Gooshays, or Cockerells,
Shellow, Rochetts, Bandish, or Pickerells,
Martins, Lambkins, or Lillyputs,
Should be his till the cart tracks had no ruts.

[3 Myfanwy][68]

What shall I give my daughter the younger
More than will keep her from cold and hunger?
I shall not give her anything.
If she shared South Weald and Havering,
Their acres, the two brooks running between,
Paine's Brook and Weald Brook,
With pewit, woodpecker, swan, and rook,
She would be no richer than the queen
Who once on a time sat in Havering Bower
Alone, with the shadows, pleasure and power.
She could do no more with Samarcand,
Or the mountains of a mountain land
And its far white house above cottages
Like Venus above the Pleiades.
Her small hands I would not cumber
With so many acres and their lumber,
But leave her Steep and her own world
And her spectacled self with hair uncurled,
Wanting a thousand little things
That time without contentment brings.

[4 Helen][69]

And you, Helen, what should I give you?
So many things I would give you
Had I an infinite great store
Offered me and I stood before
To choose. I would give you youth,
All kinds of loveliness and truth,
A clear eye as good as mine,
Lands, waters, flowers, wine,
As many children as your heart
Might wish for, a far better art
Than mine can be, all you have lost

Upon the travelling waters tossed,
Or given to me. If I could choose
Freely in that great treasure-house
Anything from any shelf,
I would give you back yourself,
And power to discriminate
What you want and want it not too late,
Many fair days free from care
And heart to enjoy both foul and fair,
And myself, too, if I could find
Where it lay hidden and it proved kind.

[*The Wind's Song*] [*Sonnet 3*]

Dull thoughted, walking among the nunneries
Of many a myriad anemones
In the close copses, I grew weary of Spring
Till I emerged and in my wandering
I climbed the down up to a lone pine clump
Of six, the tallest dead, one a mere stump.
On one long stem, branchless and flayed and prone,
I sat in the sun listening to the wind alone,
Thinking there could be no old song so sad
As the wind's song; but later none so glad
Could I remember as that same wind's song
All the time blowing the pine boughs among.
My heart that had been still as the dead tree
Awakened by the West wind was made free.

Go Now

Like the touch of rain she was
On a man's flesh and hair and eyes
When the joy of walking thus
Has taken him by surprise:

With the love of the storm he burns,
He sings, he laughs, well I know how,
But forgets when he returns
As I shall not forget her 'Go now'.

Those two words shut a door
Between me and the blessed rain
That was never shut before
And will not open again.

Tall Nettles

Tall nettles cover up, as they have done
These many springs, the rusty harrow, the plough
Long worn out, and the roller made of stone:
Only the elm butt tops the nettles now.

This corner of the farmyard I like most:
As well as any bloom upon a flower
I like the dust on the nettles, never lost
Except to prove the sweetness of a shower.

[The Watchers]

By the ford at the town's edge
Horse and carter rest:
The carter smokes on the bridge
Watching the water press in swathes about his horse's chest.

From the inn one watches, too,
In the room for visitors
That has no fire, but a view
And many cases of stuffed fish, vermin, and kingfishers.

[I Never Saw That Land Before]

I never saw that land before,
And now can never see it again;
Yet, as if by acquaintance hoar
Endeared, by gladness and by pain,
Great was the affection that I bore

To the valley and the river small,
The cattle, the grass, the bare ash trees,
The chickens from the farmsteads, all
Elm-hidden, and the tributaries
Descending at equal interval;

The blackthorns down along the brook
With wounds yellow as crocuses
Where yesterday the labourer's hook
Had sliced them cleanly; and the breeze
That hinted all and nothing spoke.

I neither expected anything
Nor yet remembered: but some goal
I touched then; and if I could sing
What would not even whisper my soul
As I went on my journeying,

I should use, as the trees and birds did,
A language not to be betrayed;
And what was hid should still be hid
Excepting from those like me made
Who answer when such whispers bid.

It Rains

It rains, and nothing stirs within the fence
Anywhere through the orchard's untrodden, dense
Forest of parsley. The great diamonds
Of rain on the grassblades there is none to break,
Or the fallen petals further down to shake.

And I am nearly as happy as possible
To search the wilderness in vain though well,
To think of two walking, kissing there,
Drenched, yet forgetting the kisses of the rain:
Sad, too, to think that never, never again,

Unless alone, so happy shall I walk
In the rain. When I turn away, on its fine stalk
Twilight has fined to naught, the parsley flower
Figures, suspended still and ghostly white,
The past hovering as it revisits the light.

The Sun Used to Shine[70]

The sun used to shine while we two walked
Slowly together, paused and started
Again, and sometimes mused, sometimes talked
As either pleased, and cheerfully parted

Each night. We never disagreed
Which gate to rest on. The to be
And the late past we gave small heed.
We turned from men or poetry

To rumours of the war remote
Only till both stood disinclined
For aught but the yellow flavorous coat
Of an apple wasps had undermined;

Or a sentry of dark betonies,
The stateliest of small flowers on earth,
At the forest verge; or crocuses
Pale purple as if they had their birth

In sunless Hades fields. The war
Came back to mind with the moonrise
Which soldiers in the east afar
Beheld then. Nevertheless, our eyes

Could as well imagine the Crusades
Or Caesar's battles. Everything
To faintness like those rumours fades –
Like the brook's water glittering

Under the moonlight – like those walks
Now – like us two that took them, and
The fallen apples, all the talks
And silences – like memory's sand

When the tide covers it late or soon,
And other men through other flowers
In those fields under the same moon
Go talking and have easy hours.

[*Bugle Call*]

'No one cares less than I,
Nobody knows but God,
Whether I am destined to lie
Under a foreign clod',
Were the words I made to the bugle call in the morning.

But laughing, storming, scorning,
Only the bugles know
What the bugles say in the morning,
And they do not care, when they blow
The call that I heard and made words to early this morning.

As the Team's Head-Brass[71]

As the team's head-brass flashed out on the turn
The lovers disappeared into the wood.
I sat among the boughs of the fallen elm
That strewed the angle of the fallow, and
Watched the plough narrowing a yellow square
Of charlock. Every time the horses turned
Instead of treading me down, the ploughman leaned
Upon the handles to say or ask a word,
About the weather, next about the war.
Scraping the share he faced towards the wood,
And screwed along the furrow till the brass flashed
Once more.
         The blizzard felled the elm whose crest
I sat in, by a woodpecker's round hole,
The ploughman said. 'When will they take it away?'
'When the war's over.' So the talk began –
One minute and an interval of ten,
A minute more and the same interval.
'Have you been out?' 'No.' 'And don't want to, perhaps?'
'If I could only come back again, I should.
I could spare an arm. I shouldn't want to lose
A leg. If I should lose my head, why, so,
I should want nothing more . . . Have many gone
From here?' 'Yes.' 'Many lost?' 'Yes, a good few.
Only two teams work on the farm this year.
One of my mates is dead. The second day
In France they killed him. It was back in March,
The very night of the blizzard, too. Now if
He had stayed here we should have moved the tree.'

'And I should not have sat here. Everything
Would have been different. For it would have been
Another world.' 'Ay, and a better, though
If we could see all all might seem good.' Then
The lovers came out of the wood again:
The horses started and for the last time
I watched the clods crumble and topple over
After the ploughshare and the stumbling team.

After You Speak

After you speak
And what you meant
Is plain,
My eyes
Meet yours that mean –
With your cheeks and hair –
Something more wise,
More dark,
And far different.
Even so the lark
Loves dust
And nestles in it
The minute
Before he must
Soar in lone flight
So far,
Like a black star
He seems –
A mote
Of singing dust
Afloat
Above,
That dreams
And sheds no light.
I know your lust
Is love.

[*Song 3*]

Early one morning in May I set out,
And nobody I knew was about.
    I'm bound away for ever,
    Away somewhere, away for ever.

There was no wind to trouble the weathercocks.
I had burnt my letters and darned my socks.

No one knew I was going away,
I thought myself I should come back some day.

I heard the brook through the town gardens run.
O sweet was the mud turned to dust by the sun.

A gate banged in a fence and banged in my head.
'A fine morning, sir,' a shepherd said.

I could not return from my liberty,
To my youth and my love and my misery.

The past is the only dead thing that smells sweet,
The only sweet thing that is not also fleet.
    I'm bound away for ever,
    Away somewhere, away for ever.

[*Sonnet 5*]

It was upon a July evening.
At a stile I stood, looking along a path
Over the country by a second Spring
Drenched perfect green again. 'The lattermath
Will be a fine one.' So the stranger said,

A wandering man. Albeit I stood at rest,
Flushed with desire I was. The earth outspread,
Like meadows of the future, I possessed.

And as an unaccomplished prophecy
The stranger's words, after the interval
Of a score years, when those fields are by me
Never to be recrossed, now I recall,
This July eve, and question, wondering,
What of the lattermath to this hoar Spring?

Bob's Lane

Women he liked, did shovel-bearded Bob,
Old Farmer Hayward of the Heath, but he
Loved horses. He himself was like a cob,
And leather-coloured. Also he loved a tree.

For the life in them he loved most living things,
But a tree chiefly. All along the lane
He planted elms where now the stormcock sings
That travellers hear from the slow-climbing train.

Till then the track had never had a name
For all its thicket and the nightingales
That should have earned it. No one was to blame.
To name a thing beloved man sometimes fails.

Many years since, Bob Hayward died, and now
None passes there because the mist and the rain
Out of the elms have turned the lane to slough
And gloom, the name alone survives, Bob's Lane.

[*There Was a Time*]

There was a time when this poor frame was whole
And I had youth and never another care,
Or none that should have troubled a strong soul.
Yet, except sometimes in a frosty air
When my heels hammered out a melody
From pavements of a city left behind,
I never would acknowledge my own glee
Because it was less mighty than my mind
Had dreamed of. Since I could not boast of strength
Great as I wished, weakness was all my boast.
I sought yet hated pity till at length
I earned it. Oh, too heavy was the cost!
But now that there is something I could use
My youth and strength for, I deny the age,
The care and weakness that I know – refuse
To admit I am unworthy of the wage
Paid to a man who gives up eyes and breath
For what would neither ask nor heed his death.

The Green Roads

The green roads that end in the forest
Are strewn with white goose feathers this June,

Like marks left behind by some one gone to the forest
To show his track. But he has never come back.

Down each green road a cottage looks at the forest.
Round one the nettle towers; two are bathed in flowers.

An old man along the green road to the forest
Strays from one, from another a child alone.

In the thicket bordering the forest,
All day long a thrush twiddles his song.

It is old, but the trees are young in the forest,
All but one like a castle keep, in the middle deep.

That oak saw the ages pass in the forest:
They were a host, but their memories are lost,

For the tree is dead: all things forget the forest
Excepting perhaps me, when now I see

The old man, the child, the goose feathers at the edge
     of the forest,
And hear all day long the thrush repeat his song.

When First[72]

When first I came here I had hope,
Hope for I knew not what. Fast beat
My heart at sight of the tall slope
Of grass and yews, as if my feet

Only by scaling its steps of chalk
Would see something no other hill
Ever disclosed. And now I walk
Down it the last time. Never will

My heart beat so again at sight
Of any hill although as fair
And loftier. For infinite
The change, late unperceived, this year,

The twelfth, suddenly, shows me plain.
Hope now, – not health, nor cheerfulness,
Since they can come and go again,
As often one brief hour witnesses, –

Just hope has gone for ever. Perhaps
I may love other hills yet more
Than this: the future and the maps
Hide something I was waiting for.

One thing I know, that love with chance
And use and time and necessity
Will grow, and louder the heart's dance
At parting than at meeting be.

The Gallows

There was a weasel lived in the sun
With all his family,
Till a keeper shot him with his gun
And hung him up on a tree,
Where he swings in the wind and rain,
In the sun and in the snow,
Without pleasure, without pain,
On the dead oak tree bough.

There was a crow who was no sleeper,
But a thief and a murderer
Till a very late hour; and this keeper
Made him one of the things that were,
To hang and flap in rain and wind,
In the sun and in the snow.
There are no more sins to be sinned
On the dead oak tree bough.

There was a magpie, too,
Had a long tongue and a long tail;
He could both talk and do –
But what did that avail?
He, too, flaps in the wind and rain

Alongside weasel and crow,
Without pleasure, without pain,
On the dead oak tree bough.

And many other beasts
And birds, skin, bone, and feather,
Have been taken from their feasts
And hung up there together,
To swing and have endless leisure
In the sun and in the snow,
Without pain, without pleasure,
On the dead oak tree bough.

[*The Dark Forest*]

Dark is the forest and deep, and overhead
Hang stars like seeds of light
In vain, though not since they were sown was bred
Anything more bright.

And evermore mighty multitudes ride
About, nor enter in;
Of the other multitudes that dwell inside
Never yet was one seen.

The forest foxglove is purple, the marguerite
Outside is gold and white,
Nor can those that pluck either blossom greet
The others, day or night.

When He Should Laugh

When he should laugh the wise man knows full well:
For he knows what is truly laughable.
But wiser is the man who laughs also,
Or holds his laughter, when the foolish do.

The Swifts

How at once should I know,
When stretched in the harvest blue
I saw the swift's black bow,
That I would not have that view
Another day
Until next May
Again it is due?

The same year after year –
But with the swift alone.
With other things I but fear
That they will be over and done
Suddenly
And I only see
Them to know them gone.

Blenheim Oranges

Gone, gone again,
May, June, July,
And August gone,
Again gone by,

Not memorable
Save that I saw them go.
As past the empty quays
The rivers flow.

And now again,
In the harvest rain,
The Blenheim oranges
Fall grubby from the trees

As when I was young –
And when the lost one was here –
And when the war began
To turn young men to dung.

Look at the old house,
Outmoded, dignified,
Dark and untenanted,
With grass growing instead

Of the footsteps of life,
The friendliness, the strife;
In its beds have lain
Youth, love, age, and pain:

I am something like that;
Only I am not dead,
Still breathing and interested
In the house that is not dark: –

I am something like that:
Not one pane to reflect the sun,
For the schoolboys to throw at –
They have broken every one.

[*That Girl's Clear Eyes*] [*Sonnet 6*][73]

That girl's clear eyes utterly concealed all
Except that there was something to reveal.
And what did mine say in the interval?
No more: no less. They are but as a seal
Not to be broken till after I am dead;
And then vainly. Every one of us
This morning at our tasks left nothing said,
In spite of many words. We were sealed thus,

Like tombs. Nor until now could I admit
That all I cared for was the pleasure and pain
I tasted in the stony square sunlit,
Or the dark cloisters, or shade of airy plane,
While music blazed and children, line after line,
Marched past, hiding the 'SEVENTEEN THIRTY-NINE'.

[*What Will They Do?*]

What will they do when I am gone? It is plain
That they will do without me as the rain
Can do without the flowers and the grass
That profit by it and must perish without.
I have but seen them in the loud street pass;
And I was naught to them. I turned about
To see them disappearing carelessly.
But what if I in them as they in me
Nourished what has great value and no price?
Almost I thought that rain thirsts for a draught
Which only in the blossom's chalice lies,
Until that one turned back and lightly laughed.

The Trumpet[74]

Rise up, rise up,
And, as the trumpet blowing
Chases the dreams of men,
As the dawn glowing
The stars that left unlit
The land and water,
Rise up and scatter
The dew that covers
The print of last night's lovers –
Scatter it, scatter it!

While you are listening
To the clear horn,
Forget, men, everything
On this earth newborn,
Except that it is lovelier
Than any mysteries.
Open your eyes to the air
That has washed the eyes of the stars
Through all the dewy night:
Up with the light,
To the old wars;
Arise, arise!

Lights Out[75]

I have come to the borders of sleep,
The unfathomable deep
Forest where all must lose
Their way, however straight,
Or winding, soon or late;
They cannot choose.

Many a road and track
That, since the dawn's first crack,
Up to the forest brink,
Deceived the travellers,
Suddenly now blurs,
And in they sink.

Here love ends,
Despair, ambition ends;
All pleasure and all trouble,
Although most sweet or bitter,
Here ends in sleep that is sweeter
Than tasks most noble.

There is not any book
Or face of dearest look
That I would not turn from now
To go into the unknown
I must enter, and leave, alone,
I know not how.

The tall forest towers;
Its cloudy foliage lowers
Ahead, shelf above shelf;
Its silence I hear and obey
That I may lose my way
And myself.

The Long Small Room

The long small room that showed willows in the west
Narrowed up to the end the fireplace filled,
Although not wide. I liked it. No one guessed
What need or accident made them so build.

Only the moon, the mouse and the sparrow peeped
In from the ivy round the casement thick.
Of all they saw and heard there they shall keep
The tale for the old ivy and older brick.

When I look back I am like moon, sparrow, and mouse
That witnessed what they could never understand
Or alter or prevent in the dark house.
One thing remains the same – this my right hand

Crawling crab-like over the clean white page,
Resting awhile each morning on the pillow,
Then once more starting to crawl on towards age.
The hundred last leaves stream upon the willow.

The Sheiling[76]

It stands alone
Up in a land of stone
All worn like ancient stairs,
A land of rocks and trees
Nourished on wind and stone.

And all within
Long delicate has been;
By arts and kindliness
Coloured, sweetened, and warmed
For many years has been.

Safe resting there
Men hear in the travelling air
But music, pictures see
In the same daily land
Painted by the wild air.

One maker's mind
Made both, and the house is kind
To the land that gave it peace,
And the stone has taken the house
To its cold heart and is kind.

The Lane

Some day, I think, there will be people enough
In Froxfield to pick all the blackberries
Out of the hedges of Green Lane, the straight
Broad lane where now September hides herself
In bracken and blackberry, harebell and dwarf gorse.
Today, where yesterday a hundred sheep
Were nibbling, halcyon bells shake to the sway
Of waters that no vessel ever sailed . . .

It is a kind of spring: the chaffinch tries
His song. For heat it is like summer too.
This might be winter's quiet. While the glint
Of hollies dark in the swollen hedges lasts –
One mile – and those bells ring, little I know
Or heed if time be still the same, until
The lane ends and once more all is the same.

[*Out in the Dark*]⁷⁷

Out in the dark over the snow
The fallow fawns invisible go
With the fallow doe;
And the winds blow
Fast as the stars are slow.

Stealthily the dark haunts round
And, when the lamp goes, without sound
At a swifter bound
Than the swiftest hound,
Arrives, and all else is drowned;

And star and I and wind and deer,
Are in the dark together, – near,
Yet far, – and fear
Drums on my ear
In that sage company drear.

How weak and little is the light,
All the universe of sight,
Love and delight,
Before the might,
If you love it not, of night.

From Diary,
1 January–8 April 1917[78]

February 13 Awoke tired and cold though it is thawing and cloudy with a breeze. No work this morning, but I pore over map and think how I may enjoy doing it when this is all over, which is not a good feeling, I suspect. Taylor says (as he makes my bed and as usual asks if he does it right): 'I am not proud, but I likes to be comfortable. I have been domesticated since I joined the Army.' Nothing to do all morning, afternoon at our position – hare, partridges and wild duck in field S.E. of guns. I feel the cold – the morning sun turns to a damp thaw wind. Letters home to Father, Mother and Eleanor. Some grass showing green through melting snow. Thorburn worries because he can't laugh at silly low talk. Evening censoring letters and reading Sonnets; others writing – when I began to talk to Rubin, the Captain said 'You get on with your Sonnets' and then all was silent. Awful fug.

14 A bad night but feeling better. All day with Horton, and then Horton and Smith, examining O.P.s above Agny and Wailly, and then between Achicourt and Beaurains. Fine sunny day – snow melting. Black-headed buntings talk, rooks caw, lovely white puffs of shrapnel round planes high up. Right Section does aeroplane shoot in afternoon. Dead campion umbels, and grass rustling on my helmet through trenches. Pretty little copse in deep hollow high up between Ficheux and Dainville, where guns look over to Berneville and Warlus.

15 With Captain observing for a B.T. [Battery Training] shoot on Ficheux Mill and edge of Blairville Wood. Fine sun but cold

in trench. With working party in afternoon. Letters arrived at 6.
We sorted them and then spent an hour silently reading. 750
letters for men; 17 for me – from Helen, the children, Father,
Mother, Eleanor, Freeman, Mrs Freeman, Guthrie, Vernon and
Haines. Evening, reading and writing letters. A quiet evening
indoors and out. Taylor says as he mends the fire, 'Well, we
have to put up with many discomforts. We are all alike, Sir, all
human.' A still starry night with only machine guns and rifles.
Slept badly again, and then suddenly with no notice got up
from breakfast on the

16th to do fire control on aeroplane shoot (only ten rounds,
observation being bad). Dull day. Left Thorburn on guns at
11.30. Bad temper. Afternoon up to O.P., but too hazy to
observe. A mad Captain with several men driving partridges
over the open and whistling and crying 'Mark over'. Kestrels in
pairs. Four or five planes hovering and wheeling as kestrels
used to over Mutton and Ludcombe. Women hanging clothes
to dry on barbed entanglement across the road. Rain at last at
4.15. This morning the old Frenchman living in this ruin burst
into our room while we were dressing to complain of our dirt
and depredation, and when Rubin was rude in English said he
was a Frenchman and had been an officer. Nobody felt the
slightest sympathy with his ravings, more than with the old
white horse who works a mill walking up and up treadmill.

17 A dull muddy day. No observation, no shooting. On guns
all day and in dug-out, writing up our fighting book. Another
letter from home. Could only just see A.P. [(First) Aid Post]. Kit
arrived late last night. I slept badly, coughing. Very mild and
the roads chalk and water, Grandes Graves 2.50 a bottle. Thor-
burn asks where he shall put the letters he has censored – decides
on the crowded table – then I have to tell him the mantelpiece
is the obvious place.

18 Another dull day down in 146 Dug-out. Afternoon to
Arras – Town Hall like Carreg Cennin. Beautiful small white
square empty. Top storey of high house ruined cloth armchair

and a garment across it left as fly shell arrived. Car to Mendi-
court and back by light of star shells. Shopping at Bellevue
B.E.F. canteen. Returned to find I am to go as Orderly Officer
to Group 35 H.A. [Heavy Artillery] in Arras tomorrow.

19 To Arras and began showing sectors and arcs on 1/10000
maps. Field Cashier's, waiting in long queue of officers to cash
cheques etc. Learning office work. Place Victor Hugo white
houses and shutters and sharpened fuller and dome in middle.
Beautiful. In class it was like Bath – retired people, schools,
priests. Gardens, courtyards, open spaces with trees. I still funk
the telephone and did not use it once today. Sentries challenge
in street and answer 'Sussex' etc.

20 Rain. To Fosseux in the car for cash and gas helmets. Rain
and mud and troops and Hun prisoners and turbaned In-
dians at a barn door holding a sheep by a rope round its neck,
all still and silent. Afternoon through Fosseux again with Col.
Witchall to Mondicourt in rain and mud and back in darkness
along main Arras Road – could usually only see 2 or 3 of the
roadside trees except when we ran into the blaze of 18-pounder
battery by roadside. Blast of 18-pounders near the billet blows
mortar from ruins against our window linen. Called at 244 for
letters – none. C/O [Commanding Officer (Colonel Witchall)]
and Berrington and Cassels as before sat up till 12.30 and I
could not get my bed before

March 11 Out at 8.30 to Ronville O.P. and studied the ground
from Beaurains N. Larks singing over No Man's Land – trench
mortars. We were bombarding their front line: they were shoot-
ing at Arras. R.F.A. [Royal Field Artillery] officer with me who
was quite concerned till he spotted a certain familiar Hun sentry
in front line. A clear, cloudy day, mild and breezy. 8 shell carry-
ing into Arras. Later Ronville heavily shelled and we retired to
dugout. At 6.15 all quiet and heard blackbirds chinking. Scene
peaceful, desolate like Dunwich moors except sprinkling of
white chalk on the rough brown ground. Lines broken and lines-
men out from 2.30 to 7 p.m. A little raid in the night . . . ,

12 . . . then a beautiful moist clear limpid early morning till the Raid at 7 and the retaliation on Ronville at 7.30–8.45 with 77 cm. 25 to the minute. Then back through 6 ins. of chalk mud in trenches along battered Ronville Street. Rooks in tall trees on N. side of Arras – they and their nests and the trees black against the soft clouded sky. W. wind and mild but no rain yet (11 a.m.). Letters, mess accounts, maps. Afternoon at maps and with Horton at battery. Evening of partridges calling and pip-squeaks coming over behind.

13 Blackbird trying to sing early in dull marsh. A dull cold day. One N.F. shoot at nightfall. I was in position all day. Letters from Eleanor, Mother and Ellis: wrote to Bronwen, Mother and Eleanor.

14 Ronville O.P. Looking out towards No Man's Land what I thought first was a piece of burnt paper or something turned out to be a bat shaken at last by shells from one of the last sheds in Ronville. A dull cold morning, with some shelling of Arras and St Sauveur and just 3 for us. Talking to Birt and Randall about Glostershire and Wiltshire, particularly Pains-wick and Marlborough. A still evening – blackbirds singing far off – a spatter of our machine guns – the spit of one enemy bullet – a little rain – no wind – only far-off artillery.

15 Huns strafe I sector at 5.30. We reply and they retaliate on Arras and Ronville. Only tired 77s reach O.P. A sunny breezy morning. Tried to climb Arras chimney to observe, but funked. 4 shells nearly got me while I was going and coming. A rotten day. No letters for five days.

16 Larks and great tits. Ploughing field next to orchard in mist – horses and man go right up to crest in view of Hun at Beaurains. Cold and dull. Letters to Helen and Janet. In the battery for the day. Fired 100 rounds from 12–1.30. Sun shining but misty still. Letter from Bronwen. The first thrush I have heard in France sang as I returned to Mess at 6 p.m. Par-cel from Mother – my old Artist boots. Wrote to Hodson. A

horrible night of bombardment, and the only time I slept I
dreamt I was at home and couldn't stay to tea . . .

17 . . . Then a most glorious bright high clear morning. But
even Horton, disturbed by 60-pounders behind his dugout,
came in to breakfast saying: 'I am not going to stay in this —
army; on the day peace is declared I am out of it like a — rabbit'.
A beautiful day, sunny with pale cloudless sky and W. wind, but
cold in O.P. Clear nightfall with curled, cinereous cloud and
then a cloudless night with pale stains in sky over where Bosh is
burning a village or something. Quiet till 3: then a Hun raid and
our artillery over us to meet it: their shells into St Sauveur, Ron-
ville and Arras. Sound of fan in underground cave.

18 Beautiful clear cloudless morning and no firing between
daybreak and 8. Drew another panorama at 7. Linnets and
chaffinches sing in waste trenched ground with trees and water
tanks between us and Arras. Magpies over No Man's Land in
pairs. The old green (grey) track crossing No Man's Lane –
once a country way to Arras. The water green and clear (like
Silent Pool) of the Moat of the Citadel with skeletons of whole
trees lying there. Afternoon washing and reading letters from
Helen and Eleanor. I did 2 shoots. News came that we are in
Beaurains and near Mercatel. Letters to Helen and Eleanor.
The pigeons are about in the streets of this Faubourg more than
ever and I could hear a lark till the Archies drowned it. Fired
600 rounds and got tired eyes and ears. Then early to bed and
up at 4 to go to O.P. on

19 Nothing to do all day at Ronville but look at quiet No
Man's Land and trenches with engineers beginning to straighten
road up. Back to sleep at billet, but preferred to return to O.P.
as I've to go to the front trench O.P. at 4 on the

20th Stiff deep mud all the way up and shelled as we started.
Telegraph Hill as quiet as if only rabbits lived there. I took
revolver and left this diary behind in case. For it is very exposed
and only a few Cornwalls and M.G.C. [Machine Gun Corps]

about. But Hun shelled chiefly over our heads into Beaurains all night – like starlings returning 20 or 30 a minute. Horrible flap of 5.9 a little along the trench. Rain and mud and I've to stay till I am relieved tomorrow. Had not brought warm clothes or enough food and had no shelter, nor had telephonists. Shelled all night. But the M.G.C. boy gave me tea. I've no bed. I leant against wall of trench. I got up and looked over. I stamped up and down. I tried to see patrol out. Very light – the only sign of Hun on Telegraph Hill, though 2 appeared and were sniped at. A terribly long night and cold. Not relieved till 8. Telephonists out repairing line since 4 on the morning of the

21st At last 260 relieved us. Great pleasure to be going back to sleep and rest. No Man's Land like Goodwood Racecourse with engineers swarming over it and making a road between shell holes full of bloodstained water and beer bottles among barbed wire. Larks singing as they did when we went up in dark and were shelled. Now I hardly felt as if a shell could hurt, though several were thrown about near working parties. Found letters from Helen, Eleanor and Julian. Had lunch, went to bed at 2 intending to get up to tea, but slept till 6.30 on the . . .

22nd (Beautiful was Arras yesterday coming down from Beaurains and seeing Town Hall ruin white in sun like a thick smoke beginning to curl. Sprinkle of snow today in sun.) A cold bright day with snow early. We fired twice. I on duty at Battery. Letters to Helen and home and Gordon and Deacon. Partridges twanging in open fields. Not much shooting to do. Several windy snow showers half-hail and then sun. Talk with Thorburn about his fate if he loses his commission. Gramophone plays Ambrose Thomas's 'Mignon' gavotte (by Raymond Jeremy's Philharmonic Quartette), 'D'ye ken John Peel', Chopin's 'Berceuse', Tchaikovsky's 'Fantasia Italiana'.

23 Frosty clear. Ploughs going up over crest towards Beaurains. Rubin back from F.O.P. [Forward Observation Post (in No Man's Land)] believes in God and tackles me about atheism – thinks marvellous escapes are ordained. But I say so

are the marvellous escapes of certain telegraph posts, houses, etc. Sunny and cold – motored to Avesnes and Fosseux to buy luxuries and get letters. Crowded bad roads through beautiful hedgeless rolling chalk country with rows of trees, some along roads following curving ridges – villages on crests with church spires and trees. Troops, children holding hands, and dark-skinned women, mud walled ruined barns. Parcels from Mother and Helen, letters from Mother and J. Freeman.

27 Rain and sleet and sun, getting guns camouflaged, stealing a Decanville truck, laying out nightlines. Letters from Hodson, Eleanor and Sgt. Pellissier. Still that aching below the nape of my neck since my last O.P. day. Sat till 11 writing letters. As I was falling asleep great blasts shook the house and windows, whether from our own firing or enemy bursts near, I could not tell in my drowse, but I did not doubt my heart thumped so that if they had come closer together it might have stopped. Rubin and Smith dead tired after being up all the night before. Letters to Helen and Eleanor.

28 Frosty and clear and some blackbirds singing at Agny Cha-teau in the quiet of exhausted battery, everyone just having breakfast at 9.30: all very still and clear: but these mornings always very misleading and disappearing so that one might almost think afterwards they were illusive. Planes humming. In high white cloud aeroplanes leave tracks curving like rough wheel tracks in snow – I had a dream this morning that I have forgot but Mother was in distress. All day loading shells from old position – sat doing nothing till I got damned philosophical and sad. Thorburn dreamt 2 nights ago that a maid was count-ing forks and spoons and he asked her 'Must an officer be present.' Letter to Helen. Tired still.

29 Wet again. Getting refuge trenches dug for detachments. Marking crests on map. How beautiful, like a great crystal sparkling and spangling, the light reflected from some glass which is visible at certain places and times through a hole in cathedral wall, ruined cathedral.

30 Bright early, then rain. New zero line, planting pickets.
Arranging for material for new O.P. dugout – old one fell in
yesterday. Clear and bright and still from 6 p.m. on. Air full of
planes and sound of whistles against Hun planes. Blackbirds
singing and then chuckling as they go to roost. Two shells fall-
ing near Agny Chateau scatter them. Letters from Helen and
Mother and parcels from Mother and Eleanor. Too late to bed
and had no sleep at all, for the firing, chiefly 60-pounders of
our own. Shakespeare's plays for 10 minutes before sleep.

31 Up at 5 worn out and wretched. 5.9s flopping on Achicourt
while I dressed. Up to Beaurains. There is a chalk-stone cellar
with a dripping Bosh dug-out far under and by the last layer of
stones is the lilac bush, rather short. Nearby a graveyard for
the 'tapferer franzos soldat' with crosses and Hun names.
Blackbirds in the clear cold bright morning early in black Beau-
rains. Sparrows in the elder of the hedge I observe through – a
cherry tree just this side of hedge makes projection in trench
with its roots. Beautiful clear evening everything dark and soft
round Neuville Vitasse, after the rainbow there and the last
shower. Night in lilac-bush cellar of stone like Berryfield. Letter
to Helen. Machine gun bullets snaking along – hissing like little
wormy serpents.

April 1 among the ragged and craggy gables of Beaurains – a
beautiful serene clear morning with larks at 5.15 and black-
birds at 6 till it snowed or rained at 8. All day sat writing letters
to Helen, Father and Mother by the fire and censoring men's
letters etc., an idle day – I could not sleep till I went to bed at
10. Letters from Helen, Baba and Deacon. A fine bright day
with showers.

2 Letter to H. K. Vernon. Another frosty clear windy morning.
Some sun and I enjoyed filling sandbags for dug out we are to
have in battery for the battle. But snow later after we had fired
100 rounds blind. Snow half melting as it falls makes fearful
slush. I up at battery alone till 9.30 p.m. Writing to Helen and
Frost. Rubin and Smith sang duets from 'Bing Boys' till 11.

3 Snow just frozen – strong S.E. wind. Feet wet by 8.15 a.m. Letters from Gordon and Freeman. The eve. Letters to Gordon, Freeman, Helen. A fine day later, filling sandbags. MACBETH.

4 Up at 4.30. Blackbirds sing at battery at 5.45 – shooting at 6.30. A cloudy fresh morning. But showery cold muddy and slippery later. 600 rounds. Nothing in return yet. Tired by 9.15 p.m. Moved to dug-out in position. Letter from Helen. Artillery makes air flap all night long.

5 A dull morning turns misty with rain. Some 4.2s coming over at 10. Air flapping all night as with great sails in strong gusty wind (with artillery) – thick misty windless air. Sods on f/c's dugout begin to be fledged with fine green feathers of yarrow – yarrow. Sun and wind drying the mud. Firing all day, practising barrage etc. Beautiful pale hazy moonlight and the sag and flap of air. Letters to Mother and Helen. HAMLET.

6 A lazy morning, being a half day: warm and breezy, with sun and cloud but turned wet. Billets shelled by 4.2: 60-pounders hit. In car with Horton to Fosseux and Avesnes and met infantry with yellow patches behind marching soaked up to line – band and pipes at Wanquetin to greet them, playing 'They wind up the Watch on the Rhine' (as Horton calls it). After the shelling Horton remarks: 'The Bosh is a damned good man, isn't he, a damned smart man, you must admit'. Roads worse than ever – no crust left on side roads. Letters from Helen, Mervyn, Mother, Eleanor.

7 Up at 6 to O.P. A cold bright day of continuous shelling N. Vitasse and Telegraph Hill. Infantry all over the place in open preparing Prussian Way with boards for wounded. Hardly any shells into Beaurains. Larks, partridges, hedge-sparrows, magpies by O.P. A great burst in red brick building in N. Vitasse stood up like a birch tree or a fountain. Back at 7.30 in peace. Then at 8.30 a continuous roar of artillery.

8 A bright warm Easter day but Achicourt shelled at 12.39 and then at 2.15 so that we all retired to cellar. I had to go over

to battery at 3 for a practice barrage, skirting the danger zone, but we were twice interrupted. A 5.9 fell 2 yards from me as I stood by the f/c post. One burst down the back of the office and a piece of dust scratched my neck. No firing from 2–4. Rubin left for a course.

[On the last pages of diary are these notes:]

The light of the new moon and every star

And no more singing for the bird . . .

I never understood quite what was meant by God

The morning chill and clear hurts my skin while it delights my mind.

Neuville in early morning with its flat straight crest with trees and houses – the beauty of this silent empty scene of no inhabitants and hid troops, but don't know why I could have cried and didn't.

Notes

1. (p. 5) This diary, which runs from 1 April 1895 to 30 March 1896, is the last piece in Edward Thomas's first collection of essays, *The Woodland Life*, published in 1897, when he was still in his teens. The diary was not meant for publication – the notes were originally made as a basis for the other essays in the book – but Thomas included it at the suggestion of his mentor, James Ashcroft Noble. In 'How I Began' Thomas observes (p. 108): 'These notes aimed at brevity; they were above syntax and indifferent to dignity.' For this reason they are much more alive and readable than the overwritten descriptive pieces that make the bulk of the collection. Thomas kept up the habit of note-taking all his life. Writing to Harold Monro on 21 December 1909 he confessed: 'I have always been a great notetaker myself yet I know I have always done best when I have forgotten my notes. I wish I had the courage to burn them all. I believe the taking of them often gives a false permanence to things striking at the moment – to the serious detriment of deeper and less superficial impressions.' These extracts should be compared with those from his war diary written twenty years later (see p. 249).

2. (p. 7) Having walked from London, Thomas stayed with his uncle and aunt in Swindon. See the extract from *The Childhood of Edward Thomas*, 'Holidays' (p. 114).

3. (p. 7) The reservoir at Coate Farm, where Richard Jefferies was born, and the scene of action in Jefferies' partly autobiographical *Bevis: The Story of a Boy* (1882).

4. (p. 11) See the poem 'It Was Upon' (p. 236).

5. (p. 17) Gordon Bottomley (1874–1948). A minor poet and writer of verse plays, Bottomley was an invalid and lived near Cartmel on the edge of the Lake District. Thomas became acquainted with him through James Ashcroft Noble. They first met in 1903, after a long correspondence. Bottomley remained Thomas's literary confidant

to the end of his life. This letter was written after Thomas had completed his first commissioned book, *Oxford*, and was recovering from one of his fits of severe depression.

6.   (p. 19) Thomas spent October 1904 walking in Wales to gather material for *Beautiful Wales*, his second commissioned book. It was written in five months to meet the publisher's deadline and appeared in 1905, illustrated with watercolours by Robert Fowler, R.I.

7.   (p. 19) Charles Haddon Spurgeon (1834–92), a famous evangelical preacher and nonconformist divine.

8.   (p. 24) This is Edward Thomas's first published poem. 'Llewelyn, the Bard' is one of Thomas's imaginary selves. Thomas told Gordon Bottomley that the poem had no Welsh original; it was one of his own.

9.   (p. 26) Helen – his wife, Helen Thomas; Mervyn – his son, aged five; Bronwen – his eldest daughter, then aged three.

10. (p. 27) Commissioned by J. M. Dent in February 1906, completed by June and published in the same year.

11. (p. 33) Commissioned in July 1908 by J. M. Dent, completed by October, and published in 1909. At the time Thomas thought it 'my worst book yet'.

12. (p. 36) See the poem 'Ambition' (p. 172).

13. (p. 36) This is one of Thomas's imaginary self-portrayals. Cf. 'The Other Man' (p. 97), and the poem 'The Other' (p. 155).

14. (p. 46) See the poem 'Words' (p. 201).

15. (p. 58) *The South Country*, published in 1909, was the first book Thomas wrote for himself. The stories and sketches he produced after that were published in two uncommissioned books, *Rest and Unrest* (1910) and *Light and Twilight* (1911). This extract from a description of a Welsh town, 'At a Cottage Door', was published in *Rest and Unrest*.

16. (p. 63) Published in *Light and Twilight* (1911). One of the best of Thomas's wry essays in self-portrayal and self-analysis.

17. (p. 68) Published in *Light and Twilight* (1911). In Helen Thomas's autobiographical classic, *World Without End*, a record of her life with Edward Thomas, the same incident is described:

> In spite of the lifting of financial cares the attacks of gloom and wretchedness had become of late more frequent and more lasting, and there were terrible days when I did not know where he was; or, if he was at home, days of silence and brooding despair. Often during this period while I was doing my housework or playing with the children or working in the garden I was straining to hear his coo-ee from the hillside, or his foot on the steps up to the gate. And often when he came I was

terrified by the haggard greyness of his face, and the weary droop of his body, as he flung himself into his study chair, not speaking or looking at me. Once in one of these fits, after being needlessly angry with one of the children who cried and ran away from him, he rummaged in a drawer where he kept all sorts of things like fishing tackle and tools, and where I knew there was also a revolver. This he put into his pocket, and with dull eyes and ashen cheeks strode out of the house up the bare hill. I watched him go until he was lost among the trees at the top. I thought 'perhaps I shall never see him again', but I knew he would not leave me like this; it would not be like this that he would save himself. Nevertheless my limbs went weak and slack, my tongue was dry in my mouth, the questions and chatter of the children were an agony to me. I wanted to be alone and listen. But I could not. I took the children down to the stream in the hollow where they could paddle and sail their boats without wanting me to join in their play. There I sat with my hands in my lap unable to sew or read or think, and while the children played I listened. I prayed too that he might be released from his agony and I from mine. When the sun set and the children got tired of their game I took them home and put them to bed. I changed my dress, made up the study fire, drew the curtains, and got the tea things ready on a little table. I was in the kitchen, ironing, when he came in.

'Hello,' I called, though the word came out like a croak. He was safe. When I could control my voice and face I went to the study. He was taking off his shoes by the fire, and I saw they were coated with mud and leaves. He did not look up.

'Shall I make the tea?' I said.

'Please,' he answered, and in his voice I was aware of all he had suffered and overcome, and all that he asked of me.

18.   (p. 74) Written in 1911. Published in *The Last Sheaf* (1928).

19.   (p. 77) Published in *Fry's Magazine* (October 1911).

20.   (p. 83) Written in 1911. Published in *Cloud Castle and Other Papers* (1922).

21.   (p. 89) Written for his children in 1911, and published in *Four and Twenty Blackbirds* (1915). See the poem 'I Built Myself a House of Glass' (p. 201).

22.   (p. 90) From *The Icknield Way*, written in 1911, published in 1913. See the poem 'Rain' (p. 215).

23.   (p. 92) Another self-portrayal: from 'The Friend of the Blackbird', written in October 1911, published in *The Last Sheaf* (1928).

24.   (p. 93) Published in *T.P.'s Weekly* (5 May 1914).

25.   (p. 97) In April 1913 Thomas bicycled from London to the Quantock Hills to gather material for *In Pursuit of Spring*, published by

Nelson later in the same year. It was this book that convinced Robert Frost that poetry, not prose, was Thomas's medium.

26. (p. 99) These extracts are taken from Chapters v and xii of *Walter Pater*, which was commissioned in 1911 and published in 1913. Half-way through it Thomas took on another commission for a similar book on Swinburne. These two studies, but particularly that of Pater, contain some of Thomas's best literary criticism. They also show how far Thomas was moving away from Pater's debilitating artificiality and towards the ideas that he and Robert Frost were to share.

27. (p. 106) Published in *T.P.'s Weekly* (31 January 1913). It is to this essay that Thomas refers in his letter to Robert Frost dated 19 May 1914:

> Don't get at me about my T.P. article, which wasn't all that even I could do, but a series of extracts from an essay I shan't do. You could do one now. And you really should start doing a book on speech and literature, or you will find me mistaking your ideas for mine and doing it myself. You can't prevent me from making use of them: I do so daily and want to begin over again with them and wring all the necks of my rhetoric – the geese. However, my 'Pater' would show you I have got on to the scent already.

28. (p. 109) In December 1913, shortly after his first meeting with Robert Frost, Thomas began writing the autobiographical fragment which was eventually published in 1938 under the title *The Childhood of Edward Thomas*. Writing to Eleanor Farjeon, he called it 'an attempt to put on paper what he sees when he thinks of himself (E.T.) from 1878 to about 1898'. Again he wrote (16 December 1913): 'My autobiography grows ... My object at present is daily to focus on some period and get in all that relates to it, allowing one thing to follow the other that suggested it. It's very lean but I feel the shape of the sentences and alter continually with some unseen end in view.'

In *The Childhood* Thomas presents his father as a somewhat stern and rigid parent, but a more genial sketch of him survives in his unpublished 'Addenda to Autobiography', now in the Berg Collection of the New York Public Library. In his *Edward Thomas*, William Cooke prints the following fragment, which Thomas should have incorporated in *The Childhood* but did not:

> Father had a few songs and comic speeches that he used to treat us to in turn when we were six or seven. He used to put on an artificial voice and expression and say 'Walk up. Walk up and see the show!

Strike up, Joe! Walk up and see the live lions stuffed with straw and Napoleon crossing the Alps in an open boat.' When we were younger he had us on his knee to sing

> Paddy from Cork he had never been
> A railway train he had never seen,
> He's off to catch the great machine,
> That runs along the railway. Whoop!

(It ended in a high whoop and a wrinkling grin of delight from my father as he tossed us up.)

29. (p. 114) Regret and yearning for something lost and not to be recovered is central to many of Thomas's poems – for instance, 'Celandine', 'The Unknown Bird', 'Snow', 'The Other'.

30. (p. 118) Written in 1919. Published in *The Last Sheaf* (1928).

31. (p. 121) Commissioned by the *English Review* and published in October 1914. To get material for this and the two following essays Thomas travelled across England, going as far north as Newcastle-upon-Tyne.

32. (p. 133) Published in the *English Review* (December 1914).

33. (p. 142) The last of Thomas's three articles in the *English Review*. Written in September 1914, this essay recalls Thomas's walks and talks with Robert Frost at Little Iddens in Herefordshire, and is a prose counterpart to his poem 'The Sun Used to Shine' (p. 232).

34. (p. 149) 'Up in the Wind'. The first of Edward Thomas's poems, completed 3 December 1914. It was based on a prose sketch called 'The White Horse', written a few weeks earlier on 16 November. This prose sketch was first published in William Cooke's *Edward Thomas* (1970). The following brief extract from it may give some idea of the transformation effected by Thomas when he changed the medium:

> 'I should like to wring the old girl's neck for coming away here.' So said the woman who fetched my beer when I found myself at the inn first. She was a daughter of the house, fresh from a long absence in service in London, a bright wildish slattern with a cockney accent and her hair half-down. She spoke angrily. If she did not get away before long, she said, she would go mad with the loneliness.

In the prose sketch it is the girl's father, the landlord, who is the chief character; but in the poem the interest is centred on the girl. In 'The White Horse', Thomas continues:

> Who 'the old girl' was, and whether she had built the house here, or what, I did not inquire. It was just the loneliness of the high-placed

little inn isolated under those tall beeches that pleased me. Every
year I used to go there once or twice, never so often as to overcome
the original feeling it had given me. I was always on the verge of
turning that feeling, or of having it turned by a natural process, into
a story. Whoever the characters would have been I do not think they
would have included either the 'old girl' or the landlord's indignant
cockney daughter.

'The White Horse' has been identified as the inn of that name at
Froxfield near Steep.

35. (p. 152) 'March'. His third poem, written 5 December 1914.
Robert Frost had referred Thomas to 'paragraphs in his book *In
Pursuit of Spring* and told him to write it in verse form in exactly
the same cadence'. That Thomas took this advice is perhaps indi-
cated by the following passage from *In Pursuit of Spring*
(compare the lines beginning 'What did the thrushes know?'):

All the thrushes of England sang at that hour, and against that back-
ground of myriads I heard two or three singing their frank, clear
notes in a mad eagerness to have all done before dark; for already the
blackbirds were clinking and shifting places along the hedge-rows.

36. (p. 153) 'Old Man'. Written 6 December 1914. William Cooke
(op. cit.) quotes a prose draft of this poem, written on 17
November 1914. The prose draft was called 'Old Man's Beard'.
The following is an extract:

As for myself I cannot remember when I first smelt that green bitter-
ness. I, too, often gather a sprig from the bush and sniff it and roll it
between my fingers and sniff again and think, trying to discover what
it is that I am remembering. I do not wholly like the smell, yet would
rather lose many meaningless sweeter ones than this bitter one of
which I have mislaid the key. As I hold the sprig to my nose and
slowly withdraw it, I think of nothing, I see, I hear nothing; yet I seem
too to be listening, lying in wait for whatever it is I ought to remem-
ber but never do. No garden comes back to me, no hedge or path, no
grey-green bush called old man's beard or lad's love, no figure of
mother or father or playmate, only a dark avenue without an end.

37. (p. 154) 'The Sign-Post'. Written 7 December 1914. The last of five
poems composed on successive days. There are similarities with
Robert Frost's poem 'The Road Not Taken', written later, which
refers to their walks together in the summer of 1914 (see note 33).

38. (p. 155) 'The Other'. See 'The Other Man', p. 97, an extract
from *In Pursuit of Spring*. In 1911, when on the point of a ner-

vous breakdown, in one of his letters Thomas referred to 'a sort of nervous conspiracy going on in it (my head) which leaves me only a joint tenancy and a perpetual sense of the other tenant and wonder what he will do'. Cf. *The Life and Letters of Edward Thomas*, by John Moore (London, 1939).

'crocketed': decorated with crockets, i.e. the carved buds or curled leaf-shapes placed on the sloping sides of spires, pinnacles and gables in Gothic architecture.

39. (p. 160) 'The Manor Farm'. Written on Christmas Eve, 1914. One of the two poems by himself that Edward Thomas included under the pseudonym 'Edward Eastaway' in his anthology *This England* (1915).

40. (p. 161) 'The Combe'. The last but one of the fifteen poems written by Edward Thomas in December 1914, nine of which are included in this selection.

41. (p. 161) 'The New Year'. Written 1 January 1915. Thomas describes the game of ' "Fly the garter" – if that is its right name' in *The Childhood of Edward Thomas*. It is an elaborate form of leap-frog. I believe its correct name is 'Flying the garter' – at least that is what it was called when I played it as a boy.

42. (p. 169) 'Man and Dog'. Written 20 January 1915. A prose counterpart of the poem is 'An Umbrella Man', from *The South Country* (see p. 52).

43. (p. 173) 'Parting'. Written 11 February 1915. On this day Thomas's son Mervyn left home to go to America with Robert Frost and his family. As with his own father, Thomas's relations with his son were not entirely happy.

44. (p. 180) 'The New House'. Written 11 March 1915. The house is the one built for Edward Thomas by Geoffrey Lupton at Wick Green in 1909, in which he lived until 1913. Several poems refer to this house – 'Wind and Mist', 'The Path', 'When First'.

45. (p. 184) 'Wind and Mist'. Written 1 April 1915. See note above. In a letter to Gordon Bottomley dated 23 February 1911, Thomas remarked: 'The garden improves but the clay breaks first the back and then the heart.' Of the house, Helen Thomas wrote in *World Without End*:

> somehow we could not love the house. The heavy oak was raw and new, and seemed to resent its servitude in beam and door, and with loud cracks would try to wrench itself free. There was nothing in that exposed position to protect us from the wind, which roared and shrieked in the wide chimneys, nor have I ever heard such furious rain as dashed vindictively against our windows. The fire of logs

burning in the hearth seemed not to respond so much to our fostering
care as to the wind which drew it up in great leaping flames and sent
sheaves of sparks into the roaring darkness. Often a thick mist envel-
oped us, and the house seemed to be standing on the edge of the
world, with an infinity of white rolling vapour below us. There was
no kindness or warmth or welcome about the house.

46. (p. 186) 'Lob'. Completed 4 April 1915. The *O.E.D.* definition
     of 'Lob' is 'a country bumpkin; a clown, lout'. In Thomas's poem
     Lob embodies the perennial English rustic, as Kipling's Hobden
     does in *Puck of Pook's Hill* and in his poem 'The Land', or G. K.
     Chesterton's drunkard in 'The Rolling English Road'. Many
     prototypes of Lob are to be found in Thomas's prose, beginning
     with his 'A Wiltshire Molecatcher' in *The Woodland Life* (1897).
     See too his poem 'Man and Dog' (p. 169) and 'An Umbrella Man'
     (p. 52). Lob probably owes something to George Sturt's *The
     Bettesworth Book* (1901) and *Memoirs of a Surrey Labourer*
     (1907), of which Thomas wrote:

     Bettesworth had fought in the Crimea, and during sixty years had
     been active unceasingly over a broad space of English country –
     Surrey, Sussex, and Hampshire – always out of doors. His memory
     was good, his eye for men and trades a vivid one, and his gift of speech
     unusual, 'with swift realistic touch, convincingly true'; so that a pic-
     ture of rural England during the latter half of the nineteenth century,
     by one born in the earlier half and really belonging to it, is the result.
     The portrait of an unlettered pagan English peasant is fascinating.

     Another model for Lob may have been David Uzzell, a Wiltshire
     countryman, a lifelong friend whom he portrayed in *The Child-
     hood of Edward Thomas.*

47. (p. 188) Sinoden Hill, Berkshire. When the editor of *Black-
     wood's Magazine* objected to this name on the ground of its
     indelicacy, Thomas substituted 'Happersnapper Hanger'.

48. (p. 189) In his anthology *This England* (1915) Thomas quotes
     from Shakespeare's *The Merry Wives of Windsor* Mistress Page's
     version of the legend of Herne the Hunter:

     There is an old tale goes that Herne the hunter,
     Sometime a keeper here in Windsor forest,
     Doth all the winter-time, at still midnight,
     Walk round about an oak, with great ragg'd horns;
     And there he blasts the tree, and takes the cattle,
     And makes milch-kine yield blood, and shakes a chain

> In a most hideous and dreadful manner:
> You have heard of such a spirit, and well you know
> The superstitious idle-headed eld
> Receiv'd and did deliver to our age
> This tale of Herne the hunter for a truth.
>
> (Act IV, scene iv)

49. (p. 190) This story, from Charlotte S. Burne's *Shropshire Folk Lore*, is also included in *This England*, under the title 'Two Shropshire Hills'.

50. (p. 190) Gotham, a village in Nottinghamshire, famous for the reputed stupidity of its inhabitants – cf. the nursery rhyme, 'Three Wise Men of Gotham'.

51. (p. 198) 'The Chalk-Pit'. Written 8 May 1915. Edward Thomas's essay 'Chalk Pits' in *The Last Sheaf* (1928) is the prose basis of this poem. 'The man of forty' is a self-portrait, and the 'girl of twenty' is Helen Thomas when they were courting (see Helen Thomas, *World Without End*).

   'Orts and crosses' = noughts and crosses.

52. (p. 201) 'I Built Myself a House of Glass'. Written 25 June 1915. At the time Thomas was making up his mind whether to go to America with Robert Frost or enlist in the army. A week or two later he joined up. See also the fable, 'People Who Live in Glass Houses Shouldn't Throw Stones' on p. 89 of this selection.

53. (p. 201) 'Words'. Completed 28 June 1915. Writing about John Clare in his *Feminine Influence on the Poets* (1910), Thomas remarked:

> Words never consent to correspond exactly to any object unless, like scientific terms, they are first killed. Hence the curious life of words in the hands of those who love all life so well that they do not kill even the slender words but let them play on; and such are poets. The magic of words is due to their living freely among things . . . Grown men with dictionaries are as murderous of words as entomologists of butterflies.

See also his remarks on Walter Pater's use of words, on p. 106.

54. (p. 205) 'Haymaking'. Completed 8 July 1915. R. George Thomas, in his *Collected Poems of Edward Thomas*, quotes some unpublished notes that Thomas made for this poem in June 1915:

> – a rick in midfield – tosser idle – men lean on rakes – old fashioned as Crome or Constable.
>
> How old it is. I seem to see it now as some one long years hence will see it in a picture.

George Morland (1763–1804) and John Crome (1768–1821) were painters of rural scenes and landscapes.

The image of the swift is drawn from a passage in *Light and Twilight* (1911): '. . . the flight of the swift which was as if the arrow and bow had flown away together'.

55. (p. 207) 'Aspens'. Written 11 July 1915. In a letter to Eleanor Farjeon, dated 21 July 1915, Thomas remarked: 'About "Aspens" you missed just the turn that I thought essential. *I* was the aspen. "We" meant the trees and I with my dejected shyness.'

56. (p. 209) 'For These'. Completed 14 July 1915, on the day he was passed fit for the army.

57. (p. 210) 'Digging'. Written 21 July 1915, his first poem after joining up. Thomas had just finished writing his *Life of the Duke of Marlborough* (1915). Blenheim (1704), Ramillies (1706) and Malplaquet (1709) were three of Marlborough's victories.

58. (p. 215) 'This is No Case of Petty Right or Wrong'. Written on Boxing Day, 1915. Thomas had visited London on leave and seen his father, with whom he had an argument about the war. Reporting this in a letter to Robert Frost, Thomas remarked, 'He made me sick.' The elder Thomas was a conventional patriot with the conventional Germanophobia of the day.

In his essay 'England', Thomas had written in 1914: 'I believe . . . that all ideas of England are developed, spun out, from such a centre into something large or infinite, solid or aëry, according to each man's nature and capacity; that England is a system of vast circumferences circling round the minute neighbouring points of home.' See also 'Tipperary' (p. 121), 'It's a Long, Long Way' (p. 133) and 'This England' (p. 142).

59. (p. 215) 'Rain'. Written 7 January 1916. The prose counterpart of this poem can be found in the extract from *The Icknield Way* (1911), printed on p. 90 of this selection.

60. (p. 216) 'The Clouds that are so Light'. Written 15 January 1916. A week later Thomas wrote to his wife: 'Fancy you thinking I might have someone in view in those verses beginning "The clouds that are so light". Fancy your being pleased at the idea. Well, perhaps you wouldn't be if there really were someone, in which case I would hardly write verses, I think.'

61. (p. 217) 'Roads'. Written 22 January 1916. To Eleanor Farjeon, in a letter dated 24 January 1916, Thomas explained: 'Helen is the lady in the Mabinogion, the Welsh lady who married Maxen the emperor and gave her name to the great old mountain roads – Sarn Helen they are all marked on the maps. Do you remember "The Dream of Maxen"? She is known to mythologists as one of

the travelling goddesses of the dusk.' 'The Dream of Maxen' is to
be found in Edward Thomas's *Celtic Stories* (1911).

62. (p. 220) 'P.H.T.' Written 8 February 1916. 'P.H.T.' are the initials of
Edward Thomas's father. The poem was not published until 1949.

63. (p. 221) 'No One So Much As You'. Written 11 February 1916.
It is addressed to Edward Thomas's mother and is obviously a
companion-piece to 'P. H. T.', written for his father three days
earlier. Some critics take the poem to have been addressed to
Helen Thomas, the poet's wife; in which case a factitious senti-
mental appeal can be read into it. See Thomas's account of his
mother in the extract from his autobiography, *The Childhood of
Edward Thomas*, on p. 110–11 of this selection.

64. (p. 224) 'Celandine'. Written 4 March 1916. Probably addressed
to Helen Thomas. In *Edward Thomas* (1978), Jan Marsh writes:

> This poem has nowhere been identified as being written about
> Helen, and in one sense, it appears to be addressed to a person now
> dead, certainly lost. But the date of its writing (4 March 1916),
> between the poems to Thomas's parents and those to his children,
> and the internal evidence of 'Her nature and name / Were like those
> flowers' – *Helen: celan*dine – point to this conclusion. And its sense
> would confirm this: Edward reproached himself for having
> destroyed with his sulks and sarcasm the bright cheerful girl he had
> fallen in love with all those years ago. Compared with that Helen,
> the woman of 1916 could be likened to a shadow or a phantom,
> existing no more or lost 'like a never perfectly recalled air'.

65. (p. 225) 'Home'. Completed 10 March 1916. This poem was
written at Hare Hall Camp. In a letter to Eleanor Farjeon, Tho-
mas remarked: 'Somebody said something about homesickness
the other day . . . The new rule about going out of camp makes
Saturday and Sunday days of imprisonment.'

66. (p. 226) 'If I Should Ever by Chance'. Completed 6 April 1916.
The first of a group of four poems addressed to his wife and
children. This one was written for his daughter Bronwen
(1902–75). Like the next two poems it exhibits Thomas's love of
place-names. See the extract from *The South Country* (1909) on
p. 33 of this selection.

67. (p. 227) 'If I were to Own'. Completed 7 April 1916. Written for
his son Mervyn Thomas (1900–1965).

68. (p. 228) 'What Shall I Give?'. Completed 8 April 1916. Written
for Myfanwy Thomas (1910–2005).

69. (p. 228) 'And You, Helen'. Written 9 April 1916, for his wife
Helen Thomas (1877–1967).

70. (p. 232) 'The Sun Used to Shine'. Written 22 May 1916. The poem is a reminiscence of his walks and talks with Robert Frost at Little Iddens, Herefordshire, in August 1914.

71. (p. 234) 'As the Team's Head-Brass'. Written 27 May 1916. At this time Thomas was making up his mind to give up his post as map-reading instructor to apply for a commission, which would involve 'going out' to the Front.

72. (p. 239) 'When First'. Written about 2 July 1916. R. George Thomas supposes that the poem was composed after Thomas had given up his hill-top study near Steep.

73. (p. 243) 'That Girl's Clear Eyes'. Written 10 September 1916. Thomas was studying as an officer-cadet at the Royal Artillery School in Handel Street, at the end of which stands the Found-ling Hospital founded by Thomas Coram in 1739. There used to be an effigy of Coram, with this date, in Brunswick Square, 'the stony square unlit', when Thomas was there.

74. (p. 244) 'The Trumpet'. Completed about 28 September 1916. In a letter to Eleanor Farjeon, Thomas wrote: 'I have written some verses suggested by the trumpet calls which go on all day. They are not well done and the trumpet is cracked, but the Reveille pleases me (more than it does most sleepers). Here is the result. You see I have written it with only capitals to mark lines, because people are all around me and I don't want them to know.'

75. (p. 245) 'Lights Out'. Written in November 1916. In a letter to Eleanor Farjeon, dated 6 November, Thomas wrote: 'Now I have actually done still another piece which I call "Lights Out". It sums up what I have often thought at that call. I wish it were as brief – two pairs of long notes.'

76. (p. 247) 'The Sheiling'. Written 23 November 1916. Thomas had been spending part of his leave at Gordon Bottomley's home, 'The Sheiling', near Carnforth on the edge of the Lake District.

77. (p. 248) 'Out in the Dark'. Written 24 December 1916. This was his last poem except for a few lines Thomas wrote in his war diary a fortnight before he embarked for France in January 1917 (published in *The Collected Poems of Edward Thomas*, 1978, edited by R. George Thomas).

78. (p. 249) Edward Thomas began his war diary on 1 January 1917 and kept it until the day before his death on 9 April 1917. It was discovered by his grandson Edward Thomas among his father's papers in 1970, and first published in 1977.

   Thomas crossed to France with his battery on 29 January 1917, and by 9 February was at the front near Arras where the build-up for the Easter offensive (the Third Battle of Arras) was beginning.

THE STORY OF PENGUIN CLASSICS

Before 1946 ... 'Classics' are mainly the domain of academics and students; readable editions for everyone else are almost unheard of. This all changes when a little-known classicist, E. V. Rieu, presents Penguin founder Allen Lane with the translation of Homer's *Odyssey* that he has been working on in his spare time.

1946 Penguin Classics debuts with *The Odyssey*, which promptly sells three million copies. Suddenly, classics are no longer for the privileged few.

1950s Rieu, now series editor, turns to professional writers for the best modern, readable translations, including Dorothy L. Sayers's *Inferno* and Robert Graves's unexpurgated *Twelve Caesars*.

1960s The Classics are given the distinctive black covers that have remained a constant throughout the life of the series. Rieu retires in 1964, hailing the Penguin Classics list as 'the greatest educative force of the twentieth century.'

1970s A new generation of translators swells the Penguin Classics ranks, introducing readers of English to classics of world literature from more than twenty languages. The list grows to encompass more history, philosophy, science, religion and politics.

1980s The Penguin American Library launches with titles such as *Uncle Tom's Cabin*, and joins forces with Penguin Classics to provide the most comprehensive library of world literature available from any paperback publisher.

1990s The launch of Penguin Audiobooks brings the classics to a listening audience for the first time, and in 1999 the worldwide launch of the Penguin Classics website extends their reach to the global online community.

The 21st Century Penguin Classics are completely redesigned for the first time in nearly twenty years. This world-famous series now consists of more than 1300 titles, making the widest range of the best books ever written available to millions – and constantly redefining what makes a 'classic'.

The Odyssey continues ...

The best books ever written

PENGUIN CLASSICS

SINCE 1946

Find out more at www.penguinclassics.com